PRAISE FOR *TAKING A STAND*

"*Taking a Stand* is essential and fascinating reading for anyone interested in the most effective strategies used by human rights defenders. Juan Méndez draws on his personal experiences as both a victim of torture and a pioneer of human rights advocacy to examine some of the most pressing issues of our day."

—José Miguel Vivanco, Executive Director, Americas Division, Human Rights Watch

"Juan Méndez, a towering figure in human rights advocacy, has written an impressively lucid and honest account of his remarkable life. For nearly four decades Méndez has been at the forefront of the human rights movement, not only in Latin America but worldwide. His unswerving commitment to the rule of law comes alive on these pages. Méndez has not only been a witness to history, but has also played a fundamental role in shaping it towards greater decency and justice. *Taking a Stand* is an invaluable contribution, told with characteristic modesty by a giant in the field who continues to inspire others through his wise reflections and outstanding example."

—Michael Shifter, President, Inter-American Dialogue

"In the field of human rights, there is no greater advocate than Juan Méndez. This thought provoking and moving book offers remarkable insight into the principles of justice and accountability. It is also a testimony to the uncompromising spirit of a man who, at great personal sacrifice, refused to remain silent."

—Mark S. Ellis, Executive Director, International Bar Association

"We can all sleep more soundly at night knowing that men like Juan Méndez take a stand to defend the rights of us all. This is a magnificent book that tells a noble story of passionate but impartial dedication to the cause of human rights. And it comes from someone who learned of human wrongs on the torture table and in jail in his native Argentina and who went on to fight for human rights across the globe. *Taking a Stand* will inspire others to follow in the footsteps of Juan Méndez and will also serve as a blueprint on how to stand up to dictators and advance true democracy."

—Robert Cox, former Editor-in-Chief of the *Buenos Aires Herald* and former President of the Inter American Press Association

TAKING

A STAND

THE EVOLUTION OF HUMAN RIGHTS

JUAN E. MÉNDEZ

WITH MARJORY WENTWORTH

palgrave
macmillan

First published in 2011 by PALGRAVE MACMILLAN® in the United
States—a division of St. Martin's Press LLC, 175 Fifth Avenue, New York,
NY 10010.

Where this book is distributed in the UK, Europe and the rest of the
world, this is by Palgrave Macmillan, a division of Macmillan Publishers
Limited, registered in England, company number 785998, of Houndmills,
Basingstoke, Hampshire RG21 6XS.

Palgrave Macmillan is the global academic imprint of the above companies
and has companies and representatives throughout the world.

Palgrave® and Macmillan® are registered trademarks in the United States,
the United Kingdom, Europe and other countries.

ISBN: 978-0-230-11233-9

Library of Congress Cataloging-in-Publication Data

Méndez, Juan E.
    Taking a stand : the evolution of human rights / Juan E. Méndez with
Marjory Wentworth.
        p.   cm.
    Includes bibliographical references and index.
    ISBN 978-0-230-11233-9
    1. Méndez, Juan E.   2. Human rights workers—
Biography.   3. Political prisoners—Civil rights.   I. Wentworth, Marjory,
1958–   II. Title.
JC571.M3995   2011
323.092—dc22
[B]

                                                                2011012449

A catalogue record of the book is available from the British Library.

Design by Letra Libre Inc.

First edition: October 2011

10 9 8 7 6 5 4 3 2 1

Printed in the United States of America.

CONTENTS

For my parents, Julio and Aurelia.
For Chichela, Juanfra, Camilo and Sole.
And for Joaquín, Anahí, Camila and Javier.

JEM

For my teachers Vincent Ferraro and Carolyn Forché.

MHW

FOREWORD

"La solidaridad no se agradece, se retribuye"—"Don't say thank you for the solidarity you received; return it." On my first-ever visit to Latin America, as Secretary General of Amnesty International in 1986, I encountered this splendid slogan on a poster for Amnesty's Uruguayan Section, many of whose members were former political prisoners. It sums up the life and career of Juan Méndez. As a political prisoner and victim of arbitrary detention and torture, he experienced the solidarity of family, friends and campaigners. As a lawyer and human rights activist, he has paid back that solidarity to others many thousand-fold.

Juan's life has taken him from being a torture victim more than 35 years ago, to being the United Nations Special Rapporteur on Torture today. His career has taken him from the grassroots to the summit of the defense of human rights. As a young lawyer, he was a local defender of political and social activists in his own country, Argentina; he made a fresh start at the grassroots in his country of exile, the United States. He went on to play major roles in leading nongovernmental organizations working for human rights and transitional justice, including an outstanding fifteen-year contribution to the development of Human Rights Watch from its early stages. Although never a staff member of Amnesty International, he consistently supported the organization that had adopted him as a prisoner of conscience and had campaigned for and assisted his release. He became a regional human rights leader,

as executive director of the Inter-American Institute of Human Rights
and president of the Inter-American Commission on Human Rights.
At the fully worldwide level, in addition to his current United Nations
torture mandate, he was the first United Nations Special Advisor on
the Prevention of Genocide. All along the way, he has been a teacher,
conveying his own knowledge and experience to other generations of
human rights lawyers and activists. His unceasing contribution to the
struggle against impunity has been both conceptual and practical.

Juan embodies the best values of the human rights movement.
Himself a person of firm political conviction, he has upheld the highest standards of impartiality in exposing the human rights violations
of the left and right. He has maintained a scrupulous regard for the
truth. While never refraining from proper public criticism and insisting on accountability and justice, he believes in the value of being open
to and seeking dialogue. He has always stayed above any kind of sectarianism within the human rights world, throughout which he com-
mands universal liking and respect. Having been a victim and worked
directly with victims, he has never overlooked the importance of campaigning for and assisting individuals.

Argentina's passage from dictatorship and repression to democracy and accountability provides one of the key stories of progress in
respect for human rights, and Juan has played a role through every
stage in this story, from which there is much to learn. The United
States has aspired to be a human rights leader, yet its claim to moral
authority has been repeatedly undermined by its inability to rise above
its political alliances, and increasingly by its own direct violations of
human rights. Juan is uncompromising in his insistence on holding his
second country to universal standards.

This book is published at a time when shifts in the balance of
global economic and political strength are rendering obsolete an approach to human rights promotion reliant on the foreign policies of
Western governments and when events in the Arab world are showing
that the yearning for respect for human dignity is indeed universal and

will be realized from within societies, not from outside. But the solidarity among those committed to human rights in the South and the North remains a powerful foundation for advancement. Juan Méndez has worked on both sides of this alliance, and his experience is an inspiration for sustaining and deepening it.

Ian Martin
London, April 2011

CHAPTER ONE

DETENTION

Throughout history, despotic governments have imprisoned dissidents and denied them the opportunity to challenge their arrest. Criticism of prolonged arbitrary detention became one of the first rallying cries that allowed the emergence of a truly international human rights movement. The designation of a victim of arbitrary arrest as a "prisoner of conscience" allowed Amnesty International, an organization that works to protect the human rights of people all over the world, to put a human face to the injustice and to recruit common men and women to fight it. I was an early beneficiary of this emerging movement; my case illustrates the arbitrariness and unfairness of prolonged detention without trial.

The first time I was detained was in 1974 in my hometown of Mar del Plata, Argentina, in front of the Catholic University Law School where I was teaching. At the time, I was known for my involvement with highly visible political cases, but I was also known for activism from my student days during the tumultuous 1960s. I tried to use my legal skills to help the poor and defend the rights of others. I was newly married to another law student, and we had two young children.

One evening I had just finished meeting with some students who had peacefully taken over the law school building. The school was across a passage from the cathedral, and both overlooked San Martin Street, the city's main commercial artery. The street was bustling with late shoppers and people going home from work. Because of the demonstration, there were even more people out than usual. Classes had been canceled due to the peaceful occupation, but the students appreciated that I, a faculty member, had gone in to talk to them about their grievances.

General Juan D. Perón was once again the president, after spending eighteen years in exile in Spain. After ten years as a democratically elected president (1946–1955), he had been deposed by a military coup d'etat in September 1955. After some skirmishes between loyalist and rebellious forces, the coup plotters gained control of the situation and Perón resigned. He took refuge on a Paraguayan gunboat and was allowed to go into exile, first to Paraguay and then to several other Latin American destinations. Eventually he settled in a tony neighborhood of Madrid, where he spent most of his years in exile. His followers, the Peronistas, remained active at home, even though their political party was banned from participating in elections. In 1973, the country held its first free and fair elections since 1955, and the Peronist candidate, Dr. Héctor Cámpora, won overwhelmingly. Later the same year, pressures from the party's right wing forced Cámpora's resignation and, in September 1973, after having returned permanently in June, Perón was elected president with his wife, María Estela ("Isabel") Martínez de Perón as vice president. By then, however, the struggle between the left and right wings within the Peronist movement was becoming violent. The left wing of the party included large numbers of young people from all walks of life, highly organized and mobilized by the Peronist Youth (Juventud Peronista). The Peronist Youth street demonstrations were peaceful, although their rhetoric was extreme. They sympathized openly with Montoneros, an urban guerrilla group that between 1970 and 1973 had isolated the military dictatorship and forced its rulers to grant the first truly democratic election in decades and allow Perón's return. Perón, however, after favoring different factions depending on the circumstances, was now clearly siding with the right, including thugs employed by the larger trade unions and small fascist student groups. By 1974, there were early signs that these right-wing groups were beginning to enjoy support from the police and the military, as they had during the military dictatorship.

Because of the atmosphere of threatened violence, some of the students occupying the law school had concealed weapons and organized regular lookout shifts. As I walked outside that evening with three friends who were political activists in the youth movement of the Peronist Party, some of the lookouts were discreetly posted at the perimeter of the block and some yards into the main square, where we were going. Fortunately, their instructions were to respond only to firearms attacks from provocateurs, so when the four of us were stopped by plainclothesmen shouting "Federal Police, hit the ground!" they did not react and simply left the area; if they had tried to defend us, there could have been many casualties.

The plainclothesmen pointed their machine guns at us as we lay on the sidewalk and then handcuffed us. They searched us, took our handguns, and asked for identification. Many of us, including me, carried guns at the time for protection. The police had no warrant and no probable cause to arrest us, as we were not breaking the law. But by 1974 the police were already aggressively and threateningly displaying weapons and flaunting the laws. Dozens of people were passing by. It all happened out in the open, as if it were something ordinary. Eventually, they piled us into the floor of their cars, then sat on us. Although they were verbally abusive and threatening with their weapons, they did not use physical violence. Since my handgun was registered and legal, I thought that I would quickly clarify the situation and we would be released. Within minutes, they took us away to the local federal police headquarters in their unmarked cars.

Upon arrival, they put us in individual cells. Each of us was taken separately to see the head of the police for interrogation. We were threatened, and my three friends were roughed up a bit. Back in our cells, I tried to give my friends legal advice through the windows, telling them to refuse to make statements and insist on seeing a lawyer. Unbeknownst to me, a uniformed cop was listening in; my words only reinforced the police's notion that I was a ringleader. We spent three nights in jail. The second night we could hear a raucous demonstration in the street; our friends in the Peronist Youth had decided to make our arrest a mobilizing event, and hundreds of young people were marching and chanting to demand our release. It was heartening to hear them, and it lifted our spirits considerably. Inside the station, the police went into high alert.

Because my arrest happened in plain sight of so many people, my wife, Silvia, also a lawyer, was notified. She went to the bar association and was lucky enough to find a meeting of its ruling board in progress. Its chairman, Reiniero Bernal, knew me because we had worked together on a sensational case involving an armed right-wing attack on students at the School of Architecture. Reiniero offered to leave the meeting and go directly to the Federal Police to inquire about my detention. He and Silvia were not allowed to enter the building where I was being held or to see the chief of the Federal Police for Mar del Plata; when they insisted, machine guns were pointed at them. Reiniero then went back to the bar association to draft a formal protest against the Federal Police, which he submitted the next day, together with the petition for a writ of habeas corpus to secure my release.

My three companions were released without charges after the third night. I was taken from my cell in the middle of the night and placed, handcuffed, in an unmarked car that made its way out of the city through deserted streets. I was driven to a penitentiary in Azul, about two hundred miles away in the interior of the province of Buenos Aires. (In 1974, there were neither federal courts nor prisons in Mar del Plata.) After I was given prison clothes and my hair was cut very short, I was taken to the courthouse to be interrogated by the federal judge.

By then, my friends and family had learned what was going on: The Federal Police claimed that the three students had small-caliber weapons, legal at the time, but that I was carrying a "war weapon"— a larger-caliber handgun, possession of which was a criminal offense that carried a mandatory prison sentence without the benefit of parole during pretrial detention. It was clear that the police switched the gun soon after my arrest. The fact that they would manipulate the evidence in this fashion made my situation seem even more precarious. At my hearing with the judge, I was assisted both by counsel and my friend Ricardo Sepe. Both were able to identify my gun and refute the charge that I was carrying a war weapon. My brother Julio had also come to help me and was stunned to see me in handcuffs and prison garb like a common criminal.

At the end of the hearing, the judge dismissed the charges and released me unconditionally. The Federal Police could not hold me after the federal courts had declared me innocent. The state of siege was not yet in effect—it was established later in 1974, after Perón had died and his widow, Isabel Perón, was president. If it had been in effect, the police would have asked the ministry of interior to place me in administrative detention, as would happen to me the following year.

I returned to Mar del Plata and expressed my gratitude to friends, family and colleagues for their support and assistance. It was clear to me, however, that the precarious balance of power that was keeping me safe in the city was irretrievably altered. Until then, all the threats against my life and liberty had come from small gangs of thugs who were not interested in upsetting that balance. But now the Federal Police had entered the growing dispute on the side of the right-wing forces. The fact that they arrested me without a warrant and deliberately distorted the evidence to keep me in prison was a clear signal that life in Mar del Plata was no longer safe for me or for my family. Silvia, who never participated in politics, was frightened most of the time. For the previous three years, the police had used tactics to intimidate and frighten me and my family, as they had on December 11, 1971, my twenty-seventh birthday, when they raided our apartment because of my participation in the case of the murdered architecture student. Other threats—in person, by phone, or through graffiti—had come from right-wing gangs. Silvia pleaded with me to be careful, but those years when Perón first returned to power were nothing resembling normal.

In retrospect, I should not have been surprised by my arrest. There had been signs, of course. In December 1971, Reiniero and I had worked on a case involving an attack allegedly by the right-wing student group CNU (Concentracion Nacional Universitaria), a national movement that was relatively strong in Mar del Plata, against a student assembly at the School of Architecture that had left an eighteen-year-old student named Silvia Filler dead and three male students wounded. Silvia Filler's family and ours were all friends, and I had always found her independent and intellectually curious. She was sitting in the middle of a classroom where a student assembly was being held when the thugs attacked. A stray bullet hit her in the forehead. The thugs were shooting wildly against the group of about 150 students, not singling her out. Nevertheless, months later, there were boasts of having killed a Marxist and Jewish student.

With two other lawyers, I represented the wounded students in the criminal investigation and eventual prosecution of their assailants, starting that same night. Reiniero and another prominent lawyer represented the Filler family. We set about to demonstrate state police complicity with the group that had stormed into the assembly while the building was under police surveillance. We gathered witnesses and brought them to court. On the basis of allegations by many eyewitnesses, twenty members of the CNU and its allies were arrested within hours of the crime. They were charged with murder and other offenses and held in pre-trial detention for almost two years. Several had been my school mates at the Catholic University Law School and often had argued with me on a variety of political issues; they were part of a tiny but vocal fringe group that the majority of students repudiated.

At dawn on Saturday, December 11, 1971, five days after the murder of Silvia Filler, the police raided my apartment. My wife and I were pulled out of bed at gunpoint. The police stayed for about an hour, going over everything in our home and taking away books, magazines, and other documents. With their guns still drawn, they played with our six-month-old son, Juan Francisco. After I insisted, they showed me a search warrant signed by a judge—the same judge who was investigating the Filler murder. He also had been a professor of mine. Silvia and I went to see him that same afternoon. He was profusely apologetic; he had signed the search warrant without knowing that it was for my home, acting in response to an anonymous letter the police showed him stating that there were weapons at my apartment. It also stated that people from other parts of the country who came to wreak havoc in Mar del Plata were staying in my home. The ease with which the police manipulated the courts to do the CNU bidding was a clear demonstration that our assumption—that the thugs had acted with police protection—was not far from the truth.

In the days that followed Silvia Filler's death, there were many demonstrations, and the police and military virtually occupied the downtown area with heavy weaponry and equipment. Things had been very unstable in Argentina for some time, and this incident brought things to a boiling point. A succession of military dictatorships had held power for almost a decade. No elections were held. Repression was escalating. There was a general crackdown on freedom of expression as well as on students and faculty at the national universities. Well-known teachers who were thought to be communists were fired from their jobs. The police presence in the streets was heavy and threatening. Student protests were met with a violent police response, and protestors were hauled away to police precincts.

At that time, however, dissidents were not yet heavily persecuted. There were only a few disappearances in 1971 and 1972. In 1971, a lawyer named Nestor Martins was the first victim of forced disappearance (*desaparecido*). He was abducted, illegally detained, tortured and ultimately murdered. All of this happened in secret; no trace of his body was found, and the government forces that took him away completely denied taking any action. Martins had a history of defending political prisoners and had charged the police with torture. The military government in power at the time (from 1966 to1973) had placed him in administrative detention under the "state of siege" (known elsewhere as "state of emergency") for several months, without trying him in a court of law; this was how the military handled leftists. Later, after his release, Martins was kidnapped by plainclothesmen as he was meeting a labor client in front of the Palace of Justice. They took the client too. No one ever found either of them.

In 1972, I became involved with the Peronist movement in Mar del Plata. I joined a coalition of left and center-left forces whose leader was Julio Troxler, a legendary Peronist leader from the 1950s. Troxler was kidnapped and murdered in Buenos Aires in 1975, in one of the most brazen and stunning crimes of the right-wing paramilitary group known as Triple A (Alianza Anticomunista Argentina). Our coalition disputed control of the Peronist party in the city, mostly in order to select candidates for office in the elections that finally took place on March 11, 1973. The infighting within Peronist ranks in Mar del Plata was so bad that once the electoral campaign started in earnest, we could not hold a single event without it ending in violence. Because of my political activism and my earlier confrontations with the CNU, I was known to many right-wing leaders and their bodyguards and thugs.

From time to time, I visited shantytowns and poor neighborhoods to offer legal services to inhabitants on all manner of legal problems: petty criminal matters, social security benefits and, most often, employment-related grievances, such as dismissal without severance pay, unpaid medical leave and workplace accidents. I was well known to the authorities because my pro bono work was part of neighborhood organizing efforts. It was not particularly controversial at first, but the fact that it was connected to political organizing with a leftist bent made it suspicious and attracted the attention of intelligence services and their servants, the right-wing thugs. One morning in the spring of 1973, I left my house to go to work after kissing my two-year-old son, who was riding a tricycle on the sidewalk. I noticed a couple of men lazily working on a house across the street. Most homes in that neighborhood were owned by out-of-towners, so they were generally closed except for the summer months. For some reason I drove back a few minutes later and took another look: I recognized the two workers as armed thugs for the right-wing trade union leaders in Mar del Plata. They were clearly conducting a stakeout of my house, possibly in advance of an attack. I got out of my car and stood on the sidewalk staring at them. They realized that I had recognized them, and that probably aborted whatever plan they had. Nothing happened at the time. My son was safe, but thirty-eight years later, I still feel like I dodged a bullet. What if I had not come back? Would they have taken my young son? My wife?

At around the same time, the head of the trade union confederation in Mar del Plata was murdered in the streets, and a small armed left-wing Peronist group claimed credit. The trade unions (especially the most powerful ones) were the arena where right- and left-wing

Peronists vied for control and power, often violently, and for political influence in the national political scene. The funeral took place at the trade union headquarters, which happened to be across the street from my law office where my name was openly displayed. During the funeral, and in the presence of police, mourners painted the whole front of my office with threats against my life: "Méndez, RIP," "assassin," "terrorist," and so on. Then they went out and painted the same threats in public places all over Mar del Plata. I repainted the front walls of my office, but the other threats remained for months: It was too dangerous to try to whitewash them. The mourners were trying to blame me for the murder because of my legal and political work in favor of progressive causes, even though they knew that the perpetrators belonged to a guerrilla group with which I was not connected.

I began to carry a gun. Once my father found the weapon in the glove compartment of my car and was upset. I explained that I was under threat and that I needed to defend myself. He said I should not enter into their fight and accused me of being crazy and misguided. In Argentina at the time those who had guns for self-defense kept them at home; most Argentines were disgusted at the spectacle of armed groups displaying weapons in public and sometimes using them in shootouts.

I was young and naive. Somehow, with the gun, I figured I would be safe. In retrospect, it was a false sense of security, but it also served as a useful coping mechanism. It is amazing how one adjusts to such stress and lives through it. I told myself that we were living through a temporary political crisis. If I could just get through this crisis, things would settle down and return to normal. I did not fully realize that the turmoil could continue for a long, long time and get more violent.

I rationalized the danger I was in by thinking that I could not be that important to people who were bent on killing and jailing adversaries; surely so many others would be higher on their lists than I. I did not realize then that there were many killers in a position to make decisions. Also, the ranks of lawyers who, like me, defended political prisoners and were better known were rapidly dwindling due to murders, arrests and exile. The country, government and society I had known for so long was rapidly deteriorating into a murderous regime that would endanger me and my family.

My wife, Silvia, and I had met at law school in Mar del Plata, a resort town where I had lived since I was twelve years old, and our two sons, Juan Francisco and Camilo, were born there. But after my arrest in front of the law school in 1974, we moved to Buenos Aires, where I was not as well known. Before my arrest, moving had been a difficult decision to make; afterward, we made the decision virtually overnight. We asked my mother-in-law and brother to pack our furniture and put the house up for sale.

My parents were living in Buenos Aires at the time, so at first we stayed with them. Later we rented an apartment nearby, and I found employment in the Buenos Aires universities as an in-house lawyer. They were still under control of the left-wing faction of Peronism, although that would not last. Soon I was doing criminal law pro bono for cases involving political prisoners. Within days of our arrival in Buenos Aires, the right-wing Triple A murdered Father Carlos Mugica, a charismatic priest who was the visible head of the activist Peronist priests. He was my friend, and I had brought him to Mar del Plata twice, to baptize each of my sons and also to speak to students and workers and organize with us. Carlos was well known and loved throughout the country, and, like many young people, I was shocked and saddened to learn of his death. He was the first of my friends to perish after the brief return of democracy in 1973, and his death filled us with fear about what the country was becoming. At his funeral and burial in Buenos Aires, I also learned that Argentina's poorest, the inhabitants of the shantytowns that surround the city, felt that they had lost their "voice for the voiceless." Their sorrow, displayed publicly and in large crowds, was especially moving.

In Buenos Aires, I continued my work in shantytowns with the Peronist Youth. The organizational work mostly consisted of helping neighborhood associations demand services and benefits from local and national governments. I also helped people find ways to participate in national demonstrations in support of left-wing Peronism, which by this time had an increasingly antigovernment agenda. More and more often, I was asked to try to find people in the early hours after their arrest, when their families were suffering intensely due to the uncertainty of the situation. I also visited prisoners in long-term custody and relayed news to spouses who could not visit them. By this time, few lawyers visited prisons; doing so had become dangerous because prison authorities shared your name and address with police and with death squads.

In November 1974, the government of Isabel Perón decreed the state of siege and suspended many constitutional rights. Beyond the legal framework, she also unleashed harsh repressive forces, including the notorious death squads of the "Triple A" and other "commandos." These were paramilitary groups that operated clandestinely though they included members of the security forces and right-wing civilians. Uniformed police were everywhere. They patrolled the streets in very menacing ways, with cars and carriers and heavy weaponry. In addition, plainclothesmen traveling in unmarked cars were common. Sometimes they were simply spying; other times they served as bodyguards for officials; and often they were simply showing force with heavy weapons and threatening attitudes. If they wanted to break through traffic jams, for example, they would point their guns (often machine guns) at other drivers to force them to yield the right of way.

The military also came out into the streets with an enormous show of force, driving huge trucks that carried about a dozen soldiers with sirens blazing and heavy weaponry. But the real terror, the kind that kept you up at night, was the realization that regular or irregular forces could kidnap you at any moment and not suffer any consequences. If you were meeting a political friend or a client at a café, you had to make sure that no one had followed you or your friend, and then you had to keep a constant watch on the door. On more than one occasion while living in Buenos Aires, I ran into right-wing students from Mar del Plata. I had to make elaborate plans to get away from them, so they would not find out where I lived or worked.

Given the conditions in which I worked, I often met clients in unusual places instead of my office. It was safer to work this way. And so, on a cold night in August 1975, I was walking down the deserted streets of Castelar, a suburb of Buenos Aires. I had no way of knowing that plainclothes policemen, who had perhaps followed me there, were hiding behind the trees. Or maybe they had set up a dragnet for somebody else and caught me. They trained their guns on me, threw me down on the floor of an unmarked car so no one could see me and took me to a nearby police station. The man in charge of the operation ordered the others not to hit me. Soon I was blindfolded and handcuffed and handed over to SIPBA (Intelligence Service of the Police of the province of Buenos Aires), an elite interrogation unit.

My family was notified as soon as I was arrested; I assume that the labor law client I was supposed to meet witnessed my arrest and told a lawyer friend of mine named Manuel Evequoz. (He is now counted among the disappeared.) Manuel immediately went to my parents' apartment, told them what had happened and asked my father to join him to try to find me at the police station. Although they arrived within an hour of my arrest, they were not allowed to speak to anyone. Instead, they were forced to leave the station at gunpoint.

With Manuel's assistance, my father filed a petition for a writ of habeas corpus with a federal judge named Carlos Molteni. Molteni immediately issued requests to the police in order to determine my whereabouts. This took about three days, but it did limit the torture to which I was subjected. Molteni—who acted in my case and in many others in faithful observance of his duties—himself was arrested on the day of the military coup—March 24, 1976—and brought to the same prison in La Plata where I was being held.

The police eventually told Molteni that I was being held in the Eighth Precinct in La Plata, about thirty miles from where I was actually detained. After another eight days of isolation, a judge finally interviewed me and allowed my family to bring clothes and food. I was then transferred to the Unit 9 penitentiary, also in La Plata, where I would be held for the next eighteen months.

At Unit 9, I was placed in one of two cellblocks dedicated to political prisoners. As we shared notes about the treatment we had received before our detention was "legalized," it became apparent that virtually everyone had been tortured, and most of us with the electric prod.

Even today I think of my eighteen months in prison as a time of utter desolation. I missed my wife and two young sons constantly, although they came to see me as often as was allowed.

Unit 9 of La Plata was one of Argentina's maximum security prisons. Located on the outskirts of the city, it was surrounded by high walls, with turrets and guard posts topped with barbed wire. Cells were designed for a single prisoner and could be locked for as many hours or days as the prison authorities wished. They had a heavy solid door locked from the outside with an opening to pass food, which the guards also used to spy on inmates. There was also a small window with thick bars overlooking a prison yard. Each cell had a sink, a toilet, an iron bed, a stool and a cement table. When the slots in the door were not locked from the outside, we could use them to communicate with those in cells across the corridor. Conditions were deplorable, and bedbugs were a constant problem. We tried to burn them with kerosene, but they simply moved to the next cell. It was hard to fill the long hours, especially when at the whim of some guard we were shut in. After the military coup, when conditions worsened, we spent much of the time in some form of solitary confinement. Despite these oppressive conditions, I also remember being inspired by the bravery and wisdom of fellow inmates and their determination to counter the rigors of prison life with the beliefs in social justice and change that had landed us all there.

In the first few weeks of my detention, political detainees were allowed "open cellblock" for about twelve hours a day and almost exclusive use of the exercise yard, a cement-paved basketball court, where we could walk and exercise. We could meet in groups or seek privacy if we wanted. Early on we were permitted two visits a week. We also had unlimited use of the prison's library and of radios and relatively uncensored access to books, magazines and newspapers that our families bought for us. Due to a history of ulcers, I was allowed what the prison doctors called the "special diet." This meant that, instead of the horrible food they gave everyone else, I got a piece of meat, often spoiled, at each meal. Everyone entitled to the "special" would share half of it with another inmate on a rotating basis. We were given four pieces of bread, and I remember resisting hunger in order to make them last the whole day.

Shortly before the end of her government, Isabel Perón decreed that those held in administrative detention and wishing to exercise the "right of option" (to leave the country rather than remain in prison) could not go to any country in the Western Hemisphere. I had a judicial order mandating my departure through a writ of habeas corpus, but my lawyers wanted to test the constitutionality of the decree and suggested that I insist on going to Peru rather than changing my destination to Europe, until we fought that legal battle. My family, however, decided that I must leave prison as soon as possible to wherever I could be free and reunite with my wife and children. My mother came to the prison on the next visit and asked to talk to me and to Ángel Georgiadis together. (At the time, we could visit with other inmates' families.) Ángel was opposition group Montonero's top-ranking leader in Unit 9 at that time, and the lawyers wanted him to make the decision about my destination. I was not obliged to follow his orders, but my fellow inmates and I wanted to make important decisions after consultation and in coordination with each other. My mother, a petite and very gentle lady, had steeled herself for a difficult conversation. To her surprise, Ángel—as kind a soul as one could imagine despite his long military experience in urban guerrilla activities—agreed and immediately communicated his decision to the outside via a smuggled message. Nevertheless, by mid-March 1976, I was still in prison, still preparing to leave Argentina with my family. We were waiting only for the court to issue a new order changing my destination and for the administrative authorities to instruct the police to take me to the airport to catch the flight that would take me and my family to freedom.

On March 24, the military junta ousted Isabel Perón. Everyone in the country had expected the coup; the military commanders had stated clearly that they were impatient with the corruption in her government and the fact that its ruthless counterinsurgency methods were only creating conditions for the insurgents to grow in popularity and power. Like many other coups in our history, this one was bloodless. Isabel was put under house arrest. The armed forces arrested a few well-known political and trade union leaders, most of them left of center, and then arrested thousands of the poor, workers, students and professionals. The army took control of Unit 9 and all other prisons. It also suspended the right of option for an indefinite period (which lasted the entire seven years of the dictatorship). Under the army's command, Unit 9 was one of several high-security prisons dedicated to political detainees. It was overcrowded because of the new influx of prisoners, and now most single-person cells held two inmates. If your cellmate shared your vision of the discipline and solidarity needed to resist, the companionship proved a buffer against loneliness and despair. I had four different cellmates through internal cellblock transfers, and although we did not necessarily share political views, each man was a source of moral support and companionship. Juan Ortiz and I had heated political discussions, but he was a good friend. The wife of another cellmate, Luis Iglesias, disappeared while he was sharing his cell with me.

All but a dozen or so common criminals were transferred out (the most subservient to the authorities and willing to act as spies, although ostensibly they were kept in Unit 9 to work in the kitchen, on clean-up details and so on), and political prisoners were transferred in from other prisons. Many came directly from the clandestine detention centers that the junta used for unacknowledged detention, if their captors felt that no further "intelligence" could be extracted from them through torture, and they were among the few who would not be killed and their corpses hidden. Others came from other political prisons. During one of those "transfers," we heard cries of pain and anguish in another cellblock where about a hundred new inmates were being beaten; the haunting cries seemed to last for hours. The open cell hours and exercise were sharply curtailed; newspapers were forbidden for weeks at a time and censored when allowed; radios were taken away; and the additional food that our families brought (and which we shared with everyone in the cellblock) was prohibited. In addition, guards who had been generally lenient or indifferent were ordered to tighten the screws. Some became physically abusive, and almost all addressed us in ways designed to provoke angry reactions so that they could punish us.

Periodically they brought in armed soldiers and shock troops from corrections headquarters and conducted unannounced, very violent searches (*requisas*) during which we were made to run through gauntlets of guards armed with batons who beat and kicked us. After hours of intimidation and frequent, random physical attacks, we would return to our cells to find that all our personal possessions—extra clothes, family photographs, letters from home, reading and writing materials and the like—had been taken away.

As the aggressive treatment grew in intensity, the guards used the punishment cells—*chanchos*—more frequently, almost always due to imaginary violations of prison discipline. At first they had been used only occasionally, but now they were turned into a specific form of harassment and cruel treatment. Many of my friends were held in these isolation cells for weeks at a time. The cells had no windows, beds or toilets, except for a hole in the ground. Inmates were held there around the clock, and food was scarce and generally inedible, even worse than what they brought to the cellblocks. Gangs of guards would enter the cells and beat inmates. I was taken to the chanchos once, together with my good friend Francisco "Barba" Gutiérrez, a young trade union leader. I still do not know why we were put into isolation; perhaps some guard thought we had not looked submissive enough when he inspected our cellblock and spewed verbal abuse at us. I was not beaten that time, but the three interminable days and nights I spent in solitary confinement was enough to give me a sense of how quickly one could be driven to despair and madness through boredom, loneliness and fear. I also missed a family visit, which made my relatives very anxious when they came to Unit 9 and were told they could not see me. Barba spent almost eight years in detention without being charged; the time we went to the chanchos together was not his only stay there.

Treatment from prison staff became progressively more violent and harsh. I was directly persecuted by one of the guards, a law student who hated me perhaps because I was a lawyer and still was willing to jeopardize my professional career out of political convictions while he was struggling with law school. Once he locked all the cells in the cellblock (thus depriving us of our daily exercise break) and called out that if anybody spoke, he would punish Méndez. Either out of fear or solidarity, not one of my nearly hundred fellow inmates in that cellblock took the bait. Other guards used beatings, threats, and isolation and curtailed benefits, such as visits. These punishments were often meted out arbitrarily against prisoners a particular officer did not like. It is important to note, however, that some decent men refused to treat prisoners in this way. I remember a certain corrections employee who honorably refused to follow the trend toward dehumanizing treatment. He never participated in the beatings and argued with other guards who yelled at or insulted us. Other guards accused him of supporting us "terrorists" and teased him about not following the instructions of their military masters. In Argentina in 1976, even a hint of sympathy toward "subversives" in La Plata was a dangerous cloud hanging over anyone, but especially over a corrections employee. And yet this honorable man never allowed himself to be dragged into inhumanity.

To pass the time, I read a lot. In fact, I read more than at any other time in my life, and more systematically. I studied the Spanish Civil War with other inmates and then discussed it in study groups. I wrote a lot of letters, of course. And I prayed, more or less reserving certain hours of the day for prayer. My experience with prayer in such circumstances is a reaffirmation of the saying "There are no atheists in the trenches." In those years, I was not yet an agnostic, as I am now, and although I no longer went to church, I considered myself a "practical Christian." I thought a lot about "liberation theology" and its focus on social justice through the church and how it helped me understand my predicament and justify my life choices.

At the end of 1976, my family and I had to face another very painful and terrifying situation: Seven lawyers who had practiced with me were captured in quick succession (all of them eventually would be listed among the "disappeared" of Argentina). Roberto Fassi, who had been my attorney early on and had loyally assisted Silvia, even as the filing of briefs in favor of political prisoners was becoming increasingly hazardous, was the last of the seven to be arrested, and we knew that he had Silvia's phone number. It was clear that the police seized appointment and contact books and followed them as leads; as a lawyer herself and the wife of a political prisoner, Silvia would surely be a target. My mother-in-law came on a visit with my parents to try to convince me to let Silvia and the boys go to Brazil and wait for me there. There was no need to convince me. I hated to see them go and would miss their visits, but I hated much more the possibility of living without Silvia if she were caught, especially now that prisoners were no longer being held in legally recognized prisons. I actually begged them to tell Silvia to leave as soon as possible. The visit was, of course, very emotional.

Silvia, Juanfra and Camilo left in December 1976 for Sao Paulo, where they waited with friends until I was allowed to go into exile. In late January 1977, my father learned through the radio that the government would allow me and six other prisoners to exercise the right of option and leave the country. I had to wait another six weeks for this to happen, and during that time, prison conditions took a turn for the worse, both for me personally and for the whole of the Unit 9 population. Army contingents made increasingly frequent visits, descending from helicopters into the prison yards and pointing machine guns at the prisoners. The authorities engineered an internal classification system of all inmates following some criterion of dangerousness and then transferred men violently from one cellblock to another. These transfers took place over several weeks, and it became apparent that officials were classifying us with the help of a few fellow political prisoners who had broken down and were collaborating with our jailers by providing intelligence about who belonged to which political organization. The information seemed quite accurate in general, and Cellblocks 1 and 2 were reserved for those known to be highest-ranking among the Montoneros and Ejército Revolucionario del Pueblo (ERP) guerrilla groups.[1]

Soon, however, it became clear that the treasonous inmates had run out of information and were trying to stay useful by making guesses. As a result, I was sent to Cellblock 1 for the last five weeks of my imprisonment, even after I had been authorized to leave the country and while my paperwork was being processed. Perhaps the prison authorities knew full well that I was soon heading for exile and wanted to give me a taste of the cruel treatment to which my friends would be subjected in the following years.

We called Cellblocks 1 and 2 death row, because periodically the army came and took inmates away. The inmates in those cellblocks were segregated from the rest of the prison population and were held one to a cell during long hours of isolation. They were allowed only short walks in a special yard each day. Days before my transfer to Cellblock 1, in January 1977, Dardo Cabo and Roberto Rufino Pirles were taken away and delivered to army officers. They were killed in the next few days; the official version—the only one published in the newspapers—was that they had tried to escape during a transfer to another prison. The murders were announced the same day that my father had come to see me. The visits had become more and more repressive; Unit 9 had no *locutorios* (booths with glass and microphones) for visits or even windows with bars, as other prisons had. Visits took place in a large room where previously inmates and families had been allowed to walk around, chat, hug. Under instructions from the army, visitors now were forced to sit on benches across from the inmates, without touching, and leaving enough room for the guards to walk by frequently.

That day, we happened to sit next to Horacio Rappaport and his father. Horacio, a young architect, had spent more than a year in the same cellblock with me, but now he was in Cellblock 1. His father, a very successful businessman in the construction industry, had just returned from a trip to the United States. Horacio was very agitated over the deaths of Cabo and Pirles and asked his father if he had tried to talk to Senator Ted Kennedy or others in Washington. He had not; perhaps he felt that such approaches would be useless. Horacio and I, joined by my father, tried to persuade him that any and all possible pleas for assistance should be made, given the inherent danger of our situation.

That same day, Horacio and two other Cellblock 1 inmates (one of them was Ángel Georgiadis) were taken away and delivered to the military. When I arrived in the cellblock, the men had been gone two or three days and no one knew what had happened to them. A few days later, we learned that the wives of Horacio and Ángel had received telegrams saying that they had committed suicide while under interrogation. The women were not allowed to see the corpses, and the families were forced to bury them right away, although they were exhumed years later, when the junta's crimes were being investigated.

The death of our friends filled all of us in death row with doom. My family was anxious and tried to accelerate my departure while also trying to ensure my safety. An acquaintance who was a centrist politician acceded to my father's request and contacted a general who told him that I would be allowed to leave as planned. When my father's friend mentioned the deaths of four inmates from the same cellblock where I was now being held and the family's fear that some underling might do the same to me, the general told him that matters of security and prisoners would not be left to underlings. Perhaps my family was momentarily reassured, but they were also convinced—as if they needed convincing, a year into the new military dictatorship— of the planned and "official" nature of the crimes being committed in the name of the struggle against subversion.

Another inmate and I were transferred out of Cellblock 1 and Unit 9 late one morning in February 1977, the weekend before Carnival.[2] We were placed in a truck with individual cells in which we were forced to stand. The cells had no windows or bars, but we could see the street through thin louvered slits. We noticed that we were escorted by two other trucks with about twenty soldiers armed with machine guns and a lead car with another soldier wielding a machine gun from a turret. I could tell that we were crossing the city of La Plata and then, to my dismay, we were turning away from the road to Buenos Aires. We entered a military compound that I surmised was Regiment 7, where Horacio's widow had been summoned to retrieve his casket, as we had learned through the visits of relatives. We were not taken from the truck, but the hour or so we spent there was the most frightful sixty minutes of my life. Eventually we were on our way again, escorted now by a helicopter as well. With sirens blaring, our caravan pushed other cars and passersby aside and threatened and intimidated them with an ostentatious display of weapons. When we reached Buenos Aires, in a lower-middle-class neighborhood and during a traffic jam, the soldiers threatened an old man, forcing him to run inside his house, and then laughed at his reaction.

Another family visiting an inmate that day was able to tell my family that I had been taken away. My parents spent the whole four-day weekend trying unsuccessfully to find out where I was. Unit 9 authorities confirmed only that the army had taken me away. Silvia and my two sons had left for Brazil three months earlier, so she learned about all of this, including the deaths of our friends, only when we were reunited. My parents preferred not to share their anxiety about my whereabouts during those four days. On Wednesday after Carnival, they finally learned that I was in Villa Devoto, the main federal prison in Buenos Aires. In Villa Devoto I was in open cells and I had asked a nonpolitical detainee if his visiting family could call my parents. That same day I was transferred to Federal Police headquarters in downtown Buenos Aires, where my parents could visit with me. A few days later, after my family presented my renewed passport and an airline ticket, I was taken to Ezeiza Airport by three police officers. Family and friends came to see me off, and a female police officer was kind enough to stand by and let me talk to them before the plane departed. My passport was given to the pilot, and I did not get it until I arrived in Paris, where I would await Silvia's arrival. Paris was a great destination for a reunion of this sort, but in fact the site was chosen for us by circumstances: the prohibition to go to a country in the Western Hemisphere, enacted by Isabel Perón, was still in effect.

I was nervous about arriving in France and being presented to an immigration officer with my passport being held by the airline and an indication that I was being expelled from my own country. I knew that when one inmate had arrived in Mexico, he was returned and spent several more months in prison. Thankfully this was not a common occurrence. As it happened, the commander of the Argentine Airlines flight was a good friend of another pilot whose son had just disappeared, so he invited me to sit in first class in the relatively empty plane, to see if I had something to tell him that would help his friend. Unfortunately, I did not. On the second leg (Madrid–Paris), there was another crew, but by then they knew about me. The flight attendants were union leaders and also wanted to talk to me. In the end, they radioed the Argentine Airlines ground crew in Paris, and they gave me my passport before I passed, uneventfully, through immigration and customs. Then I was all alone. I had an address in Paris to go to, but I did not know who was there. I spoke no French and, in addition to very light baggage, I had about $150 in my pocket. Silvia had sent me that one address via my parents, but due to security concerns, names had been omitted. I spent that night in a small hotel, and the next morning I made contact—I don't remember how—with friends living in Paris. A few days later, Silvia arrived from Brazil with my two sons. A friend of mine had taken me to Orly Airport to meet them, and even he was overwhelmed by my emotion in being able to hug my family again. Later that day, Silvia and I walked around a quaint suburb, and I told her the dire news about the murders of Ángel and Horacio, husbands of the two best friends she had made during the painful visits to Unit 9.

During the eleven months after the coup, judges had issued at least three orders directing the Ministry of the Interior to allow me to go into exile. Prosecutors had signed off on those orders, which were based on the fact that the suspension of the right of option could not affect my right to leave; before that suspension, I had received final judicial decisions allowing my travel, and those decisions were, in legal parlance, *res judicata*, nonreviewable. Yet the government ignored those warrants even after my family made reservations on flights leaving for Europe. I should have been able to leave within days or weeks; as it happened, it took almost a full year before the matter reached the supreme court. But before the court could decide, the minister of the interior reversed his position and allowed seven of us—out of nearly eight thousand prisoners held under the state of siege—to leave the country. In contrast, my friend Barba, whose case was proceeding at a similar pace as mine before the coup, had decided to follow the advice of our lawyers and test the constitutionality of the decree prohibiting travel to Western Hemisphere countries. At the time of the coup, his judicial warrant was still subject to appeal. Because of this twist of fate or legal technicality, he spent eight years in administrative detention

without charges. Others spent an average of four years before being
released or allowed to leave for exile.

During my imprisonment, Silvia and my extended family attempted
to conduct as normal a life as possible. In addition to the pilgrimage
through courts and Ministry of Interior offices, where they also faced
long waiting hours and denigrating treatment from petty bureaucrats
and military officers, they had to meet with friends and lawyers in
conditions of increasing insecurity, at coffeehouses where waits for another person of longer than ten minutes could lead to arrest. Some dear
friends turned their backs on Silvia (and on me, indirectly), but most
gave us their love and loyalty at some personal risk, even when they did
not agree with me on fundamental political issues. For example, close
friends stored books and magazines for me when we feared searches
and those publications would have compromised our security.

Before becoming a lawyer, I had played rugby in Mar del Plata
for many years and made many lasting friends. Among them, Ricardo
Sepe, an economist, stands out. As mentioned, he testified at my pretrial hearing that ended my first short-term arrest. He was in Buenos Aires on business when news came of my second arrest, and he
dropped what he was doing and drove my relatives and lawyers on
urgent trips to La Plata to file writs of habeas corpus to try to "legalize" my detention. He was the only friend (other than family members)
who visited me in prison, despite the fact that by doing so his name
could have been recorded as having visited political prisoners. During
the years I spent in prison, he went to Rome to ask an Argentine cardinal (Eduardo Pironio, formerly the bishop of Mar del Plata, who had
been called to the Vatican to save him from right-wing threats against
his life) to intercede on my behalf. Ricardo lived for some years in London and kept regular contacts with Amnesty International (AI), thus
ensuring that I would be adopted by AI as a "prisoner of conscience."

I also had support from far away. I had lived with an American
family named Hutchison in Iowa from 1961 to 1962 during a one-
year foreign exchange program through the American Field Service.
Since that time, I have maintained frequent and loving contact with
my American family. The Hutchisons were not particularly political

people and most certainly not activists. But they were sincere and ethical, and they were passionate about helping me. As soon as the brother closest to my age, John, by then a pharmacist, learned of my predicament in Argentina, he started a campaign to get me out of prison, even though he had not seen me in fifteen years. In addition to feeding to Amnesty International information that he received from my family in Argentina, he secured the support of several senators and members of the U.S. Congress from both sides of the aisle, who wrote letters to the State Department and to the Argentine embassy in Washington inquiring about me.

IN ARBITRARY ARREST, the uncertainty about how long detention will last cuts both ways: On one hand, it allows the inmate to hope that the ordeal will end sooner rather than later. Knowing that there is a fixed, long term ahead must be heartbreaking for inmates and for their families. But *not* knowing when it will end and understanding that there is no effective remedy that can be sought through the courts to end the detention is also nightmarish. In addition, the inmate knows that his captors are aware of his innocence; otherwise, they would file charges. Of course, I mean "innocence" here in the sense of the criminal law; I was well aware that for the military dictatorship—and for the right-wing government of Isabel Perón that had originally placed me in administrative detention under the state of siege—I belonged to a category of persons who were guilty of what they called "subversion," a concept that was much broader than any criminal activity and for which there was no need to have judicial determinations.

About 80 percent of the political prisoners in Argentina (not including the much larger number of the disappeared) between 1974 and 1983 were held under PEN (Poder Ejecutivo Nacional) detention, that is, at the discretion of the executive branch due to the state of siege. Habeas corpus supposedly was available, but the government always responded to judicial inquiries with the same formula—"This person's detention is necessary for the peace and security of the nation"—and judges failed to demand a reasonable standard of evidence.

The remaining 20 percent of prisoners were held under charges before federal courts or—in a smaller number—by military courts that the junta had endowed, against the constitution, with jurisdiction to try civilians. Even those prosecuted under civilian courts were not getting fair trials, since courts refused to throw out evidence obtained under torture, and virtually every political prisoner was tortured.

Arbitrary arrest takes a toll on the inmate and on his family. That is why international law recognizes it as a violation of human rights. Major human rights treaties do allow governments to suspend certain rights during emergencies that endanger "the life of the nation," and the right to be free from arbitrary arrest is one of those derogable rights. Many constitutions allow the same; the Argentine constitution does so in Article 23, but immediately qualifies the severe powers awarded to the executive branch through the "right of option," which I mentioned earlier: The executive can arrest persons and transfer them around the country unless they choose voluntarily to leave the country. Treaties authorize governments to detain persons without charges during emergencies, but that power is surrounded by strict guarantees, such as the ability to seek judicial review of the reasons for the state of emergency and for each specific measure applied to individuals under such powers. International human rights law establishes a very fundamental "right to a remedy" by which governments must afford victims of any violation access to courts to review the action and correct the problem. The right to a remedy or, more plainly, the right to justice cannot be suspended even in times of emergency. In implementing the right to a remedy against arbitrary arrest, judges are bound to demand specific reasons from the executive and to scrutinize them carefully; the longer the period of incarceration, the higher the burden on the executive to show that the emergency justifies detaining the individual. Arbitrary arrest is a serious violation of human rights; prolonged arbitrary arrest, if conducted in large numbers and as a matter of policy, ranks even higher. Indeed, together with disappearances, torture, extrajudicial executions, forced deportations and the like, prolonged arbitrary detention constitutes a crime against humanity that the international community vows to investigate, prosecute and punish if it is conducted in a widespread or systematic fashion.

I can only imagine how much worse the suffering was for Silvia, my children and my parents and siblings. For a three-week period right after the coup, no visits were allowed at all and no communication of any sort was possible. Once visits were allowed, family members had to endure demeaning searches every time they visited, along with long trips to another city and then long lines and long waits. They had to go back to Buenos Aires at the end of the visit with the sorrow of seeing me in prison, even if I tried to cheer them up and reassure them that my spirits were high. I learned later that my son Camilo, four years old, cried for the whole one-hour trip back to Buenos Aires with my father, saying that he (Camilo) knew that we would never go to France or anywhere else and that I was never going to be released from prison. My father never forgot that somber trip back from a prison visit. My family also had to read my letters (mostly smuggled out) and imagine how I spent my days and what I was really thinking regarding my chances to leave the country.

In my work as a staff attorney at Human Rights Watch from 1982 to 1996, I had many occasions to investigate arbitrary arrest and dire prison conditions in many countries. I visited prisons in the United States, Nicaragua, Guatemala, Mexico, Honduras, Peru, Brazil, Argentina and Venezuela. My colleagues and I researched and published reports on those countries plus Chile and Cuba. We designed protocols regarding what to look for in detention centers and insisted on interviewing prisoners whom we selected ourselves, without witnesses, a procedure pioneered by the International Committee of the Red Cross. We advocated for the immediate release of those who had not been charged and for judicial review of detention orders.

There are many ways in which governments violate the international law prohibition against prolonged arbitrary arrest. An arrest can be arbitrary even if it is cloaked in some legal formalities. For example, an arrest is arbitrary if a person is thrown in jail on trumped-up charges and courts refuse to offer redress or if the charges are not trumped-up but themselves violate a fundamental right, such as freedom of expression or association. Such is the case of Chinese dissident

Liu Xiaobo, who is currently serving an eleven-year term for publicly petitioning the government for democratic changes. His Nobel Peace Prize for 2010 is a great step toward worldwide awareness of the need to uphold the prohibition against prolonged arbitrary arrest, even when it concerns a powerful country.

Other times, persons are arrested on reasonable grounds, but courts allow them to linger in prison for long periods without bringing them to trial; this was the case with about 130,000 Rwandans accused of participating in the 1994 genocide. Years later, the number of those imprisoned dwindled after many of them were subjected to the so-called gacaca courts (community-based trials) and others were finally released. Pretrial detention is supposed to be the exception, not the norm, according to human rights instruments. Unfortunately, due to underdeveloped judicial structures, it is all too frequent throughout the world.

Another form of prolonged arbitrary arrest happens when states invoke a state of emergency, as Argentina did during the time I was imprisoned. Thanks in large part to the efforts of the worldwide human rights movement, detention under a state of emergency is much less frequent nowadays. Its injustices are easy to document, and states that practice it are stigmatized.

In addition to the types of arbitrary detention already described, we must consider the cases in which inmates are held—whether preventively or after sentencing—under criminal charges based on evidence obtained unfairly, particularly if gathered by investigators who use torture as the preferred method of investigation. If courts do not exclude evidence obtained under torture, trials themselves are unfair, and the resulting detentions are arbitrary.

Another category of prolonged arbitrary arrest has gained some attention recently and presents a serious challenge to the human rights movement: States that are involved in an international conflict now arrest and detain "enemy combatants" for the duration of the hostilities. As will be seen in chapter 7, the Geneva Conventions authorize such detentions as "prisoners of war." In fact, it is a reasonable and humane way to deal with the consequences of combat, and it is part of the obligation of states to refrain from killing enemy soldiers who have been captured and are out of combat due to wounds or surrender. Unless they have committed war crimes, enemies so held must not be prosecuted but should be returned to their country at the end of hostilities. A serious human rights problem arises because states are now defining "hostilities" in ever-broader and more elastic ways. Consider arrests by the Israel Defense Forces of Palestinians who are not accused of crimes but are held in indefinite detention on suspicion that they are armed activists who resist the occupation of the West Bank and Gaza. Some have been held under that status for many years, since the "war" between Israel and Palestinian armed organizations has been going on for decades, with no end in sight. The U.S. government held hundreds of prisoners in Guantanamo Bay under this rubric after 2001 in the so-called war on terror. The Obama administration has released some but not all of these prisoners. As of 2011, the U.S. government is not incarcerating others in Guantanamo and continues to insist that its goal is to close down the detention camp. It is sending some prisoners to be tried in federal courts, releasing others to countries that will accept them and submitting others to trial by military commissions (under less-than-complete due process and fair trial guarantees). Unfortunately, in March 2011 the Obama administration announced that it will institute some form of indefinite detention without trial for a number of prisoners it will never release, under a still-undefined legal basis that presumably extends beyond the legitimate category of enemy combatant. If so, individuals captured in non–combat-related situations, and against whom no charges will be filed, will be held by the United States in prolonged arbitrary detention. Some periodic review of their status is contemplated, but not full-fledged judicial protection against arbitrary deprivation of freedom.

There may be a sound legal basis to hold "high-value" detainees captured in combat until the end of hostilities, whether held in Guantanamo or at prisons at the theater of war, provided the "hostilities" are reasonably defined in terms of geographic scope and duration. But others captured in law enforcement operations (by American or other forces) should be charged or released. The concept of "hostilities" that can justify holding enemy soldiers should not be used as a rhetorical device to abuse the principle of personal freedom. A "war" has to have a temporal and geographic dimension, and "hostilities" and "combat" should be understood in terms of the laws of armed conflict, not as rhetorical analogies. The "war on terror" cannot be an open-ended struggle involving both military and law enforcement operations against vaguely identified and shifting terrorist organizations without making a mockery of the prohibition on prolonged arbitrary arrest.

It is clear that arbitrary detention comes in many forms, and all must be considered when looking for ways to counter its practice in states and regimes around the world.

CHAPTER TWO

TORTURE

On September 29, 2010, the president of the United Nations (UN) Human Rights Council appointed me the Special Rapporteur on Torture and Other Cruel, Inhuman or Degrading Treatment or Punishment. The mandate of the special rapporteur dates back to a 1985 resolution issued by the former UN Commission on Human Rights, and it has become one of the most effective and respected of the Geneva-based human rights protections.[1] It is also enormous in scope, as it includes prison conditions that may amount to torture or cruel, inhuman or degrading treatment, and because some form of torture or mistreatment is happening at any moment in at least half the countries of the world. The special rapporteur acts on complaints about torture, examines conditions and treatment in prisons and detention centers, conducts on-site country visits and formulates recommendations to prevent torture and to strengthen national protections against it. His reports to the UN Human Rights Council and to the General Assembly are widely disseminated and discussed.

It is particularly significant to me that I was chosen from among a large list of very capable candidates as the first Latin American and the first torture victim to occupy the position. I hope to bring to the job a special empathy with victims and that my approach to prevention and punishment of the crime of torture will be victim centered.

The prohibition against torture and cruel, inhuman or degrading treatment or punishment has a special place in the human rights canon. It is widely accepted that torture is illegal and immoral, yet it is practiced in many countries, either as a routine method of investigation of crimes or "justified" by exceptional circumstances.

Descriptions of torture can shock the conscience and mobilize those confronted with its insidious nature into action. Soon after I was tortured, in the late 1970s, I joined a worldwide Amnesty International (AI) campaign against torture premised on the notion that, with a consistent, determined effort by democratic governments and international organizations supported by common men and women across borders, torture could be abolished in our time just as the African slave trade had been abolished a century earlier.

All national sections of the worldwide movement staged rallies, lobbied their governments, publicized detailed accounts of torture inflicted on prisoners and proposed measures to be adopted against regimes that practiced torture and individual torturers. As part of that campaign, I visited many U.S. cities and college campuses describing my experience and offering some suggestions as to what could be done. On my first U.S. appearance, in Chicago in 1978, I heard the South African poet Dennis Brutus describe conditions in Robben Island and heard for the first time the name of Nelson Mandela. Although there certainly have been important victories in this campaign and its successive incarnations, the sad fact is that the practice of torture and of cruel, inhuman or degrading treatment or punishment still is widespread. It is used as a method of interrogation or as incidental to hard labor or, as in China today, to force prisoners to renounce religious beliefs like the Falun Gong or to force Tibetans to denounce the Dalai Lama.

Two factors account for the continued use of torture in our world. One factor is the neglect that incarcerated men and women face in prison systems in most countries, even in wealthy countries. In international law, cruel, inhuman or degrading treatment or punishment and torture are ranked by severity; the term *torture* is reserved for treatment that causes greater pain or suffering, either physical or psychological. For that reason, harsh conditions of detention generally are considered cruel, inhuman or degrading treatment. In extreme cases—which unfortunately are not rare—prison conditions are so brutal that they amount to torture even without deliberate infliction of bodily harm. Overcrowding can be so severe that inmates lose all privacy and are subjected to inmate-on-inmate violence, often promoted by guards. In some poor countries, prisoners have to take turns sleeping, and the lack of sanitary facilities means that they constantly are exposed to stench, filth and disease. In most prisons around the world, juveniles and children are not adequately separated from the adult prison population. In Equatorial Guinea, women are not separated from men, resulting in rape and sexual violence. In extreme cases, food and water are so scarce that malnutrition becomes an added penalty.

The other factor is the attempt by some to rationalize the use of what they euphemistically call "enhanced interrogation techniques" or, worse, to redefine certain cruelties as not constituting torture and thereby pretend they are legal or at least not punishable. In truth, the torments men and women face under techniques such as waterboarding, sleep deprivation and stress positions were shocking in the Middle Ages and must be included in today's definition of torture. What the proponents of enhanced interrogation techniques do not tell us is that they generally are applied in combination and in increasing intensity; something that may seem relatively mild in and of itself is actually very brutal when implemented. The real harm of this linguistic ploy is that it persuades large segments of the public that torture is acceptable and a small price to pay for security. For as long as victims of this treatment are persons whose names we cannot pronounce and whose faces we refuse to see, the human rights movement will face an uphill challenge.

In Latin America, torture was used by military dictatorships that— no matter how tight their grip on power—always were conscious of the need to persuade at least a segment of the population that what they were doing was morally sound. Those regimes refused to admit that what they did was torture and demanded that the public accept a level of brutality in order to feel secure against "subversion" and "terrorism." But societies pay a high price for the state-sponsored torture of suspects. Soldiers and law enforcement officers are demeaned and discredited, and the population grows to distrust the government and its institutions. Even long after the perceived threat is gone, rebuilding trust is very difficult because the relationship between citizens and the armies and police is one of fear, not confidence. States that have engaged in torture also have a very hard time regaining the respect and trust of the international community.[2]

Because of these debates about what is and is not torture, I have been thinking more frequently of the torture to which I was subjected in 1975, when I was thirty years old. I still do not know why I was arrested by plainclothes policemen as I was going to meet with a potential client. Perhaps I was their target, or perhaps they were setting up a covert checkpoint to arrest people who seemed out of place in that remote suburb. My family learned of my arrest almost immediately; their efforts on my behalf did not obtain my immediate release but certainly limited the amount of torture to which I was subjected. After the initial arrest, I was turned over to a special group of interrogators who drove me around, blindfolded and on the floor of a car, to undisclosed locations where for the next forty-eight hours I would be savagely tortured. As they drove, they spoke incessantly in menacing tones and made it clear that I was in their power and that there was nothing anyone could do to protect me. During those car rides, I tried to prepare myself for what I knew was coming; my defense work had made me familiar with the torture methods applied against persons suspected of "subversive activities."

I thought about my friend and colleague Manuel Evequoz, who like me defended arrested activists as soon as they were remanded to courts. Manuel was concerned with how much information actually was conveyed by the victims to the torturers and had drafted a memo on what he called "defensive combat." He thought that many young people were ready to give up their lives in shoot-outs with the oligarchic army or police but were not prepared to resist when they were under enemy control. He advocated complete silence; torture victims should supply only minimal information, something akin to the name, rank and serial number that soldiers are instructed to give when captured, and then remain absolutely silent. His main point was that all activists should be prepared to withstand torture. I had been skeptical that such preparation was possible, but on that fateful night of August 26, 1975, I found myself trying to follow his advice.

In at least four different places in the suburbs of Buenos Aires, I was interrogated under beatings and application of the electric prod called the *picana* on my genitals, other sensitive areas and ultimately all over my body. The picana was invented specifically for enhanced interrogation. The tool makes a whizzing sound before it is applied, and the operator regulates the intensity of the discharge as well as the length and frequency of each application. I was tied up, spread-eagled on a table (which they called the *parrilla,* or grill), nude but blindfolded and facing up the first time and down on the next session, so as to ensure that not an inch of my body was spared. The pain I suffered with each discharge was so intense that my whole body tensed up; my muscles ached for days afterward. When applied in the mouth, face or head, the shock can cause the victim to black out. Needless to say, I screamed at the top of my lungs; the interrogators assured me that no one could hear me. I received five sessions of the electric prod, each lasting about a half hour or more, during the course of what seemed to be twenty-four hours. The torturer let up intermittently to allow the interrogator to ask a question and me to answer. If the answer was considered inadequate, the prod was applied again, with increased intensity and violence and in a more sustained fashion. More than once I begged my torturers to kill me. They said they would, but later. Years later I think about it and wonder if I really meant it. I think I did, at the time.

I was subjected to psychological pressure as well. My interrogators and torturers talked to me all the time, insulting and threatening to inflict all kinds of harm on me and my family and friends. At least twice they pretended they were executing me by placing a gun to my head or inside my mouth and clicking the trigger. Another time they opened a bottle of natural gas and pretended to rush away because I would be blown up. All of this paled in comparison to the picana, except when they mentioned my children (then three and four years old) and told me they would torture them in my presence. As it happened, my family had not been captured, but I did not know that. There are several well-documented cases of relatives—pregnant wives, elderly parents and even children—being tortured in front of prisoners or nearby, where the prisoners could hear their screams. Twice I was examined by police doctors, mostly to make sure that I was not about to die and could endure more torment. Although I could not see them and they hardly spoke to me, I tried in vain to persuade them to conduct a thorough examination of my wounds and prevent the continuation of torture on medical grounds. I was deprived of sleep, food and water during the whole period of interrogation.

At the end of the fifth session, my torturer told me, in his brand of gallows humor, that he had pumped so much electricity into my body that if he put a lightbulb in my mouth, I would turn it on. Later I was dumped in a cell, still handcuffed and blindfolded, and left there for what seemed like another day or two, during which I had nightmares. They did not allow me to use the bathroom and refused to give me water despite my requests. This was to ensure I would not die; apparently, a person can go into shock if he or she drinks water within hours of being subjected to the picana. At the same time, the passage of electricity leaves one with tremendous thirst. I was not given water or food until the fourth day of my captivity, when my arrest had already been acknowledged. I was held for another eight days, alone and incommunicado, at the Eighth Precinct of La Plata, where I was no longer mistreated.

During those long and lonely days while I awaited transfer to a penitentiary, I was seen briefly by a judge, and my family was allowed to bring in food and medicines for me. I knew from my professional experience that I would not be tortured again after the judge had seen me and my arrest was "legalized." I concentrated on preparing for the coming hearing at which I would be indicted or released. The police had legalized my arrest by claiming that I had been driving a stolen car and carrying weapons. As it turned out, they had not bothered to invent much evidence for those charges. The owner of the stolen car did not recognize me in a lineup, although the police encouraged him to do so. The police also claimed that they had destroyed the weapons I had with me in the process of testing them. This, of course, meant that there was no *corpus delicti* (physical evidence that a crime had been committed). This sloppy police action was more or less standard operating procedure at the time. The security forces were more interested in gaining "intelligence" leading to other persons and were not particularly concerned with gathering evidence for criminal prosecutions. Nevertheless, they had forced me to sign a seizure document in between torture sessions, admitting to possession of illegal weapons. When I was taken to the court to render my first judicial declaration, I was seen by a court doctor, who certified that the marks in my body were consistent with electrical torture; thereupon, the seizure admission was invalidated. A few weeks later, my case was dismissed, but I remained in prison under administrative detention without charges nonetheless.

I tried to take stock of what I said while being tortured, my "defensive combat." Fortunately, I had not given my torturers any clue that they could use to arrest any friends or colleagues. In moments of weakness, I had acknowledged my participation in the Peronist Youth and that, as a lawyer, I took on cases of recently arrested persons and acted in their defense in court as needed. Through their own records, my torturers discovered that earlier, in Mar del Plata, I had denounced police torture and persuaded courts to bust a couple of houses in which the police interrogated prisoners clandestinely. Their need for revenge made them redouble their efforts to break me. Although I had not stuck to the version of name, rank and serial number that Manuel had envisioned, I took solace in the fact that I had not caused the capture and torture of others. In this I had been lucky: I was captured alone, so the police had no way of playing my statements against anyone else's. I had also fallen into a trap or a checkpoint by my mistake, so initially the police did not know what to ask me, other than about my actions as a lawyer. Finally, because Manuel and my parents had acted so quickly after my arrest, the interrogators knew that they were under pressure to produce me alive in the next several hours, a fact confirmed by the petitions for habeas corpus that my family and lawyers presented while I was in clandestine detention.

When I reached the Unit 9 penitentiary in La Plata, I compared notes with my fellow inmates. It turns out that almost everyone had had a similar experience. In those days, detainees were held "in the air," meaning that their arrest was not acknowledged for about a week, during which time they were tortured twice a day. In my case, the period of unacknowledged detention was reduced to seventy-two hours, but I was tortured five times in twenty-four hours. Although picana was the torture method of choice in Argentina, several other prisoners also were "submarined" (had their heads plunged into a bucket of water until they nearly drowned). About a hundred women held in nearby Olmos prison (with whom we communicated through relatives who visited both prisons) took a survey of the torture they had suffered as of late 1976: almost 100 percent had been physically and mentally tortured, and of all those tortured all had been raped.

Through conversations with other torture survivors, I was able to determine that my torturers belonged to the Servicio de Informaciones of the Police of Buenos Aires (SIPBA), even though during the torture sessions, they addressed each other with military ranks to make us believe we were in the hands of the military. This roving "intelligence-gathering unit"—a euphemism for a torture squad— was allowed to use clandestine facilities in different parts of the greater Buenos Aires area, including police facilities. I figured out the site of at least one place where I was tortured, because I could hear fast traffic at a nearby highway, and at the time there were only two such highways in the city and its surroundings. The site is now a car depot for the police, next to the road connecting the city with the Ezeiza International Airport. I see it every time I arrive in my country and every time I leave.

The "colonel" who led the torture team also handled the picana and gave orders to all other interrogators and torturers. He had a very distinct, coarse voice. Although I do not have any firm evidence, years later I was able to guess his identity: Comisario Miguel Etchecolatz, former chief of SIPBA. In the 1980s, Etchecolatz and others were convicted of torture, disappearances and murder of several victims in the only case, other than the 1985 trial of the junta commanders, to reach that stage before the pseudoamnesty laws interrupted the prosecutions and he was released.[3] According to a newspaper article, at the time of his sentencing in 1986, Etchecolatz shouted obscenities to the court in his characteristic coarse voice. In the most recent cycle of prosecutions after 2005, Etchecolatz was again convicted of other crimes against humanity. He was sentenced to life in prison and is serving his term in the Marcos Paz penitentiary north of Buenos Aires.

Later, when I worked professionally in human rights monitoring and advocacy, I focused on the need to abolish torture. I interviewed countless victims of the Central American wars who had been tortured or mistreated by forces of opposing ideological positions. I remember especially testimony I received in 1984 from Inés Consuelo Murillo, a beautiful young Honduran lawyer who was being held in the country's only women's prison. I was part of a joint mission to the country by Human Rights Watch (HRW), the Lawyers Committee for Human Rights (now Human Rights First) and the Washington Office on Latin America. The authorities had insisted that we visit the prison in the company of the Honduran first lady, because the prison was under her jurisdiction. We asked to interview Inés Consuelo in private. An advisor to the first lady objected and claimed that he was a journalist so he could not be excluded. After a long and tense negotiation, Inés Consuelo was brought before our mission, the first lady, the advisor and the prison authorities. I explained to Inés Consuelo that her case was known to us in the international human rights movement and that we had asked to meet with her in private. Under the circumstances, we would understand if she chose not to talk to us. Inés Consuelo, a very brave woman, volunteered to tell us her story anyway. For the next half hour, the wife of the president of Honduras listened in uncomfortable silence to a harrowing story of torture and abuse, including sexual abuse, committed against Inés Consuelo in secret detention centers run by Battalion 316, the Honduran army's interrogation and murder squad.

The rebels in El Salvador and Guatemala and the Sandinista government in Nicaragua publicly claimed that they would not torture their enemies because they themselves had been tortured, and they recognized how important it was for their cause to distinguish themselves from "the enemy" on this important moral issue. It is true that these groups did not use the picana or waterboarding as a matter of policy, but Sandinista security agents did apply vicious psychological pressure on detainees and in some cases also brutal physical mistreatment.

The Convention Against Torture (CAT) of 1984, ratified by more than 100 countries, including the United States, establishes the state's obligation to exclude from judicial proceedings confessions and statements obtained under torture; to afford detainees a quick judicial remedy against mistreatment (usually via habeas corpus); and most especially to investigate, prosecute and punish every act of torture. During the "contra war" of the 1980s, the Sandinistas could rightly claim that they did in fact investigate and punish cases of human rights violations; before leaving office after being voted out in 1990, however, they too passed a broad and unconditional amnesty for themselves, just as Augusto Pinochet in Chile, the Argentine junta and other dictatorships had done.

The CAT was followed in 1985 by an Inter-American Convention to Prevent and Punish Torture, which establishes very similar standards and was ratified by virtually all Latin American countries and some other members of the Organization of American States, but not the United States. The prohibition against torture also is included in human rights treaties of a more general nature, such as the International Covenant on Civil and Political Rights (1966) and the European and American Conventions on Human Rights (1950 and 1969, respectively). The prohibition on torture and the state obligations that flow from each violation, as mentioned above, have long been considered peremptory rules of international law that are binding on all countries, whether they have signed a treaty or not.

At AI and at HRW, I learned that an effective way to fight torture is to monitor and report it. Pressure on governments to prevail on other governments to abolish the practice can only come from concerned citizens who are moved by the stories they read, see and hear about the many manifestations of mankind's cruelty toward other human beings. The stories have to be realistic and even graphic, but not sensationalistic or exploitative. In addition, they have to be credible and as internally consistent as possible. They have to begin with a very personal account from the victims. In order to secure those narratives, one has to be able to establish a rapport with victims and question them in nonaggressive but probing ways. One also needs to seek ways to corroborate the stories as much as possible while at the same time

ensuring victims' and witnesses' safety. It is also important to confront
authorities with the stories and give them a chance to show that the
stories are inaccurate or that some remedy has been put into place by
those in a position to correct the wrongdoing. Field researchers for
human rights organizations have mastered these techniques and apply
them even in the most dangerous situations.

At HRW, we recognized the importance of institutional remedies
(mandated by international law) and researched and reported on their
effectiveness as a deterrent against torture. As a lawyer in Argentina, I
frequently made applications for the writ of habeas corpus on behalf
of recently detained persons. I knew that, properly used, habeas corpus
applications could be an effective tool against torture. I would file petitions even at irregular hours because my colleagues and I knew that if
we waited until the courthouse opened the prisoner would suffer long
hours of nightmarish torment; sometimes we would wake up a judge
in the middle of the night and urge him to communicate with police
immediately to find out the whereabouts of recently detained persons.
Of course, judges' receptivity to being awakened varied widely, but
the Argentine legal culture did accept that habeas corpus cases were,
by definition, urgent. In Central America, I worked with lawyers and
judges to strengthen the effectiveness of habeas corpus and tried to
instill legal reform through our HRW critiques and recommendations.

I also endeavored to bring the exclusionary rule into the law and
practice of Latin American nations. That rule, developed by U.S.
courts, says that evidence obtained in violation of procedural restrictions cannot be used against a defendant in criminal cases. Documents
and physical evidence found in the course of an illegal entry into a
home are therefore not admissible. Only evidence obtained pursuant to
proper search warrants issued by a court can be used in criminal cases.
In the United States, the exclusionary rule is extended via the "fruit
of the poisonous tree" doctrine, which excludes evidence obtained in
an illegal search or seizure as well as all other evidence originated in
that illegal search, even if produced through a regular one.[4] Several
countries have adopted these rules via legislation or judicial decision.
In international law, the rule is similar but less comprehensive: The
Inter-American Convention to Prevent and Punish Torture and the UN

Convention Against Torture both establish that states must exclude from judicial proceedings confessions and statements established as having been obtained under torture, except in cases against a torturer, and then only to show that the statement was made.

In order to exclude confessions or statements obtained under torture, however, courts first must establish that the statement was indeed obtained under torture, which places the burden of showing torture on the defense. It would be better to extend the exclusionary rule to statements obtained under cruel, inhuman or degrading treatment as well (which is not the case under these treaties) or else to apply it to statements obtained in violation of procedural safeguards against self-incrimination, like the well-known Miranda warnings, which is the way the exclusionary rule applies in the United States. The U.S. exclusionary rule is explicitly meant to induce law enforcement officials to respect the law by discouraging illegal behavior. If police officers know that they jeopardize prosecution if they torture offenders, they will strive to obtain evidence and intelligence by legal means.

The moral and practical value of the exclusionary rule is particularly relevant to the debates in the United States. The policies of the George W. Bush administration resulted in many human rights violations. The very fact that proponents of torture feel the need to use the euphemism "enhanced interrogation techniques" for waterboarding, stress positions and sleep deprivation is an admission of the immorality of torture.[5] And yet these same proponents accuse critics of the Bush administration of grandstanding on false moral grounds. Harvard Law professor Alan Dershowitz, for one, defends torture by resurrecting the "ticking bomb scenario."[6] Yet he does not explain how to justify torturing detainees when there is no bomb ticking and the information sought has nothing to do with preventing a deadly attack. To date, no ticking bomb scenario has been involved in the enhanced interrogation of any suspect held during the war on terror since September 11, 2001. The scenario was used to justify torture in the 1970s in Argentina by proponents of the "dirty war" waged by the military against its opponents, but it was widely considered an invalid argument even then. The fact is that in Argentina in the 1970s everyone knew that fear of a ticking bomb is not why torturers torture.

Later the argument surfaced again in Israel to support a deliberate Israel Defense Forces policy to extract intelligence and confessions from Palestinians suspected of terrorism. Dershowitz revives those arguments to propose that judges be allowed to issue "torture warrants." In 1999, the Israeli supreme court declared torture illegal and explicitly rejected the ticking bomb scenario as an argument in a decision about interrogation practices by the General Security Service (GSS) that included shaking, forcing detainees to crouch on their toes for five minutes at a time (the "frog crouch") and forcing them to sit for long periods in a tilted-forward low chair with a sack covering their heads to cause near suffocation and sleep deprivation.[7] The Israeli supreme court declared all these techniques illegal because they are meant to cause unnecessary and cruel suffering. With respect to the "necessity" claim made by the Israeli government, the court said that if interrogators believe in good faith that they are avoiding a greater harm by torturing, they may be covered by a defense of necessity if prosecuted; but the ticking bomb scenario cannot justify an administrative order or practice of torturing all interrogation subjects.

Despite the Israeli supreme court decision, in June 2007, former Bush administration official David Rivkin, blaming administration critics for the fact that the United States could no longer engage in renditions or enhanced interrogation, asked, "Is it inherently the problem of those techniques or is it the fault of the people who drove the debate, who polarized the debate, who postured it in such a way that it is all horrible and inherently evil?"[8] He went on to say that eliminating stressful interrogation techniques was equivalent to eliminating all forms of coercion in our society—from drill sergeants, to parents yelling at children. Rivkin carefully avoided use of the word "torture" in his argument. Comparing the "coercion" applied by parents and drill sergeants to the cruel and deliberate infliction of pain and suffering on a helpless detainee is not only absurd, it is an insult to the intelligence of listeners.

In 2010, it was revealed that several Guantanamo detainees who should be prosecuted and punished for violent acts against the American population will not be tried because their cases have been tainted by torture. In October 2010, a federal district court judge declared a witness's testimony inadmissible because the government discovered his existence as U.S. agents were interrogating the defendant under harsh treatment. To its credit, the Obama Justice Department announced that it would not challenge the ruling; it went ahead with the trial, confident that it had other evidence that was not tainted by torture. The defendant was acquitted of most counts but convicted of one and sentenced to life in prison without parole.[9]

Fortunately, an important difference between the United States since September 11, 2001, and Latin America in the 1970s is that civil society organizations—such as the American Civil Liberties Union, HRW, AI of the United States, Human Rights First and others—resisted the Bush administration's drift toward repression and illegality very effectively from day 1. I have been proud to join these organizations in writings, public statements and testimony as a torture survivor. I also joined the International Center for Transitional Justice in its program on U.S. accountability; I and others revealed the experiences of many other societies and confronted the legacies of abuse by means of truth telling, prosecutions, reparations to victims and institutional reform. Torture has a special place among human rights violations in the canon of international law. Like genocide, war crimes and crimes against humanity, torture is an *international* crime, meaning that its prevention and punishment is a concern of the international community. Torture can be a war crime if committed in the context of armed conflict, whether a civil or international war; it also can be a crime against humanity if committed as part of a widespread or systematic attack on a civilian population.

Significantly, however, a single act of torture also gives rise to state responsibility under international law and to the state's obligation to investigate, prosecute and punish perpetrators. If the state fails in this responsibility, other states can judge acts of torture under the rules of universal jurisdiction; or torturers can be tried by international criminal courts with appropriate jurisdiction. A very important way to fight torture—along with habeas corpus and the exclusionary rule—is to insist on the investigation, prosecution and punishment of every case. Impunity for torture simply encourages repetition and condemns the security forces to an endless vicious cycle of brutality and corruption.

Punishment of each case of torture, especially if done consistently and through fair trial and due process, establishes the principle that those who break the rules of proper law enforcement or military behavior must pay a price. Fundamentally, a society prosecutes and punishes torturers because it considers the prohibition of torture a fundamental value that sustains the kind of society it is or wants to become. Argentina's efforts to complete the cycle of truth and justice for the mass atrocities perpetrated during the years of the dirty war are important for this very reason.

President Obama is to be lauded for issuing, on his first day in office, an executive order banning torture by U.S. agents and restoring the full effectiveness of the Uniform Code of Military Justice (UCMJ). The UCMJ governs disciplinary and criminal cases heard by military courts. In line with international law, the UCMJ prohibits and criminalizes torture under all circumstances. The previous administration had declared the UCMJ inapplicable to actions in the war on terror. In the two-plus years since Obama's executive order, no new cases of torture have been reported. The president not only prohibited torture, but also the use by the Central Intelligence Agency of clandestine detention and torture centers abroad, commonly known as black holes, and extraordinary renditions of detainees to countries where they will be tortured.[10] It appears that those prohibitions are being followed, although it is hard to be certain due to the covert nature of the acts. But the fact that torture may not be practiced now by U.S. agents is not enough.

Like all other nations, the United States is obliged to investigate, prosecute and punish all cases of torture. Yet, in its war on terror, in the few cases where penalties have been imposed, the United States has scapegoated only minor figures. In the best-known scandal of mistreatment—Abu Ghraib prison in Iraq—no senior officer has been investigated for any acts of torture, even though it is clear now that the Bush administration—and President George W. Bush himself, according to his own statements—ordered enhanced interrogation techniques as a matter of policy.

There have been some serious congressional inquiries into some aspects of this problem, but the Obama administration has made efforts to limit them.[11] It is essential, however, that a commission be established to get to the bottom of detention practices and the effect of the infamous torture memos issued at the request of the Bush administration (which disavowed and withdrew them when they were discovered).[12] The United States has a moral and a legal obligation to discover and disclose the truth about torture committed by its agents and to investigate and prosecute those against whom evidence can be found. In addition to these moral and legal obligations, the United States has an obligation to conduct these inquiries in order to restore its standing among the law-abiding nations of the world and its leading role in the promotion and protection of human rights everywhere. If the United States fails in these obligations, it invites other nations to follow the U.S. example of impunity for torture and provides rogue regimes with a ready-made excuse for rejecting international community concerns about their own abuses.

CHAPTER THREE

DISAPPEARANCES

"Disappearances" are by far a more terrifying phenomenon than arbitrary arrest and imprisonment. In Argentina, disappearances were the preferred form of repression in the military's war against subversion after the ousting of Isabel Perón on March 24, 1976. The very night of the coup d'etat, the military implemented a plan based on disappearances, carried out by task forces that included members of various security units under the command of military or naval intelligence. At least thirty thousand persons were arrested, and about half of them were disappeared "temporarily": Their detention, at secret locations, was not acknowledged initially. At least twelve thousand and perhaps as many as fifteen thousand people remain today as the permanent desaparecidos of Argentina: Although they are presumed to be dead, their fates are unknown to this day. The junta used at least 340 clandestine detention centers throughout the country, mostly in police stations or military quarters. Several centers became notorious because of the high number of persons held and tortured there and because they were used for several years. Later it was established that thousands of the disappeared were exterminated when they could no longer provide useful intelligence. The task forces used several methods to hide their corpses: Bodies were thrown from planes into the ocean or into lakes; crematory

ovens seem to have been used in some places; most victims, however, were buried in clandestine cemeteries or in sections of public
cemeteries as "N.N." (name unknown).

Victims who were "temporarily" disappeared were interrogated
under torture; after weeks or months, they were either quietly released
or recycled into the system of "legal" (acknowledged) detention under
the state of siege. A smaller number of such victims were held for more
than two years under harrowing conditions, with their captors trying
to "turn" them into collaborators by getting them to reveal the identities or location of comrades or make appointments with them so that
they could be captured. Under torture, some did succumb to pressure
and served as *dedos* (fingers). Others were forced to cooperate with
their captors in providing political analysis of events. An even smaller
number openly betrayed their previous cause and offered their enthu-
siastic services to the military in its "struggle against subversion." Several were released and sent into exile, where they eventually testified
about their incarceration and revealed details of the practice. With the
return of democracy, other survivors—the temporarily disappeared—
added their own testimonies to the public knowledge of this sinister
policy.

At the time of the 1976 coup d'etat, disappearances were new to
Argentina, but the method had been used for some years as a feature of
repression in Guatemala, Brazil and Chile. More recently, the method
has been used in Turkey, Sri Lanka and the Philippines; it has become
a frequent tool in the arsenal of counterinsurgency. By late 1977, I
was becoming active in the worldwide human rights movement as an
Argentine exile; and since disappearances were the central feature of
the murderous regime in my country, I tried to learn as much as I could
about them. Amnesty International (AI) and other organizations had
received information about an alarming number of persons arrested
at their homes or places of employment and whose relatives were desperate to establish what had happened to them. I met Argentine expatriates who had brothers, sisters and even children caught up in the
junta's action. I was also receiving news of friends and colleagues who
did not escape it. Families of the disappeared traveled to Washington
seeking aid and information about their loved ones, and the network

of exiles in Europe and Latin America circulated testimony from survivors. I carefully studied each account, desperately hoping to learn the fate of dear friends who had disappeared and to try to make sense of the machinery of death that the junta had set in motion.

The practice of forced disappearance defied the tried-and-true methods of the human rights movement to convince governments to release political prisoners. Letter-writing and meetings in embassies were less effective when authorities refused to acknowledge they were holding anyone. Activists had to devise new techniques of advocacy and mobilization more suitable to the characteristics of disappearances.

The first challenge for the human rights movement was to define the practice of forced disappearances in a manner that distinguished it from other human rights violations, such as torture or arbitrary detention. To make some sense of the practice, it was necessary to determine why a government resorts to disappearances as opposed to detention. The deliberate attempt to circumvent any institutional controls, including those of courts, is meant to facilitate interrogation under torture without "interference," but it also has an obvious impact on the rule of law and on the legitimacy of state institutions, such as the military and police. The definition also had to describe how disappearances affect and may even be designed to punish relatives and friends of the targeted person and eventually to terrorize wide sectors of society.

In its simplest form, a disappearance is an unacknowledged detention. It differs from a kidnapping only in that it is perpetrated by one or more state agents acting in an official capacity. A detention also may be unacknowledged because of the malicious intent of a single official or even through negligence; in those cases, the temporary disappearance ends after a few days when the detention is recognized. When the cases of disappearances are numerous and even routine, and when the refusal to acknowledge the location of the person is prolonged or permanent, the phenomenon is very different. Widespread or systematic disappearances are a crime against humanity. Here is my own working definition of disappearances as a policy or practice: The security forces arrest the victim without a warrant. Even when there are multiple witnesses (relatives, fellow workers, passersby), the fact of the arrest is denied from the start, including in response to judicial inquiries. Victims are taken to clandestine detention centers where they are interrogated without limits either in time or in intensity of the torture inflicted. Eventually they are murdered by their captors, and their remains are hidden. Their captors and their superiors are intent on ensuring that the fate and whereabouts of victims will never be known.

In Argentina, the "task forces" conducting these arrests operated in plain clothes and unmarked vehicles, and sometimes in disguise. They were able, however, to turn a clandestine operation into a "legal" one by flashing their credentials if they encountered a regular police patrol. In most cases, the military commanders of the task forces first ordered a "free area" (*area libre*) near where the abduction would take place, and the local police would not interfere with the operation even though they knew it to be an abduction. Relatives who made inquiries at police stations and military barracks were told that their loved ones had not been arrested. Resort to courts and the writ of habeas corpus (which we lawyers had used earlier to locate prisoners and prevent their torture) were also useless. In previous years, judges acting on a petition for habeas corpus would inspect detention centers unannounced in order to locate a prisoner and ensure his or her safety and the legality of the arrest.

After March 1976, no judge anywhere in Argentina attempted to inspect a detention center to verify whether a detainee was there. Such inspections, if they had been conducted within hours of an arrest, would have made a difference in some cases. But because the task forces knew that no judge would inspect the premises, they took victims to clandestine detention centers usually within military or police compounds or remote facilities with easily restricted access. There victims were subjected to even more extreme forms of torture than that applied to "legalized" prisoners. After being held in appalling conditions, the desaparecidos of Argentina generally were murdered and their corpses were disposed of, so their fate and whereabouts would remain secret forever. The experience was terrifying for the families. After initial inquiries did not provide any information, they made endless pilgrimages to offices of the Ministry of Interior or used contacts with military officers to seek assistance. They went to priests and bishops for help. Even if religious leaders were sympathetic—and some were—they had little or no influence over the military government. Those priests and bishops who did maintain good relationships with the government generally tried to persuade the families of the disappeared to stop looking and resign themselves to their fate.

Many of my closest friends and colleagues were caught in this machinery of death in Argentina during the dictatorship, and even today their fate and whereabouts remain unknown. Among them is Manuel Evequoz, who was so helpful to my family after my arrest. Fernando Hallgarten, the young law student arrested with me in Mar del Plata, is among the disappeared, as is Roberto Fassi, who represented me when I was brought before a judge on trumped-up charges and then advised Silvia on the administrative appeals and habeas corpus writs to secure permission for me to leave the country. Mario Yacub, the prominent lawyer whose son, Ivan, is now an immigration attorney in Virginia, is another desaparecido. When I arrived in the United States in 1977, I was obsessed with the need both to prevent harm to my fellow Unit 9 inmates and to find the disappeared. In some cases of better-known victims, early and very loud denunciation in Argentina and abroad had forced the government to "legalize" the detention and specify the charges. In a very few cases, the person was released.

An especially troubling case for me was that of Guillermo Díaz-Lestrem, a good friend and one of the smartest, most creative attorneys I have ever known. He had been a clerk and a public defender in the federal court system and, because he was well known for his progressive views, his career was stalled even before the junta took power. He helped me write defense briefs for clients accused of subversive activities, although of course his name would not appear. His wife, Nelly Ortiz, had been a prosecutor before the dictatorship and had exposed corruption among big companies that were stripped of assets. In the early days of the dictatorship, Guillermo was dismissed from his post, arrested, tortured and placed in administrative detention. While he was being held in Sierra Chica prison, Nelly was abducted in November 1976 and became one of more than one hundred lawyers among the desaparecidos. Their son was under ten years old at the time. Eventually,

Guillermo was released, but instead of fleeing the country, he chose to stay in Buenos Aires and practice in the city's most prestigious criminal law firm. One night in May 1978, a task force came to his apartment. Guessing that this was a clandestine operation, he refused to open the door, made some frantic phone calls and generally made such an uproar that a right-wing judge who lived in the same building took him into custody under his own protection. The judge took him to the court-house holding cells in downtown Buenos Aires; when no government agency offered reasons for arresting Guillermo, the judge released him after a few days. Soon after, Guillermo was abducted, probably from the streets. His bullet-riddled body was found one morning in the wooded Palermo parks.

In Mar del Plata, one of the worst episodes of disappearances af-fected my colleagues and former law school mates. The event is known nationally as *la noche de las corbatas* (the night of the neckties) be-cause lawyers are supposed to wear neckties all the time. The perpetra-tors of this tragedy used that name themselves, in a show of gallows humor. An earlier case in La Plata, where high school students were made to disappear, was labeled *la noche de los lápices* (the night of the pencils) by the abductors themselves; eventually a stunning and terribly sad motion picture of the same name was produced.[1] These labels were references to "the night of long knives" in Nazi Germany before World War II and to the raids on national universities in Ar-gentina during an earlier military dictatorship, in 1966, which still is remembered today as *la noche de los bastones largos* (the night of long sticks). In Mar del Plata, the victims were Norberto Centeno, one of the country's best-known labor lawyers and an intellectual author of the nation's labor laws, and five young lawyers, all of whom had been friends of mine. Centeno's body, showing signs of horrendous torture, was found in a desolate location; all but one of the other men are among the disappeared. The children of Tomás Fresneda, whom I knew better than the others, are now lawyers themselves and active in the trials against the perpetrators of junta crimes.

At first, disappearances were not publicized, as the major Argentine newspapers and other media would not publish anything about repres-sion that was not officially sanctioned by the junta. Only two smaller newspapers, *La Opinión* and the Buenos Aires *Herald,* published accounts of these clandestine detentions. Robert Cox, then editor of the *Herald,* testified, at a trial in Buenos Aires in November 2010,[2] that he decided to publish accounts of disappearances brought to him by desperate mothers and wives because, in his experience, doing so sometimes forced the captors to acknowledge the detention. Unfortunately, it happened in very few cases; the larger papers, as well as television and radio outlets, preferred to follow the government's instructions.

The editor of *La Opinion*—Jacobo Timerman—and of the *Herald* eventually paid dearly for their courageous stands. Timerman became a desaparecido himself; his detention went unacknowledged for weeks while he was held in at least two notorious detention and torture centers in the suburbs of Buenos Aires; his newspaper was confiscated and—after his detention was "legalized"—he was held under house arrest for a long period before being forced into exile. Cox was briefly arrested at Federal Police headquarters, where he said he saw a huge swastika painted on a wall. He and his young family suffered terrifying threats and had to leave the country.

As mentioned, the relatives of the disappeared also sought the help of other powerful institutions outside government. The Catholic Church, unfortunately, offered little of value, save for the occasional consolation and suggestion that the families stop looking. Most Catholic bishops refused to comment on human rights altogether, although a handful did join the Argentine human rights organizations. Two progressive bishops in the provinces were murdered by government agents. Among foreign embassies, however, there were many examples of heartening support from diplomats and several democratic governments.

F. A. "Tex" Harris, a political officer in the U.S. Embassy in Buenos Aires, was among the most energetic and imaginative supporters for the relatives of the disappeared, even though he often faced restrictions from his own superiors in Buenos Aires and in Washington. Tex would grant interviews to all who came to see him and would even visit relatives of the disappeared in their own homes; he would take careful notes and then seek information from Argentine authorities. He reported meticulously to his superiors at the embassy and at the State Department in Washington. Tex would arrange for relatives of the victims to hold conversations with high-ranking officers. In a memorable Fourth of July party at the U.S. Embassy, Tex introduced Emilio Mignone, a well-known jurist and educator whose twenty-four-year-old daughter Mónica had been taken from his house and subsequently disappeared, to Admiral Eduardo René Fracassi (now under indictment in Argentina). Exasperated, Fracassi admitted, before many people, that the government detained the people listed as disappeared and did not intend to reveal their whereabouts. Tex is now in retirement after a distinguished career; his heart is still very much with the victims of the Argentine dictatorship, and the Argentine government has publicly and very deservedly recognized his efforts.

Eventually, the search for the disappeared took the relatives abroad, especially to Europe, the United States and Canada. In 1977, I had just arrived in Washington and, understandably, the U.S. capital was a frequent destination. In the process of helping the relatives as much as I could, I learned quite a bit about disappearances and was able to help define and devise a strategy to counter this devastating practice.

One of the most influential groups protesting the disappearances at this time was the Mothers of Plaza de Mayo, who paraded silently wearing white headscarves once a week in front of the Argentinean government house in Buenos Aires. They became an international symbol of the cruelty of the dictatorship, but at home the main press ignored them. During the World Cup of Soccer played in Argentina in 1978, the Dutch team, at that time the best in the world, visited the Mothers one afternoon, thanks to an intensive campaign in Europe by AI and other human rights organizations. Some of the movement's founders were themselves the victims of disappearances, as were two French nuns. In 1977, the early group of Mothers was infiltrated by a young man posing as the brother of a desaparecido. He turned out to be Lieutenant Alfredo Astiz, a young naval intelligence and operations officer and a member of the task force that ran the country's largest clandestine detention and torture center in the infamous Navy Mechanics School (Escuela de Mecánica de la Armada–ESMA), a facility in the city of Buenos Aires. Authorities contend that, in late 1977, his team of torturers raided the Catholic Church of the Holy Cross as the group was meeting and took away several members, including Azucena Villaflor de DeVincenti, who has been credited with the idea of organizing the Mothers movement. Not knowing who had given them up, all of the members of the group wanted to protect Astiz and urged him not to appear in public with them; in their experience, young people were much more likely to be targeted for repression than housewives.

The French nuns who accompanied and supported the Mothers were last seen in the ESMA detention center by those who survived the ordeal. The bodies of the nuns and many others were thrown from planes into the River Plate. Sister Leonie Durquet is said to have gone to her death worrying about the fate of the young man she had known only as Angel Rubio ("Blond Angel"), the false identity Astiz had used to infiltrate the group. When the French government made stern diplomatic inquiries about the nuns' fate, some Argentinean navy officers are said to have commented sardonically, at cocktail parties, about the "Flying Nuns." After many fits and starts, justice is finally being done in Argentina; in 2011, Astiz is one of the principal defendants on trial in Buenos Aires in the case that deals with ESMA kidnappings, torture and murders.[3] Eventually the Mothers became the most visible part of a home-grown human rights movement that spearheaded the resistance against the dictatorship.

Emilio Mignone and Augusto Conte MacDonnell, along with their wives, two founding members of the Mothers of Plaza de Mayo, were parents of disappeared children. Both men were well-known, successful professionals in Argentina; the fact that their children were among the disappeared reminded those who knew them that this tragedy could strike even influential middle-class families.

Mónica, Emilio's twenty-four-year-old daughter, was taken from their home in Buenos Aires by a task force pretending to be members of the regular police. Mónica, active as a Catholic catechist and social worker in a Buenos Aires slum, was part of a group of young Catholics who worked for the poor under the direction of a progressive priest. Several of her friends and coworkers were also taken that night; none of them was involved in violent activities. Later on it was established that they were taken to the ESMA detention center; they disappeared from there forever. Augusto's son, Augusto María, was in the middle of performing his mandatory year of military service, although the army probably knew that he had been active in student movements before being drafted. He is one of dozens of conscripts who are counted among the disappeared.

Driven by this traumatic event, Emilio and Augusto first joined the broad-based Permanent Assembly for Human Rights and then founded the Centro de Estudios Legales y Sociales (CELS–Center for Legal and Social Studies), a more dynamic arm of the human rights movement and one geared more toward legal action and documentation. The Permanent Assembly for Human Rights was tolerated (but just barely) by the junta because it consisted of a few political leaders of democratic parties, religious leaders of different denominations and a few well-known jurists and "public citizens." The composition of the Permanent Assembly was of course a protection for its members, but it also meant that all decisions had to be reached by consensus. Through CELS, Augusto and Emilio used the courts creatively in a succession of "collective" petitions for habeas corpus on behalf of thousands of disappeared persons called *Pérez de Smith I, II, III,* and *IV,* in which the main named plaintiff was the wife of a well-known disappeared trade union leader. Although the courts were slow to act, the four cases produced evidence of the pattern of disappearances, and CELS managed to get the reluctant major dailies to publish that information.

During one of his trips to Washington, Augusto wrote a seminal analysis of disappearances from evidence then at his disposal, calling it "a system of global parallelism." According to Augusto, the junta had created a secret chain of command to run the disappearances, effectively circumventing all institutional controls, even as they remained in existence on paper. CELS eventually published Augusto's tract; years later, the evidence produced by the National Commission on Disappearances of Persons and at the trial of the junta members completely validated his findings. With Emilio's guidance, CELS also collected materials for the most important documentation center in existence in Argentina at the time and made sure its contents were safe from military seizure. I helped him buy a huge microfilming machine and later helped him transfer copies of the microfilm archives out of Argentina. Today, CELS is one of the most effective and professional human rights organizations anywhere in the world.

Thanks to the way in which the Mothers bore witness to their plight during their trips abroad and to CELS' documentation and legal analysis, the truth about the nature of the military dictatorship eventually was known and recognized abroad. The international isolation of the junta resulted in the quick erosion of the support it enjoyed among some sectors of Argentine society. In November 1977 (the same month in which the Mothers were kidnapped at the Holy Cross Church), U.S. Secretary of State Cyrus Vance visited Argentina and delivered to the junta government a list of the names of fifteen thousand detainees and disappeared persons, requesting information about their fate, whereabouts, charges against them and reasons to hold them. In this fashion, Vance put into practice the announced policy of the Carter administration to set human rights at the center of its relations with the rest of the world. Of course, it had taken careful work by American citizens and their institutions, such as AI, the National Council of Churches and the Washington Office on Latin America, to urge Congress and the State Department to translate stated policies into concrete action. Argentine exiles and expatriates in the United States found in those organizations of civil society a sympathetic channel to the U.S. government. They obtained names of the detained and disappeared and dates on which they were captured and submitted them to the State Department. Credit is due to Patricia Derian, the first assistant secretary of state for human rights, not only for Vance's initiative but for maintaining the pressure on the Argentine military regarding its human rights record. And of course such pressure could have occurred only because of Vance's personal, deeply held belief in justice and human dignity. Years later, I was privileged to meet Vance when he was asked to investigate human rights abuses at the beginning of the wars in the former Yugoslavia.

In 1978, the Carter administration reduced the amount of military aid to Argentina because of human rights violations; in response, the junta angrily rejected all aid (for that year). Undisturbed by that outburst, Congress passed the Humphrey-Kennedy Amendment to the

Foreign Assistance Act, cutting off all military aid, sales and training to Argentina and Chile. Also in 1978, U.S. Vice President Walter
Mondale extracted from General Jorge Rafael Videla, then the junta-
appointed president of Argentina, a promise to let the Inter-American Commission on Human Rights (IACHR) of the Organization of
American States (OAS) conduct an on-site visit in Argentina, in exchange for extending credit for a dam to be built on the Paraná River.

The disappearances campaign was most intense in Argentina during 1976 and 1977. By mid-1978, the number of new cases was considerably smaller, in part because by then the left-wing opposition had
been all but destroyed and also because the soccer World Cup was
played in Argentina in June of that year and the regime had to make
itself more presentable to the world. The regime and its friends abroad
presented this reduction in new cases as proof of "improvements" in
the human rights situation. In response, Argentine and international
human rights activists began to insist that disappearances were a
"continuing offense," at least for as long as there was denial and an
attempt to force society to forget about the disappeared.

The human rights community demanded that the regime report
in exhaustive detail about the fate and whereabouts of each person
detained and then disappeared. In 1979, the IACHR finally conducted
its on-site fact-finding mission, and the following year, it produced
the most significant report on disappearances ever published in international law.[4] It was also one of the most stinging indictments of
the junta ever published, and it was circulated and publicly discussed
at the General Assembly of the OAS in November 1980. After this
pioneering work by the IACHR, the United Nations (UN) created the
Working Group on Disappearances in 1982. The Working Group,
still in existence today, no longer displayed the exaggerated respect
for state sovereignty that had characterized the UN's earlier position.
The regime's representatives in Geneva staunchly opposed the Working Group; its creation was a signal defeat for the dictatorship and a
measure of its isolation in world affairs.

By 1982, the number of new disappearances in Argentina was down
to a trickle, but the demand for information about the thousands still
unaccounted for was growing. In addition, the Working Group became

a powerful instrument to contain the practice and to obtain redress
for victims of disappearances and their families in many other countries. In time, the Working Group on Disappearances and others like it
have made the human rights machinery of the UN more relevant to the
needs of victims and nongovernmental organizations, although much
improvement needs to be made. Starting in 1982, the procedures of the
UN human rights protection mechanisms were no longer confidential
or subject to votes by member states of the UN Commission on Human Rights; they now were entrusted to independent experts who were
better shielded from political pressures. Over the years, these "special
procedures," as they are called in the United Nations, resulted in the appointment of other working groups and special rapporteurs on a variety
of issues as well as with country-specific mandates.

In 1981, the Reagan administration made it clear that human
rights would no longer be central to the foreign policy of the United
States. Among other things, the State Department went to Congress
to push hard for the lifting of the Humphrey-Kennedy Amendment to
the Foreign Assistance Act (section 620[B]) and other restrictions. Secretary of State Alexander Haig announced that human rights would
yield to concerns about fighting terrorism,[5] among other strategic U.S.
interests. The U.S.-based human rights movement promptly reacted to
defend the former policy. In the movement's first major victory, Reagan's appointee as assistant secretary of state for human rights, Ernest
Lefever, failed to be approved by the Senate after a dramatic hearing in which Jacobo Timerman, who had just recently been released
from detention and forced into exile, denounced the idea of "quiet
diplomacy" that Lefever and others proposed. Within the year, the
Reagan administration switched gears and decided to push for human
rights, but on its own terms. Lifting restrictions on aid to Chile and
Argentina was still very much a part of the agenda. Throughout 1981,
I testified in Congress, introduced Argentine human rights leaders to
congressmen and assisted in drafting legislation opposing the change
in policy. In a compromise, the Humphrey-Kennedy amendment was
not repealed but amended: The president was authorized to renew
military sales and credit to Argentina if he found that the junta had
clarified the fate and whereabouts of the disappeared.[6]

In early 1982, I joined Americas Watch (now Human Rights Watch [HRW]); its leaders had been instrumental in bringing Timerman to Washington and in opposing Lefever. At a meeting with our leaders and staff, Elliott Abrams, then assistant secretary for human rights in the Reagan administration, told us that he intended to certify that Argentina had met the condition established by Congress. We pointed out that the dictatorship had done nothing to clarify the fate or whereabouts of even a single victim of disappearance, and he answered that the congressionally imposed condition "depended on how you interpreted it." We made it clear to him that we would challenge any interpretation that allowed the junta criminals to get away with not revealing what had happened to each desaparecido and what would be done to investigate the practice of disappearances fully.

On April 2, 1982, General Leopoldo Fortunato Galtieri, by then the third junta-appointed president of Argentina, took the ill-fated decision to invade the U.K.-occupied Malvinas (Falklands Islands), long an anticolonial rallying cry for all Argentines. Having to choose between two "friends," the Reagan administration naturally sided with Margaret Thatcher and the United Kingdom and abandoned any interest in renewing military assistance to the regime. During frantic weeks of negotiation to avoid war, the United Kingdom trumpeted the vicious nature of the military dictatorship (although the Thatcher government had remained silent about human rights until then); the world finally knew more than it ever wanted to know about the disappeared of Argentina. The humiliating Argentine defeat suffered in the short winter war (late May to mid-June 1982) accelerated the end of the military dictatorship. The regime began to plan its retreat and a transition to democracy, but its loss of prestige rendered it unable to impose conditions on future democratic governments, such as complete impunity for the crimes of the "dirty war." By late 1983, democracy again was in force in Argentina, and the country has remained a democracy for twenty-eight years, the longest period of true democracy in its history.

In the post-Malvinas period and in the early days of this democracy, the Mothers and the human rights groups in general became the most respected institutions in Argentine society and were able—

through their moral courage but also thanks to the clarity and political wisdom of some of their members—to transfer their agenda to wider circles of the public. Chief among the items on that agenda was the insistence on knowing the fate and whereabouts of the disappeared.

In addition to campaigning over disappearances and other human rights violations in Argentina, my first tasks for Americas Watch (later HRW) took me to several conflicts in Central America. At that time, the civil wars in El Salvador and in Guatemala were already raging, and the Reagan administration's "contra war" against the Sandinista government was just beginning. There were many cases of disappearances in El Salvador and Guatemala, but it was hard to campaign about them because, in both countries, massacres of civilians, destruction of villages and forced displacement of indigenous communities dominated the concerns of the human rights movement. The Reagan administration argued that everything evil was due to the Salvadoran and Guatemalan guerrillas and their ally, the Nicaraguan government, while the U.S.-supported contras (Nicaraguan rebels fighting the leftist Sandinista government) were freedom fighters. The administration claimed that the contras and the armed forces of El Salvador and Guatemala were democratic "friends of the U.S." and were wrongly accused of human rights violations. They also echoed the excuses of the Guatemalan and Salvadoran governments—for example, that missing persons actually had deserted their families to live with a mistress or lover abroad. In fact, the Guatemalan military governments had practiced large-scale disappearances for years before the dictatorships of Brazil, Chile, Argentina and Uruguay adopted the method. The practice had been less visible than in Argentina only because the victims were generally poor and indigenous inhabitants of the highlands.

Honduras managed to live in the middle of these wars without experiencing a large insurgency of its own. Because of its geography, however, leftist forces from El Salvador and Guatemala used Honduras for arms trafficking, as a safe haven for wounded guerrillas and as a refuge for peasant families escaping military operations. Later, the United States would use Honduran territory as training camps and launching grounds for the Nicaraguan contras. In mid-1982, I visited Honduras for the first time, to investigate initial complaints of disappearances there. It was known, but largely not documented at that time, that with covert U.S. support, the Argentine military was providing training to Central American security forces, including those of Honduras. There were already indications of the use of clandestine prisons by secret units and clear efforts to prevent courts from inquiring about the fate of the missing persons.

After HRW published my report in 1982,[7] the U.S. Embassy in Tegucigalpa tried to discredit my findings that the Honduran armed forces were applying "the Argentine method." A few years later, I represented the families of the Honduran disappeared in the first case to come before the Inter-American Court of Human Rights. I had met the family of Angel Manfredo Velásquez, an economics student, during my first trip to Honduras, and eventually they and other victims persuaded the Inter-American Commission to send their cases to the Inter-American Court of Human Rights, a new OAS body sitting in San José, Costa Rica. *Velásquez-Rodríguez v. Honduras,* decided in 1988, became the first adversarial case to be heard by this court, and its decision would break new ground in international law.[8] Conscious of the fact that disappearances are meant to be the perfect crime, my fellow attorneys and I set about to prove that the disappearance of these victims was part and parcel of a larger pattern. We wanted to show that similar actions, deliberately and systematically conducted by the Army of Honduras, caused about two hundred citizens to disappear over the course of three years. Through witnesses, including an army deserter, we established the existence of a clandestine unit in the Honduran army, reporting directly to the high command, called Battalion 3-16. In acknowledging its existence, Honduran military leaders claimed that it was only an intelligence-gathering and capacity-building unit. But this battalion actually conducted intelligence operations—abductions—and frequently used clandestine prisons and eventually murdered the victims and disposed of their remains.

The Inter-American Court produced a wonderful decision, finding Honduras responsible for crimes against humanity. The decision, still quoted throughout the world more than twenty years later, described the phenomenon of disappearances and concluded that they unmistakably constitute crimes against humanity. This decision marked the first time that an intergovernmental organ stated that disappearances gave rise to the obligation by the state to investigate, prosecute and punish those responsible; to discover and disclose the truth about them to the families and to society; and to offer reparations. These obligations had to be performed in good faith and with "due diligence," a standard that has since been used to judge whether states are living up to their solemn international obligations to human rights, acquired when they sign and ratify treaties.

It is worth noting the similarities between disappearances and the George W. Bush administration practice of "extraordinary renditions" and use of "black sites" by the Central Intelligence Agency after September 11, 2001. Both extraordinary renditions and disappearances keep the identity of the person being detained and the location of the detention center a secret and do not acknowledge transfers to another jurisdiction. As of this writing, most of the known victims of the U.S. government's policy of extraordinary rendition have survived the experience, and that may be an important difference from disappearances: In most countries, the overwhelming majority of disappearances end in the murder of the victim. Nevertheless, the conscious decision to avoid institutional controls and prevent the intervention of courts is central to the practice of renditions. And decisions as to who will be subject to renditions are adopted in secret and by unaccountable authorities, which make those decisions inherently arbitrary. In addition, the whole purpose of both renditions and disappearances is to interrogate under torture. Both practices put rendered and disappeared detainees in the harrowing situation of being held in secret for prolonged periods, without recourse to family, friends or judges, and completely at the mercy of interrogators bent on destroying their morale and personality through torture. Denial by the authorities holding them also punishes the next of kin of the rendered and disappeared alike by placing them in a state of prolonged uncertainty about their loved ones' fates, of self-doubt about whether they are doing enough to find their relatives and of not knowing when or how to mourn them and get on with their lives.

Today it is a lot harder for repressive states to get away with unacknowledged detentions and subsequent denials, in large measure because the human rights movement has succeeded in calling disappearances by their name and attaching to the practice a very clear stigma. Nevertheless, disappearances still are used in a broad spectrum of regimes across geographic, cultural and ideological boundaries.

States now have an obligation to the victims and families of the disappeared. Truth seeking and truth telling have become major objectives of policies of redress; originally they arose from the desperate need of loved ones to know the fate and whereabouts of the disappeared. Similarly, the families insisted on justice—in the form of truth telling but also of prosecution of those responsible for disappearances and features that accompany them: torture, execution and denial.

The obligation to break the cycle of impunity is the reason why it is not enough to put an end to the practice: It is also necessary to investigate it, reveal it and let justice run its course. After *Velásquez,* the international community recognized that disappearances are a crime against humanity and that that categorization carries with it specific legal and policy effects. In this regard, the Obama administration and Congress cannot expect the problem of extraordinary renditions simply to go away because they have ended the practice. A thorough inquiry is necessary, including who designed the program, who gave the orders and who executed them. If crimes have been committed, criminal prosecutions should follow.

CHAPTER FOUR

IMMIGRATION

I n the late 1970s, Argentine exiles were received with compassion almost everywhere. Unless they had previous academic or business connections, however, they had to survive doing menial jobs or selling trinkets in the subways of major cities. My experience, fortunately, was very different. My family and I stayed with the Hutchisons, the family I had lived with during high school, in Mount Carroll, Illinois, who had generously offered to help us start a new life. Silvia and I and our sons, Juan Francisco and Camilo, stayed there for about three months while I looked for a job and we learned how to remain in the United States legally. The offices of U.S. senators and congressmen that had helped my friends campaign for my release also provided good advice on employment and immigration.

A year after I got my first job, I applied for asylum and eventually became a permanent resident. I went back to law school at the American University in Washington, where I now teach, and by 1981, I was licensed to practice law in the United States. Since that first job, I have not gone a single day without work in these thirty-four years. Early on, however, I realized that such good fortune was not what most immigrants in the United States could expect.

Because my detention without trial and subsequent torture in Argentina was well documented, my family and I had little difficulty in obtaining asylum and eventual permanent residence in the United States.

Asylum seekers are foreigners who cannot go back to their countries due to a well-founded fear that they would be persecuted upon return because of their ideas or political activities. They are by definition refugees, except that in U.S. immigration law, refugees arrive in the country after their status has been determined by a U.S. consular official and they have been awarded a refugee visa. Asylum seekers enter the country with a different visa (as my family and I did; we had tourist visas) or even without a visa and then request that immigration authorities recognize their well-founded fear of persecution. A year after asylum is granted, they can become permanent residents.

My first job in the United States, in 1977, was to serve a large Mexican and Mexican American community in Aurora, in northern Illinois, through the Centro Cristo Rey program run by the Catholic Church. The community included U.S. citizens, either by birth or by naturalization; immigrants who had obtained permanent residence through family relations or because they had been certified as holding jobs that made them eligible for permanent stay in the United States; and a number of undocumented aliens, who had entered without visas or had let their initial visas expire. My boss, Father Philip Reilly, was a very compassionate and eminently practical man, and he wanted his program to expand his pastoral duties by offering social services as well. He and other priests and nuns offered masses, confessions and other liturgical services, and I coordinated courses, seminars, and discussions related to neighborhood organizing, employment and immigration rights and ensured that our clients had access to legal and social services. On the basis of his job offer, I obtained a temporary nonimmigrant visa that allowed me to work and be paid for it. Silvia and the children obtained temporary visas linked to mine. I could not change jobs while holding that visa, which was valid for one year. Before it expired, I applied for asylum and obtained a more flexible work permit. After asylum was granted, I waited another year and then we all became permanent residents.

Father Reilly told me that he appreciated that my family and I were willing to live in the community that was being served, given the fact that Silvia and I had been professionals in Argentina and had likely enjoyed a middle-class life. In fact, however, starting from scratch with a family of four and with a single salary from a nonprofit organization, we did not have much of a choice. Still, raising children in a working-class and immigrant neighborhood was a great learning experience for us. We fretted about our kids growing up among street-smart kids in run-down areas of Aurora, a far-western suburb of Chicago. Fortunately, we were allowed to enroll them tuition free in first grade and kindergarten, respectively, at the parochial school next door to the center for immigrants where I worked. They received a good education, and the nuns and priests and laypersons of the parish and center formed a loving, welcoming community for us and our children. A year later, when we moved to Washington, DC, we also lived in a poor area of town.

Our sons did not forget their immigrant experiences. As high school students at Sidwell Friends School in Washington and during the summers while at college, they did community service work in immigration service centers and soup kitchens and shelters. As a young lawyer in a big New York firm, our oldest son, Juan Francisco, took a pro bono case from a human rights organization and successfully litigated an asylum claim for a Colombian woman. Camilo has gone on to work on microcredit; he lives with his family in Lima, Peru, and his work brings him into contact with the working poor in all of South America. Our third child, Soledad, born in Washington in 1981, is an architect who works for a midsize firm in New York. Three years after graduating from Notre Dame, she left the firm for two years and obtained a master's in urban planning from the Massachusetts Institute of Technology, in order to expand her professional horizons from high-end residential projects to work benefiting communities as a whole. In the meantime, she has traveled to Kenya as a volunteer with Engineers Without Borders, to design and build a school in a poor village midway between Nairobi and Mombasa. Clearly, my three children were profoundly and permanently affected by the immigrant experience, and in turn each one of them has benefited the society in which they have grown up, precisely because of that experience. Each one of them is motivated by a larger sense of community, and I am extremely proud of them.

AFTER I GOT TO THE STATES, I immediately got in touch with the U.S. branch of Amnesty International (AI). As noted, after about a year in Illinois, we moved to Washington; I was eager to be in a place where I could be more helpful to the cause of human rights in Argentina. My friends at the Washington office of AI helped me find a job as a paralegal on the Alien Rights Law Project in a public interest law firm, the Washington Lawyers' Committee for Civil Rights Under Law. I learned a lot about immigration law and policy through this legal service and policy-oriented program, which allowed me to serve immigrants and refugees from all over the world.

In Washington, Silvia and I went back to law school part time and eventually obtained admission to the bar (I in DC in 1981, Silvia in Virginia in 1985). Silvia has worked in immigration and refugee matters for much of her professional life in the United States. She worked for specialized firms in private practice and later in the Alien Rights Law Project after I had moved on, and she often provided pro bono services through faith-based and other charitable organizations. In the 1990s during the Clinton administration, Silvia joined the federal government's Immigration and Nationality Service as an asylum adjudicator. At the time, the law had changed to favor a process of asylum meant to honor U.S. obligations under international law. Soon, however, because of widespread abuse of the asylum process, the bureaucracy started discouraging favorable disposition of petitions. Her Valley Stream, New York, office rejected about 50 percent of all the claims heard, and its approval rate was one of the highest in the country. In spite of the pressure to dispose of claims quickly, Silvia took her job seriously. She rejected petitions only after it was clear to her that the person had not satisfied the conditions to obtain asylum; the same person would have another shot at it before an immigration judge. If asylum was granted, the person and his or her family were legally in the country and on the road to permanent residence and an opportunity to start a new life, just as we had done. Silvia has always maintained that her job as an asylum officer is the most gratifying professional experience she has ever had.

In the years that have elapsed since my family and I arrived in the United States, the developed world has turned much more hostile and unwelcoming to people who leave their countries and need to settle in a foreign land. This is true in all of Europe as well as in Canada and the United States. Xenophobia and nativism are not limited to wealthy societies; the competition for natural resources creates conditions for ethnic hatred and discrimination in poor countries as well. However, some young democracies tend to be generous and welcoming. For example, citizens of the countries in the trade agreement known as Mercosur—Argentina, Brazil, Paraguay, Uruguay and Venezuela—can travel, work and establish residence in every other member country.

Argentines have had to emigrate only in the last thirty or forty years. Now that they themselves have experienced anti-immigrant sentiment abroad, they are beginning to recognize that poor Bolivians, Paraguayans and other neighbors—and more recently Korean and even African immigrants—are victims of discrimination in our homeland. Perhaps because the numbers of immigrants are still relatively small, hostility and rejection is sometimes evident but it does not yet affect public policy toward immigrants.

In the United States, policies have been established to control borders and discourage illegal immigration, generally without doing violence to the basic principle that the country is the product of waves of immigrants who traditionally have been welcome because their contributions are acknowledged. The stated objectives of immigration law continue to encourage orderly processing of immigrant visas, reunification of families and entry of new immigrants into labor markets without exploitation. But over the years the policies have become more restrictive and limited, with a greater emphasis on enforcement than on service, and with many local police departments taking it upon themselves to enforce the law without adequate training. Silvia and I have both practiced immigration law in the United States, and we remain interested and engaged in immigration policy. We have witnessed the hardening of laws and attitudes toward immigrants and the gradual development of a "scorched earth" approach to immigration control. Examples of scorched earth tactics include sanctions on employers who hire undocumented aliens, refusal of health care benefits except emergency care, denial of drivers' licenses or identity documents and authorization of police bodies to stop foreign-looking persons and demand proof of legal residence. These practices are intended to make life in the United States difficult for those who are here illegally, but they also discourage people who may qualify from seeking legal status. These measures penalize hardworking people who come looking for opportunity and make their lives difficult and dangerous.

In addition, political realities in some parts of the U.S. have fueled anti-immigrant sentiment that appears closely linked to racism and prejudice against persons of certain national origins. The southwestern border of the United States has seen a rise in vigilantism, whether promoted by restrictive policies or in response to a perceived lack of adequate controls, which shows the worst in Americans.

In uncertain times, newcomers are easy scapegoats for all that is wrong with the economy, even if it can be demonstrated that they create wealth and are not a burden to the state treasury. Still, politicians become popular by attacking newcomers. The result is bad policy, such as the statutes promulgated in Arizona that make it a crime to be there without valid immigration papers. The face of Sheriff Joe Arpaio of Maricopa County, Arizona, who has become a celebrity by arresting and detaining persons he considers "illegal aliens," is now the public image of American anti-immigrant attitudes.

To be sure, there are still organizations of civil society that bravely swim against the tide and try to help immigrants through legal and humanitarian means, in much the same way as the Sanctuary Movement of the 1980s protected refugees from the Central American wars. Today, faith-based local organizations, immigration attorneys and clinics in many law schools do their best to defend the rights of foreign workers.

Immigration advocacy in the United States and other developed nations has become more urgent than ever, even as the odds seem all the more stacked against sound and humane policies. It is gratifying to see that the movement to defend immigrants has become stronger and capable of showing some street strength in recent years and that Hispanic Americans, particularly the young, have taken the lead. I am especially impressed with the quality of the work of lawyers and activists in the Southwest United States, who organized to denounce and counter the policy of the Department of Homeland Security to build walls and barbed-wire fences in long segments of the land border with Mexico, which forces incoming immigrants to take more dangerous routes through deserts where they are subject to exploitation by *coyotes* (people smugglers) or to attack by anti-immigrant goon squads.

In the decades following my family's flight into exile, anti-immigration sentiment has grown in most developed countries, and it has resulted in backward policies with regard to asylum and the admission of refugees. The return of persons with well-founded fear of persecution to places where they will be persecuted (known as *refoulement*) happens today with terrifying frequency, despite the fact that it violates a principle that has long been considered central to human rights and refugee law.

The Committee Against Torture (CAT; a United Nations treaty body that supervises compliance with the UN Convention Against Torture) now dedicates most of its efforts to individual case complaints regarding democratic countries' practice of sending back persons to places where they face the prospect of being tortured. Right after September 11, 2001, even Sweden was found in violation of the convention when it sent an Egyptian dissident back to Egypt, where the CAT found that he was indeed tortured.[1]

Despite the efforts of CAT and many nongovernmental organizations, the return of refugees and asylees to where they may be persecuted, and of anyone to where he or she may be tortured, continues unabated. Democratic governments have crafted new policies to discourage entry of refugees and asylum-seekers—persons who in previous times would have been received generously because they are clearly deserving of protection. One such practice is the automatic detention of migrants who enter without visas or who request asylum at the entry point; in the United Kingdom and Greece, for example, such people can be assured of a long detention in prisons or in camps before their claims for asylum or protection from torture are reviewed and adjudicated. Another practice that violates the non-refoulement principle is the returning of persons—after obtaining "diplomatic assurances" from the reentry coutry—to countries where they might be tortured or persecuted. Those assurances are not worth much; Sweden had received such assurance from Egypt, yet the dissident was tortured upon return to his native land.

The Obama administration sent an Algerian detained in Guantanamo back to Algeria against his will in 2010, after receiving diplomatic assurances from Algeria, even though the man feared persecution or torture from nonstate agents and the government's ability to protect him from those agents was in question. The State Department claims that it is monitoring the man in Algeria and that so far he has not suffered any violation of his rights; it is also true that in this case his return is defensible as a step in the direction of closing down the Guantanamo Bay prison. But it is still the case that the prohibition against refoulement—the "expulsion of persons who have the right to be recognized as refugees"[2]—is absolute; it cannot be sidestepped with diplomatic assurances.

At the Alien Rights Law Project, we advocated for the rights of "boat people" from Haiti and Cuba to have their claims for asylum heard and fairly adjudicated. Later, in the course of field investigations for Human Rights Watch from 1982 to 1996, I visited refugee camps for Salvadorans and Nicaraguans in Honduras. In some of the countries we covered, internal displacement due to civil war or other violence was common. Internally displaced persons (IDPs) are not technically refugees because they are still in their native countries. But they might as well be refugees, because they live in deplorable conditions in makeshift camps or shantytowns near large cities. International law has begun to recognize their plight. The problem was especially acute in Colombia when I was doing field research for Human Rights Watch in the early 1990s. IDPs left their homes to escape violence from rural guerrillas, from right-wing paramilitary forces supported by the Colombian army (whose paramilitary leaders also stole their land) and even from drug lords. State institutions were, to put it charitably, slow to respond to their plight. Over the years the problem has not abated, but Colombian organizations of civil society contribute much-needed material support and policy advocacy on behalf of these IDPs.

In Brazil in the late 1980s, I had occasion to visit with IDPs forced to flee their homes not because of war but as victims of the struggle for land and the use of "private armies" that large landowners hired to prevent invasion of unexploited land by large groups of peasant families. "Landless peasants" thus became not only destitute but also displaced. I chatted with some of them in makeshift camps by road-sides. They had been forced to flee their places of origin under the threat of violence by armed thugs. Now they lived with their families in tents or in cars and old buses, mostly waiting to settle on unused land. The Sem Terra (landless people's) movement, supported by some Catholic priests and laypersons, tried to organize them at a time (as Brazil emerged from a military dictatorship) when state and federal authorities did little to meet their needs.

During my four years as a member of the Inter-American Com-mision on Human Rights (IACHR) of the Organization of American States—2000 to 2003—I was the Special Rapporteur on the Rights of Migrant Workers and Their Families, a post that allowed me to return to the themes of how best to protect the rights of those who leave their countries in pursuit of a better future for themselves and their loved ones. I visited border crossings in Central America, Mexico and the United States and interviewed undocumented immigrants held in detention centers awaiting deportation. The increasing restrictions had not made a dent on the incessant flow of immigration; if anything, they had led to the spread of organized criminal gangs engaged in traf-ficking in humans, conducted with growing violence and exploitation. In a facility in Mexico's capital, I talked to a Honduran young woman who had lost a leg during her journey as the coyotes hustled her to board a moving train to avoid detection.

IN MY CAPACITY AS COMMISSIONER in charge of the rights of migrant workers, I litigated two important cases dealing with Haitians in the Dominican Republic and the discrimination they suffer, along with Dominicans of Haitian origin whose rights as citizens are routinely ignored. One was a request for provisional measures from the Inter-American Court of Human Rights to freeze mass deportations conducted by the Dominican government.[3] The public hearing in 2001 produced vibrant exchanges with government representatives who resented the implication that their policies were inspired by racism.

The other case was a petition on behalf of two young Dominico-Haitian girls who had been denied birth certificates and, later, access to schools, to health services and the like, as well as the opportunity to prove that they had in fact been born on Dominican soil. I represented the commission in negotiations with the Dominican government, and some improvements did occur; for example, the girls were issued birth certificates and the government instituted a general policy that no school-age child would be turned away for lack of a birth certificate. The case continued before the Inter-American Court after I had left the commission and resulted in a landmark 2005 decision finding the Dominican Republic in violation of the American Convention on Human Rights for its treatment of Dominico-Haitians.[4] Unfortunately, rather than complying with its international obligations, the Dominican Republic has reinterpreted its constitutional norm on *jus soli* (anyone born in the territory is a citizen by birth) to exclude those who are born there while their parents are in transit and to consider "in transit" any immigrant who cannot prove that he or she has been admitted legally into the country. An example of human rights practice: Victories are hard fought and often won, but new challenges appear, and Sisyphus-like human rights activists must start again to push the rock upward. How can we persuade Dominican leaders to institute more liberal and humane policies toward Haitians and Dominico-Haitians when members of the U.S. Congress seriously propose to deprive persons born in the United States of citizenship if their parents are not here legally?

IN MY ANNUAL REPORTS as the Special Rapporteur on Migrant Workers and their families, I proposed detailed standards of due process in the determination of status and in deportation or exclusion proceedings.[5] Laws and practices vary widely in the Americas, and the lack of uniform standards means that any law enforcement official can detain persons they deem to be foreigners and order them thrown out of the country without much opportunity to state a claim. The IACHR has developed a rich jurisprudence on the international standards of due process applicable in criminal trials and other proceedings, and I proposed their application to immigration law and procedure. Some states have indeed improved their internal legislation and even the management of their immigration detention facilities; but the pressure to use detention as a means to discourage population movement is great, and the setbacks are more frequent than the partial victories.

The movement of people across borders has continued to grow despite the restrictive and shortsighted policies of receiving countries. Today it presents issues not only in the destination countries but also in the "sending" countries and those through which migrant workers transit. It generates mafias set up to conduct trafficking of persons while evading immigration controls, and which exploit the vulnerability of migrants, especially of women and children. In turn, the same gangs diversify and use their brutal methods to force victims into child labor, prostitution or sexual slavery. Receiving countries' obtuse and intolerant policies that shut borders ignore the tragic developments that they generate on both sides of those borders.

There have been efforts to systematize the rights of migrant workers and their families, notably by way of a UN convention on the matter.[6] Unfortunately, it has been signed and ratified mostly by sending countries and has been rejected even by the most progressive and liberal receiving countries in northern Europe. Drafting and ratifying multilateral treaties to disrupt and prevent smuggling and trafficking in persons has become much easier than developing treaties to protect the rights of migrant workers.[7] North and South countries agree on the need to break up networks of organized crime that exploit the special vulnerability of poor people who move across borders seeking work and opportunity. Human rights activists also recognize that coyotes are the enemies of immigrants' rights. In addition, the human rights movement supports the disruption of trafficking networks.

During my tenure at IACHR, I held many meetings with U.S. State Department officials, representatives of other governments and international organizations on the efforts to curb human trafficking, including a high-level conference in Santiago, Chile, in 2003, sponsored by the International Organization on Migration. It was plain to see that the main motivation of governments was to control migration flows; at the same time, it was impossible to deny that the victims of trafficking were and are the same persons whose rights and dignity I wanted to defend. I emphasized the need to concentrate on organized crime and to ensure that sweeping anti-trafficking regulations were not directed at individuals and organizations that helped migrants at or near borders out of a genuine humanitarian impulse and not for private gain. My colleagues and I were able to see some of these immigration activists at work near the borders. Their organizations, some faith based and all mostly volunteer, are shoestring operations by any standard. But their commitment and dedication to their clients is inspirational. Many of these organizations are turning their attention to issues of trafficking of women and girls for sexual slavery, and their efforts are beginning to show results in the concerns expressed by the international community about this widespread and not well-understood phenomenon. Because sexual slavery and forced prostitution are mostly run by organized crime, anti-trafficking activists face great danger; their bravery should be rewarded with attention and support from the rest of us.

IN MY OWN WORK with IACHR, I insisted in treating immigrants as victims of trafficking, not as witnesses to be compelled to testify, at considerable risk of retaliation to themselves or their families, much less as accomplices or participants in trafficking crimes. Undocumented immigrants are guilty of an administrative infraction, not a crime. They may not have a right to remain in the country where they arrive, but their presence in that country is not a criminal offense. Unfortunately, the very term "illegal alien" leads people to believe that immigrants and their families are criminals to be persecuted.

This attitude toward undocumented immigrants is common in many parts of the world, and today it is harder than ever for immigrants to obtain legal status in countries that have traditionally welcomed them, such as the United States, Canada and all the European nations. In the years that have elapsed since my family and I arrived in the United States, the developed world has turned much more hostile and unwelcoming to people who leave their homelands and need to settle in a new society.

CHAPTER FIVE

SOLIDARITY

As I have mentioned, my time in prison in Argentina was shortened considerably due to international pressure. My adoption as the first Amnesty International (AI) Argentine "prisoner of conscience" in 1976 facilitated the decision of several U.S. senators and congressmen to write to the Argentine government on my behalf. At the time, Jimmy Carter had put human rights at the center of U.S. foreign policy concerns, and my American "brother," John Hutchison, had maintained a steady stream of letters and phone calls to Washington, DC, from his home in Illinois. If it sounds unlikely that letter writing and inquiries from the United States would force the Argentine military to release me, it must be said that it was. Mine was an isolated case, but it also shows that determination, patience and insistence by common men and women can produce results in the struggle for justice.

In the meantime, thousands of prisoners and disappeared persons who did not have international support remained in Argentina under intolerable conditions. Eventually, campaigns on behalf of other prisoners and disappeared persons became a flood that persuaded the world about the true nature of the Argentine dictatorship.

AI's decision to adopt me as a prisoner of conscience was the result of careful and painstaking research. The researcher for Argentina, Tricia Feeney, corresponded with John Hutchison and through him with my Argentine family. She proposed my adoption after verifying through court documents that I was in detention without trial or charges as a result of my work as a lawyer and that the government was refusing to honor court orders to let me travel abroad, warrants actually issued by judges appointed by the dictatorship. That careful research by Tricia, and her consultation with sources in the Argentine diaspora in Europe, was decisive in the relatively quick resolution of my case. As was the regular process in those years, my case was also assigned to an AI "adoption group" in Uppsala, Sweden. This was one of hundreds of adoption groups in several countries comprised of volunteers who worked on many cases of unjustly detained prisoners around the world. The Uppsala group continued to conduct these tasks for the next thirty years. Weeks after my adoption, Tricia conducted AI's only mission to Argentina during those years, in November 1976. She and her fellow mission members used my file as a demonstration case in their conversations with the government. Although the Argentine government admitted no wrongdoing in my case, within three months of those discussions I was able to fly into exile.

Silvia and the two boys joined me in Paris only a few days after I got there. On arrival we received support from fellow exiles and from AI and from generous French citizens who provided us a place to stay in the suburbs while we awaited visas to travel to the United States. After my family and I arrived in the United States, I traveled to Washington to express my gratitude to congressmen and senators who had responded to John's requests. I met with Americans working for human rights in Latin America through organizations like AI and the Washington Office on Latin America (WOLA). Their curiosity about events in the hemisphere and their selfless solidarity with my friends who were still in prison were very impressive. Many people at that time were working hard and long on these issues, including the Reverend Joe Eldridge, a Methodist minister who founded the WOLA to add Latin American voices and perspectives to the debates on U.S. policy toward the region. Sister Joan McCarthy, who had narrowly escaped being arrested in Cordoba, Argentina, and the Reverend Bill Wipfler, who was then the human rights director of the National Council of Churches, were immensely resourceful and full of ideas about how to get political prisoners released. They formed part of a loose but eventually very effective network of people and organizations that welcomed Latin American exiles, supported them morally and made sure their stories were told.

In the United States, I encountered many people like the Hutchisons, whose solidarity with victims of human rights abuse is selfless and sincere and who act in practical ways to alleviate suffering and to afford redress. To be sure, I have also witnessed acts of solidarity in many other countries and cultures, and early on I was a beneficiary of them. You come to expect solidarity from your family, and I received it from mine in many ways with no questions asked. You also expect assistance from your companions in the struggle: My fellow inmates at Unit 9 exhibited extraordinary solidarity on a daily basis—we had to trust each other, and we knew we had a common enemy. As a lawyer in Argentina, I witnessed solidarity from the public in ways that can be explained only by the generosity of the human spirit: In one case, a friend and client of mine was pregnant at the time the police entered her apartment. The police wanted to stay there to capture whoever else came in but got scared when she said she would miscarry. They called an emergency medical service. A doctor she did not know examined her and, although he realized she was not in any danger, told the police that he needed to take her to the nearest hospital and would not allow them to interfere with his medical duties. My friend was detained without charges for years and had her child in prison; nevertheless, the doctor's solidarity with her plight saved her from what would have surely been some savage sessions of cruel torture.

There were even risky shows of support for me and my family from friends who did not share my political convictions—from hiding books and papers, to defending me when others attacked me. One such person was my friend from my rugby-playing days, Ricardo Sepe, mentioned in the introduction.

At one point, however, I had occasion to see ideology and political rivalry come before solidarity. I had been in Paris for only two weeks when I attended a major rally at a downtown theater in support of political prisoners in Argentina. I was desperate to help the twenty-five inmates left behind in Cellblock 1 of Unit 9. I had memorized their names by using memory exercises. All of them were Peronists and Montoneros. The rally had been organized jointly by Argentine exiles and French leftist groups and had been carefully negotiated in terms of format and content. One of the French organizers (who sympathized with some Argentine groups but not with Montoneros or the non-Peronist guerrillas of the Ejército Revolucionario del Pueblo (ERP, People's Revolutionary Army) told me that he could not allow me or anyone else to tell the story of the recent killings in Unit 9 or call for solidarity with the inmates in the prison's death rows. Since that time I have been less than impressed with human rights work performed out of a sense of political or ideological identity and all the more admiring of those who are ready to help even those with whom they share nothing in terms of politics or ideology.

During the Carter administration, there were voices calling for a more realistic approach to human rights violations in Argentina, one that would give lip service to human rights without risking important U.S. interests abroad (mostly military or investment related). Dictatorships hired lobbyists and public relations firms, which in turn sponsored trips to Argentina and other countries for journalists and opinion makers to defend the junta and deny reports on human rights violations. Jeanne Kirkpatrick, a Georgetown professor who went on to be U.S. Ambassador to the United Nations (UN) for the Reagan administration, and others led the charge against the human rights policy with the view that only left-wing dictatorships should be the subject of U.S. sanctions, not American "friends." In the late 1970s, former president Richard Nixon criticized the Carter human rights policy and attempted to protect the Shah of Iran by saying, "You don't grease the skids for your friends." Kirkpatrick and her acolytes accused the Carter administration of applying a "double standard" in assessing the behavior of right-wing dictatorships. Indeed, Kirkpatrick used that phrase in a flawed but influential tract she titled "Dictatorships and Double Standards."[1] The double standard critique was particularly unpersuasive because its proponents actually argued that critiques and sanctions should be pursued aggressively against "totalitarian" foes of the United States, such as the Soviet Union, but not against "authoritarian" friends, such as the Argentine military. Their rationale for the different treatment was that totalitarian regimes closed down the possibility of change while authoritarian ones, because of their preference for open markets and trade with the West, would inevitably become less intolerant of dissent if only we remained friendly with them. It bears saying, however, that these cold war theorists missed their mark by a wide margin: They failed to predict that the Iron Curtain would crumble in only a few years, and they still cannot explain why China remains authoritarian and totalitarian despite its remarkable openness to international trade and investment.

To combat this dangerous ideology, I joined the Argentine exile community and contributed information and analysis to AI, WOLA and other organizations. Information collected by an Argentine exile group in New York called the Argentine Information Service Center was presented to the State Department before Secretary of State Cyrus Vance went to Argentina in November 1977. As noted, Vance provided the junta with the names of fifteen thousand persons whose fate and whereabouts were of interest to the United States. The following year, the Department of State announced a reduction in military aid to Argentina because of its human rights record; in response, the junta rejected all aid for that year. In the meantime, Congress passed the Humphrey-Kennedy amendment, which suspended all military aid and sales to Argentina and Chile.

The human rights policies of the Carter era were a welcome change from the overbearing "superpower" policies of earlier years. It is safe to say that the policies were applied most consistently, and with better outcomes, in Argentina than anywhere else. The visits by Vance and later by Patricia Derian, the first assistant secretary of state for human rights, were remarkable in their insistence that the junta could not expect "business as usual" with the United States unless it released prisoners in prolonged arbitrary detention and came clean about the disappeared. Such diplomatic demarches were backed up with legislative action conditioning U.S. aid on human rights performance and with concrete administrative steps to enforce or threaten sanctions on trade and access to financial institutions. This relentless insistence on human rights had the effect of putting the junta on the defensive in international arenas and of shaking Argentine confidence that their government was on the right track.

Implementation of the policy, however, was undermined from time to time by measures and initiatives meant to help the Argentine government. Unfortunately, Ambassador to Argentina Raúl Castro and Assistant Secretary of State for Inter-American Affairs Terence Todman were primarily interested in stable relations with the junta. The pro-government press in Buenos Aires filled the front pages with statements from Todman and Castro that seemed to contradict the State Department's policies regarding human rights.

Nevertheless, there were courageous U.S. officials fighting for political prisoners at that time, such as diplomat F. A. "Tex" Harris, whose support of the relatives of the disappeared was mentioned earlier. His confidential cables were declassified years later. They presented clear evidence for military complicity in disappearances and for the junta's mendacity in claiming that human rights violations were at worst the product of "excesses" by a few rogue elements. Often his cables included moving encounters with mothers of the disappeared and their attempts to obtain information from callous officials in the government and judiciary. Harris faced internal pressures to silence him, and he was unfairly removed from his position. Later he served in equally courageous ways as a consular official in apartheid-era South Africa. Eventually he received richly deserved recognition from his peers in the Foreign Service Association for his efforts to promote U.S. interests while upholding universal human rights values.

The fight against human rights policies was not only within U.S. government agencies. In Washington in those years, arguments about why the Argentine junta should be defended, even if its methods to combat subversion were not palatable to Western and Northern sensitivities, were common. On human rights grounds, the Carter administration instructed Eximbank, a federal agency that promotes foreign trade, to refuse a guarantee to the turbine manufacturer Allis-Chalmers in its bid to build a thermoelectric dam in the Paraná River in northeast Argentina near Paraguay and Southern Brazil. For years it had seemed that no one cared about human rights in Argentina; then all of a sudden the matter rose to the top of the Washington agenda.

Allis-Chalmers mobilized the U.S. Chamber of Commerce and conservative legislators to argue that human rights concerns were harming U.S. business. I witnessed an event at a Washington law firm in 1978 in which State Department officials were grilled by business academics and their students; their argument was that human rights were not so bad in Argentina and that, in any event, "development" was more important to the Argentine people than human rights.

It is amazing how quickly proponents of U.S. "exceptionalism" and superiority can turn to cultural relativism to explain away the indefensible actions of their allies abroad. And although now it is not fashionable to acknowledge it, in those years, the Argentine henchmen were indeed the allies abroad of important American interests. To its credit, the Carter administration did not budge. Vice President Walter Mondale met with General Jorge Rafael Videla in Europe and obtained his promise to let the Inter-American Commission on Human Rights (IACHR) conduct a fact-finding mission by a certain date, and then Allis-Chalmers got its loan guarantee. (The dam, however, was never built.) It might seem that not much was gained in return for favoring foreign investment in Argentina. Undoubtedly, the participation in bids by important U.S. firms gave the junta a veneer of respectability. But the visit by the IACHR would be—and effectively was—a major turning point in international condemnation of the junta's practices. The Carter administration's initiatives on Argentina proved that it was possible—indeed necessary—for the government to reflect the values of the American people by standing with the victims of mass atrocity. They also showed that such a stand did not adversely affect other legitimate American interests of a political, diplomatic or economic nature. In fact, long-term U.S. interests in the region were served by a human rights–oriented policy, as it was much easier to have relations of mutual respect and cooperation with Latin America once young democracies that were equally interested in human rights succeeded dictatorial regimes.

The junta hired Burson Marsteller, an expensive public relations firm, to improve its image. One of the most significant initiatives of this effort was to organize a press and legislative junket to Buenos Aires with columnists such as William Buckley and several prominent senators and congressmen. Key U.S. legislators presented themselves in the Argentine press as "understanding the true nature" of the debates about Argentina. Since that time, stricter ethical rules have been established regarding what U.S. legislators can accept from lobbyists paid by foreign governments. Upon his return to the United States, Buckley wrote a syndicated column purporting to show that human rights violations were not as bad in Argentina as pictured abroad and should not—in any event—be an obstacle to normal relations between that regime and the United States. In the mid-1980s, when the true scope of the tragedy of disappearances was revealed in the "Nunca Mas" (Never Again) report of the National Commission set up by President Alfonsín and in the trial of the junta members, Buckley wrote another column acknowledging that he had been wrong.[2]

In the early 1980s, with Reagan ascendant (he too had published a column defending the junta),[3] the Argentine military and its allies in the United States tried to have the Humphrey-Kennedy amendment repealed. U.S. businessmen came back on the offensive, and the then-leader of the junta, General Leopoldo F. Galtieri, decided it was time to travel to Washington and New York to promote business. Fascinated by the dream of opening Argentine markets, key U.S. business leaders gushed. They pronounced themselves bullish about Argentina and called Galtieri a "majestic" general. Even though soon after they were profoundly embarrassed by their guest's disastrous invasion of the Malvinas Islands, they provided no explanation or even a minor correction on their views about the Argentine dictatorship. At hearings on repeal of the Humphrey-Kennedy amendment, serious geostrategic experts would explain that Argentina was so strategically placed in the middle of important sea lanes that the United States could not afford to have a bad relationship with its government.[4] No one asked why this was an important consideration in the late twentieth century, when both commerce and war were conducted with technologies that made geographic position nearly irrelevant.

Starting in 1978, I was in Washington when debates over the best way to promote and protect the rights of others, including those in Argentina, were central to U.S. foreign policy issues. The interest in human rights was truly bipartisan, even though it was never fully freed from ideological moorings. Some liberal and progressive politicians and some nongovernmental organizations (NGOs) spent more time and energy criticizing right-wing governments, and conservative members of Congress did the same with left-leaning governments while accusing human rights movements of a double standard.

With respect to so-called authoritarian regimes (read: dictatorships considered friends of the United States), Kirkpatrick et al. advocated "quiet diplomacy" as opposed to public condemnation of torture, murder and disappearances. Today it would sound embarrassing to call the military dictators of Latin America "friends of the United States," but neoconservatives had no compunction to call them that or to argue for good relations with right-wing despots. An early report by Human Rights Watch (HRW) critiquing the intentions of the Reagan administration to restore aid to those regimes, and starkly documenting the regimes' human rights records, was very appropriately titled *With Friends Like These*.[5] After his release from prison and his arrival in the United States, Jacobo Timerman famously testified in Congress at the beginning of the Reagan years that, in the face of the atrocities committed by Latin American military regimes, "quiet diplomacy" was no less than surrender.[6]

The double standards critique could be applied to some advocates on either side of the spectrum. However, on the matter of where one chooses to dedicate time and energy, I do not think there is anything wrong with concentrating in one country, especially if one has links of nationality or cultural affinities with it. I would never criticize Miami Cubans for caring more about what is happening to victims of repression in Cuba; and of course the same is true for Salvadorans, Nicaraguans and Guatemalans living in the United States as well as exiles from the Southern Cone. What is unacceptable is for anyone to distort the facts to suit their own political agenda. This distortion sometimes results from exaggeration or from concealment of some relevant fact; it is even more egregious when it results from deliberate and knowing dishonesty about the facts or from placing an exceedingly high standard of evidence on the allegations that one tries to discredit. This happened all the time on Capitol Hill during human rights hearings in the early 1980s. Whenever conservative members were unable to discredit the mounting evidence of right-wing atrocity, they chose to discredit the bearers of bad news by imputing to them political or ideological motives. At hearings on El Salvador and Nicaragua, for example, Republican members publicly criticized Catholic nuns; their embrace of liberation theology somehow made their reports of what they had seen with their own eyes not credible.[7]

The exercise of constantly having to prove our assertions ultimately had a salutary effect on human rights advocacy. It caused AI and HRW to sharpen their arguments, to demonstrate the reliability of their fact-finding methodology and to confront head-on the issue of what had happened to whom and by whose responsibility. I was excited to be a part of these debates—I had begun working for HRW in 1982—and particularly in relation to the facts of the Central American wars. A Swedish diplomat in Nicaragua once told me that he found the HRW reports on Nicaragua (which I had written) particularly useful because they provided crucial human rights facts and used reason and evidence to attack readers' doubts and skepticism. The Washington debates about human rights in Latin America were indeed a turning point for the human rights movement.

Central to those debates was the question of sanctions for human rights violations. Unilateral sanctions for such violations in other countries had been written into U.S. law. The Foreign Assistance Act incorporated the Harkin Amendment, passed in 1975, establishing that foreign states that engaged in a pattern of gross and consistent human rights violations were not eligible for certain forms of assistance from the United States. In the mid-1970s, the anti–Vietnam War movement had brought to Congress new members intent on preventing U.S. complicity in human rights violations abroad, prompted by, among other things, revelations of the committee chaired by Senator Frank Church about Central Intelligence Agency assassination plots. Tom Harkin (D-IA), now a senior senator, authored legislation to amend the Foreign Assistance Act by conditioning aid to foreign countries on human rights performance. His amendment established an exception for aid destined to fulfill basic human needs. In addition, other statutes required that military sales and training programs would be similarly restricted, that the United States Trade Representative would deny "most favored nation" status to countries that abused the rights of workers and unions and that U.S. representatives to international financial institutions would be required to vote against loans to such regimes. Enforcement of these statutory restrictions was left largely to the discretion of the president, but they lent important authority to the State Department in conducting relations with abusive governments and in some situations were a factor in obtaining significant improvements. They also allowed for serious public debate in Congress and in the media about human rights violations in foreign countries.

In addition, there were a number of country-specific restrictions, such as the Humphrey-Kennedy amendment, which for several years cut off military assistance, sales and training to Argentina and Chile. Later versions of country-specific prohibitions, such as the one on El Salvador enacted in 1982, contained a "certification" clause that allowed the executive branch to waive the prohibition if in its judgment there was sufficient progress in the human rights situation. This escape clause allowed the Reagan administration to manipulate facts, figures and analysis and continue to support the murderous military regime in El Salvador. But it also opened the door to significant debates on the Hill that allowed human rights organizations to demonstrate the fallacy of the administration's findings of "progress" among the Central American military forces.

I was and still am very much in favor of sanctions, even unilateral ones, and not only because of the significant effect that Humphrey-Kennedy had on the Argentine situation. Nevertheless, sanctions for human rights violations pose significant moral and political questions. European human rights activists, for instance, have expressed doubts about sanctions because they are most effective precisely when they reflect the dramatic imbalance between rich and poor nations and because they tend to accentuate that imbalance. I understand that concern, but we should not renounce a powerful tool for human rights protection for that reason. After all, despotic leaders of less powerful countries abuse their positions and shield themselves behind notions of sovereignty and nonintervention for the worst possible purposes: to commit atrocities against the most vulnerable within their societies. In that context, separating the United States and other democratic countries from dictatorial regimes is right not only for practical reasons (it objectively weakens the regimes' power grip within their countries and isolates them from the international community), but for moral reasons as well: It is a way to side with the poor, the disenfranchised and the vulnerable. In any event, sanctions really are "conditions" for U.S. assistance. Conditionality is an important part of all international economic relations; trade benefits are granted or denied depending on a country's willingness to accept impositions by more powerful states or by international financial institutions. Conditions that limit the choices of poor countries to decide how best to feed their people are a particularly unhealthy and unfair aspect of international relations. It seems to me that a case can be made that countries should enjoy normal relations with the rest of the world if they are willing to respect fundamental norms of human rights behavior; they jeopardize those normal relations if they commit atrocities against their own people.

Still, for conditionality and sanctions to be morally justified, some fundamental principles should be respected.

1. Suspensions of aid should not affect assistance for basic human needs, such as food, health care and emergency relief.
2. There should be an order of ascending gravity of sanctions depending on the regime's behavior and its willingness to introduce real, measurable improvements. Military and police aid should be the first targets for sanctions, because ordinarily the armed and security forces are the instruments of repression. Similarly, treasury-to-treasury transfers of aid could be cut off or suspended because receiving countries can use the cash for any purpose; therefore, such funds subsidize security forces. Trade sanctions, however, are more of a blunt instrument that affects larger circles of citizens and economic sectors, some of which are not

only innocent of human rights violations but could well be
counted among their victims.

3. It always is preferable to apply sanctions on a multilateral
   basis rather than by the decision of a single very powerful
   nation.

4. One always should be ready to advocate the abandonment
   of sanctions if it appears that they are not effective in curb-
   ing human rights violations and instead cause more harm
   than good, especially to the innocent.

Such was the case with the multilateral sanctions against Iraq, ordered
by the UN Security Council after the first Gulf War, in the early 1990s.
These sanctions were more far-reaching than any other example in recent history, as they allowed the UN to seize and administer all the oil
revenues produced by one of the largest exporters of petroleum in the
world. For years there was no consensus about lifting the sanctions,
even though serious research showed that Saddam Hussein's grip on
power in Iraq was undiminished while the population suffered crush-
ing reductions in living conditions. This finding highlighted the very
real possibility that sanctions in fact do more harm to the innocent
than to the guilty and gave rise to the theory of "smart sanctions" that
can be applied dynamically and adjusted to changing circumstances.
In the era after September 11, 2001, the international community has
attempted to impose sanctions on individuals rather than on states, by
means of seizing assets, prohibiting travel and other measures. Unfortunately, the individual sanctions regime is fraught with problems of
fairness and due process and is rightly attacked for its lack of transparency. Although sanctions or their threat always will be part of the
human rights arsenal, it is undeniable that they present very grave
moral choices.

In discussing sanctions, it is important to remember one good example in which they produced a desirable outcome. UN-imposed multilateral restrictions eventually isolated and helped bring down the
apartheid regime in South Africa. In this case, the overtly racist practices
of that regime and its atrocities against the majority of its population
easily rallied the solidarity of the rest of world. Opponents of apartheid

in South Africa, especially Nelson Mandela, were seen clearly to occupy the moral high ground, and they publicly supported sanctions; the multiracial opposition made it clear to the world that trade sanctions, restrictions in military aid and even prohibition of South African participation in sports and entertainment were in fact helping to bring about the demise of the regime. Yet multilateral sanctions were not easy to enforce; the regime had many ways of violating the embargoes and the white supremacists never lacked for strategic supporters. Israel, for example, continued to give military and intelligence assistance to the regime. The Reagan administration embarked on a policy of "constructive engagement" with white-dominated South Africa, which in fact eased the pressure on the state. In the end, the regime fell not because of economic pressure but because the sanctions contributed to its moral and political isolation in the world as well as internally. The sanctions—in this case multilateral ones—eventually isolated and brought down the apartheid regime in South Africa. That is why the argument that sanctions are an instrument of powerful nations against poor nations, and thus should not be used, is wrong.

I OPENED THE HRW OFFICE in Washington on January 1, 1982. My tasks were fact finding and reporting on the Americas as well as advocacy before the U.S. Congress and administration. In advocacy, our office represented not only Americas Watch (now the Americas Division of HRW) but also its sister organization, Helsinki Watch, dedicated at that time to human rights in the Soviet bloc. We could hardly be accused of an ideological bent in our human rights advocacy since—like AI—we were equal opportunity critics: We condemned dictatorships of the left and right equally, as the situation warranted. Nevertheless, Washington-based supporters of various dictatorships that proclaimed themselves anticommunist still tried to discredit us, especially during the Central American wars between the late 1970s and early 1990s.

HRW built a highly successful program of human rights advocacy in Washington in only a few years. We were able to draw interest from members of Congress and from senators and persuade them to take action on behalf of victims as well as to insert human rights concerns into major foreign policy issues. The State Department became responsive to our inquiries, since our capacity to mobilize congressional support was implicit. Our influence on both the executive and legislative branches of government was bolstered by a deliberate strategy to disseminate our issues through the press, by cultivating foreign correspondents in countries where we worked, by aggressively disseminating our reports and by frequent and well-argued opinion pieces that we were able to place in major newspapers. Press strategies and dedicated staff—and more recently smart use of digital communications technology—are now standard with all advocacy-oriented organizations, but I have always thought that at HRW, Aryeh Neier and Susan Osnos early on took that strategy to the level of an art and obtained results far beyond what could be expected from what was then a relatively small and underresourced organization. Under Ken Roth, who succeeded Aryeh as executive director of HRW, the organization continues to be a source on human rights quoted daily in the worldwide press. Beyond HRW's evident success in dissemination of its reports, its strategy to focus on press attention has contributed to making human rights a central issue in all discussions about international affairs.

In our advocacy in Washington, Holly Burkhalter played a key role. She came to our organization after having worked in the House of Representatives and befriending many human rights leaders in the city. She was able to mobilize us quickly to participate in every major human rights endeavor on the Hill, at first mostly on Central American issues but soon on matters as diverse as Soviet dissidents, African famine and mass atrocities and persecution of opponents in China. What made Holly so effective was that she was eminently practical. After hearing ten minutes of a human rights story, she could figure out whom to call, what to propose in terms of action and what human rights activist to introduce to Washington decision makers.

In the 1970s, during the presidency of Jimmy Carter, human rights became a central tenet of U.S. foreign policy. Most important, American citizens of many political persuasions embraced the idea with enthusiasm: Concern for the plight of political prisoners, campaigns to end torture and demands to know the fate and whereabouts of disappeared prisoners captured the imagination of common men and women. I was the beneficiary of this remarkable change in Americans' view of the proper role of a major power in international relations, which began in Congress during the presidency of Gerald Ford and was made officially a part of U.S. foreign policy with Jimmy Carter. My American "brother" organized a campaign on my behalf from a small rural town in the Midwest and with the help of AI succeeded in obtaining support for my release from prison from Republican and Democratic members of Congress, as well as from the State Department and from churches and NGOs in Washington. This new human rights policy was questioned from the start by those who preferred a return to either U.S. isolationism or the pursuit of human rights only when they served a different, more strategic interest of the nation abroad. Despite those attacks, the power of the idea survived Carter's electoral defeat in 1980. Dictators in Latin America celebrated Ronald Reagan's electoral victory because the new administration initially vowed to make human rights concerns secondary to other U.S. interests, particularly the fight against terrorism. Early in the first term, however, congressional and civil society's emphasis on human rights prompted the Reagan State Department to embrace human rights as an idea, even if applied selectively and more in rhetoric than in reality.

In 2009, Republican members of Congress defended the coup plotters in Honduras, despite clear evidence of the detention, torture and killing of supporters of the deposed president, Manuel Zelaya. This is part of the recent trend of the United States abandoning its leadership position in the world as a promoter and protector of human rights, especially since September 11. The world, of course, is worse off. That leadership, begun in the 1970s and not forsaken in later years, was essential to the growth of a vibrant worldwide network of organizations and persons that is sometimes called the human rights movement. But human rights as part of foreign policy have been taken up by other countries, especially newly democratic ones—including Argentina, South Africa and Chile—and European nations. Human rights are now more firmly entrenched in the doctrine and protection machinery of the UN and regional organizations like the Organization of American States, the Council of Europe, the European Union and the African Union. In fact, the United States itself is hurt by its abandonment of the moral high ground in favor of expediency and the pursuit of short-term power and influence. A major superpower needs to rely not only on military and economic might but also on prestige and ethical leadership in order to exert positive influence over world events. During the Reagan and Bush (Sr.) years, even with contradictions, the foreign policy of the United States still served important humanitarian purposes. Members of Congress from both sides of the aisle continued to lend their influence on important committees to put pressure on tyrants abroad. For example, it was Senator Richard Lugar (R-IN), who accused Ferdinand Marcos of scandalous electoral fraud in the Philippines and started him on the road to isolation and eventual fall from power in the 1980s, even while then Vice President George H. W. Bush praised Marcos's "democracy."[8] During the Clinton presidency, reputed activists joined the State Department in key human rights positions, although there were some notable failures to take action, particularly the decision not to rescue 800,000 Rwandan Tutsis from genocide.

Already in the 1990s, the deep polarization in American politics resulted in a complete lack of interest among Republicans in pursuing human rights anywhere for their own sake (Republicans would not refuse to use human rights and democracy arguments if they served to buttress initiatives to extend U.S. power abroad). The absence of bipartisan support considerably diminished the weight of any human rights initiatives. After September 11, the issue again returned to the purposes announced by Alexander Haig when he became Reagan's secretary of state in 1981: Concern for human rights would be replaced by efforts to fight terrorism.

Yet, as the United States abandons human rights in foreign policy, the rest of the world has borrowed a page from the Carter years. Although the human rights movement has new friends, it still is absolutely vital that the United States joins the struggle. The Obama administration's renewed engagement with the International Criminal Court is one positive change, and the engagement has not been easy, given the hostility to the court by neoconservatives in the United States. The prohibition on the use of torture and restoration of the application of the Uniform Code of Military Justice to all anti-terror operations were also welcome changes at the beginning of the Obama presidency. Since then, however, progress has been slow and not without important setbacks. Failure to close the prison at Guantanamo Bay despite the promise to do so during Obama's presidential campaign is only the most glaring of those backward steps. The refusal to investigate human rights violations by U.S. agents is similarly disappointing. Inevitably, there have been similar setbacks in the international sphere. U.S. criticism of the report of a UN team led by Richard Goldstone on Israeli actions in Gaza is one such misguided action.[9] The abandonment of democratic principles in support of the coup plotters in Honduras is another; in this case, the problem is compounded because the only reason to break with Latin American democracies on this issue was to defuse Republican opposition to the appointment of Arturo Valenzuela as assistant secretary of state for Latin America and the Caribbean.

It may be impossible to return to the era when U.S. foreign policy had as a central tenet the defense and protection of human rights everywhere. U.S. economic might is not what it used to be; today the threat—even implicit—of consequences for trade with the United States immediately becomes a threat to the U.S. side of the equation. But it is nonetheless essential that we insist on the implementation of human rights standards. Even with contradictions, that policy did serve genuine U.S. interests all over the world and, most important, offered the hope that a powerful actor in international relations would stand by courageous human rights leaders and victims of abuse no matter what regime oppressed them. The natural solidarity of individual men and women in the United States and in other developed countries is still very much present. The challenge to the human rights movement is to come up with new ideas and strategies to turn that solidarity into positive action.

CHAPTER SIX

LAW

I first became involved with political protest as a young law student in Argentina in the tumultuous 1960s. I did relatively well in law school and graduated in 1970, but my first few years as a solo practitioner were uninspiring and economically not very profitable. I worked as a staff attorney at City Hall in Mar del Plata and, though the pay was meager, I actually enjoyed administrative law better than run-of-the-mill litigation. In fact, my only serious professional satisfaction came from the many lawyerly things I did on a pro bono basis: offering legal advice to the poor and disenfranchised and, increasingly in Argentina in the early 1970s, defending political prisoners. I can still see the face of the mother of a friend when I told her that her son would be released. She evidently expected a long prison term or at least lengthy pretrial detention for her son, and her face was ashen as she waited at the police precinct waiting room. The investigative magistrate had found no evidence linking her son to the bank robbery and other crimes under investigation and had ordered his immediate release, and I was the defense lawyer who brought the good news to her. Her face lit up and she shed a few tears of joy before thanking me. But like so many of my "clients" at the time, only a couple of years later, her son, Rolando Jeckel, would be counted among the disappeared. Years later we learned he had been held and then killed at the infamous Navy Mechanical School clandestine detention and torture center.

Once in exile in the United States, I rediscovered my main interest: seeing how the law could be put to use to solve injustices and to support the poor and disenfranchised. In Washington, DC, between 1978 and 1981 I worked as a paralegal in a public interest law firm set up to address racial and other forms of discrimination through litigation and advocacy. I went back to law school at American University, and after two years of night classes I was able to pass the bar examination in the United States, and I went straight into full-time human rights work: I took a position with Americas Watch (now Human Rights Watch, HRW) on January 1, 1982, scarcely six months after I had been admitted to the bar.

Since then I have worked on cases from Argentina and other Latin American countries arising from repressive military dictatorships and involving numerous issues, including torture, disappearances, arbitrary detention and extrajudicial executions. Over the years, my work has expanded to include global efforts to prevent genocide and provide accountability for mass atrocities; I am fond of some contributions I have made to the development of protections for freedom of expression and fair elections. Democratic principles must be nurtured and maintained in order to ensure the rights of all people, but in particular women, indigenous peoples, ethnic minorities, migrant workers and refugees. The law, and the role that it can play in the creation and implementation of international systems of protection against all manner of human rights violations, has been and continues to be an important focus of my work.

An important achievement of the human rights movement has been the creation of international institutions for the protection of human rights to which victims and activists can resort when national institutions fail. But while in the last fifty years there has been a marked improvement in the effectiveness of the European Court of Human Rights, the Inter-American Commission on Human Rights (IACHR) and the Inter-American Court of Human Rights, the African Commission and the new African Court of Justice and various "treaty bodies" and Charter-based procedures created by the United Nations, originally they got off to a rocky start. Each one of these bodies had to establish its legitimacy and prestige through decisions on hard cases, and often they had to withstand pressures from governments that were unhappy about those decisions.

In the late 1970s, around the time when I started engaging in human rights advocacy, human rights organizations based in the United States did not want to waste much time or energy bringing concerns to regional or universal bodies for the protection of human rights—especially the ones set up by the United Nations and based in Geneva—because they were considered slow, inefficient and hopelessly dominated by political considerations. Instead, efforts to mobilize public opinion in the world capitals and to engage democratic governments were thought to yield better results. At the beginning of the Carter presidency in 1977, many human rights advocates believed that Congress and the State Department offered the most fertile grounds for advocacy on human rights issues.

There were important exceptions to this rule, however. One group that was already effective at this time was the IACHR, created by the Organization of American States (OAS) in 1959. The IACHR was surprisingly ready to criticize repressive practices in powerful Latin American countries governed by military dictatorships, starting with Chile, but also including Brazil and later Uruguay and Argentina. The IACHR consists of seven commissioners elected by member states of the OAS. They serve up to two four-year terms, and they are chosen in their capacity as independent experts on human rights. The IACHR has a professional staff and Secretariat that is based in Washington, DC, at the headquarters of the OAS. Despite the fact that many Latin American governments were repressive military dictatorships, there were enough democracies on the continent to appoint serious-minded commissioners and to force serious discussions of IACHR reports at inter-American diplomatic and political forums, such as the annual OAS General Assembly, despite efforts of military dictatorships to suppress them. Besides often comprehensively analyzing the situation in a given country, these reports also included abundant cases as illustrations of patterns and practices and surprisingly tough language. In addition, by the early 1980s, the IACHR was beginning to present case complaints, particularly in cases of arbitrary detention, disappearances, political murder and torture.

In Washington beginning in 1977, my Argentine friends and I approached the IACHR Secretariat to describe various cases and to assist human rights leaders coming from Argentina to document cases of disappearances and political imprisonment. The IACHR lawyers worked on a variety of cases, including those of Jacobo Timerman, the Argentine newspaper editor who had been arrested and tortured and was then under house arrest, and the disappearance after arrest of Emilio Mignone's daughter. Eventually they produced a report, finally released in 1980, that became the most devastating indictment of the Argentine junta written to that date; it also represented the high point of the IACHR's investigation and monitoring of human rights violations.[1] The report was the main subject of debate at the OAS General Assembly in Washington in November 1980. Unfortunately, because President Carter lost his campaign for reelection that same month, the Argentine diplomats succeeded in eviscerating the ensuing resolution and suppressing important information from the draft report that identified some perpetrators by name. Nevertheless, and owing in large part to the quality of that report on Argentina, the IACHR retained a high level of credibility among human rights practitioners, victims' groups and democratic leaders in the whole region.

In 1979, the same year as its on-site visit to Argentina that led to that report, the IACHR released an important report on Nicaragua that contributed mightily to the isolation of the Somoza dictatorship and accelerated its downfall.[2] In later years, it also forcefully criticized the human rights practices of the Sandinista government that replaced Somoza, during the so-called contra wars supported by the Reagan administration. In the 1980s, as many repressive governments were yielding to emerging democracies, the IACHR acquired even greater prestige and legitimacy. Grateful for its contributions in their darkest hours, the newly democratic governments were more prepared to cooperate and engage with the IACHR.

By then, the Inter-American Court of Human Rights was in operation, and individual cases could be brought through the IACHR to this new judicial forum. In the late 1960s, as the work of the IACHR grew, it became apparent that an individual's rights when state institutions fail would be better protected by a fully judicial process to complement the promotional and quasi-judicial actions of the IACHR. The IACHR itself drafted and promoted a treaty that would give a firmer normative basis to its condemnation of the actions of some governments, and the result was the American Convention on Human Rights, which all Latin American states have now ratified.[3] In addition to its substantive norms, the Convention creates a system of case complaints that petitioners can bring before the IACHR for initial investigation. If the IACHR finds a violation of rights under the Convention, it submits the case to the Inter-American Court for a full adversarial process involving the state, the IACHR and the petitioners and victims. The court was established in San José, Costa Rica, in 1979 and initially issued only a few advisory opinions. By 1982, when I joined HRW, the IACHR and the Inter-American Court were promising but relatively untested forums to which we could bring cases that we developed as a result of our fact finding on the ground in Latin American countries. Our colleagues in domestic human rights organizations in Latin America urged us to join them in litigating cases before this venue. That led to our involvement in representing victims in the historic *Velásquez Rodríguez v. Honduras* case that resulted in a landmark decision in 1988, one that to this day is cited frequently for its major contributions to the advancement of international law.[4] In this case, the Inter-American Court held highly publicized hearings on the practice of disappearances in Honduras and gave that state ample opportunity to defend itself. The court found Honduras responsible for the disappearance and presumed murder of two Honduran activists and ordered the payment of reparations to their families. More important, the decision described disappearances in detail, established that they constitute crimes against humanity and ruled that the state is obliged to investigate, prosecute and punish the perpetrators and to reveal the truth of the fate and whereabouts of each disappeared person to the families and to society.

This first exercise of human rights justice in the Americas offered us the opportunity to urge the court to apply procedural rules so as to allow victims and civil society organizations to participate extensively in the proceedings; to clarify standards of evidence to be used in this kind of *sui generis* litigation; and to interpret international law expansively regarding absolute prohibitions and the legal effect for the state of their violation. The court did in fact create valuable precedents for the future. We presented expert witnesses, survivors of disappearances and defectors from security agencies, and we developed arguments on their admissibility, on the nature and scope of reparations for the victims and on the content of the state's obligations. We prepared thoroughly to cross-examine witnesses presented by the state, including some military officers suspected of direct involvement in disappearances. At the request of the Honduran government, these officers testified at a closed hearing, but the court afforded us ample opportunity to cross-examine them. We also needed to react to developments on the ground, such as the murder of witnesses: one who had been the first to testify in San José and one (a police officer) who was to testify at a later hearing at the court's insistence.

During the *Velásquez* hearings but especially after the decision, many Latin American nongovernmental organizations wanted HRW to help process cases through the IACHR (before reaching the court), so I was inundated with cases. This led in 1991 to my founding, with Chilean lawyer José Miguel Vivanco, of the Center for Justice and International Law (CEJIL), dedicated to litigating cases before the IACHR and the Inter-American Court on behalf of victims of human rights violations. At first CEJIL shared office space with HRW, but soon had its own office in Washington. A few years later it established an office in San José, Costa Rica. The Washington office processes cases before the IACHR in the initial stages; only after the IACHR rules on the merits of the case—and assuming the state rejects or ignores its ruling—can the IACHR choose to submit the case to the court. Litigation, therefore, can only be effective if it takes place assiduously in both Washington and San José, where the court sits. CEJIL has gone on to become a unique human rights organization in the hemisphere, partnering with domestic human rights groups all over the continent that represent victims of human rights abuse. Its litigation activities have resulted in new landmark judgments. To mention only one recent example, in December 2010, CEJIL and two Brazilian organizations won a major decision in a case called *Guerrilha do Araguaia*.[5] In this case, the Inter-American Court declared that the Brazilian amnesty law passed by the military dictatorship in the 1970s was contrary to international law and therefore could not be invoked as an obstacle to investigate torture, disappearances and murder.

Commissioners and judges for the IAHCR and the Inter-American Court are elected based on their expertise in human rights issues, and only for fixed terms (four years for the IAHCR, six for the court) that are renewable just once. They are not supposed to represent any country, although they are elected by the member states of the OAS. (In the case of the court, they are elected only by those states that are also parties to the American Convention on Human Rights.) As expected, those elections are seldom free of political maneuvering or pressure from states that wish to clip the wings of bodies that issue troubling pronouncements about human rights practices. Fortunately, because the court has been around only since the early 1980s, is limited to judicial proceedings and sits in Costa Rica, it is comparitively more isolated from undue political pressures.

In contrast, the IAHCR has been around for upward of fifty years, is based at the seat of the OAS in Washington and—in addition to individual cases—also conducts on-site visits and issues comprehensive reports on the human rights situations of OAS member states. For that reason, political pressure on the IACHR is constant. Diplomatic missions to the OAS in Washington participate weekly in meetings of the Permanent Council, where some try to use the muscle of that organ to influence IACHR decisions and thereby affect its impartiality and reduce its independence. Occasionally they ask the secretary-general of the OAS to lean on the IACHR for similar purposes. As the IACHR is dependent on the Secretariat for budgetary and administrative matters, opportunities for undue pressure are rampant. Fortunately, diplomats from democratic countries often come to the defense of the independence and impartiality of the IACHR and the court. At the time when commissioners and court judges are nominated and elected, however, those pressures can be very strong. The IACHR has developed some procedures that effectively blunt the effect of such pressures. For example, individual commissioners are barred from participating in decisions affecting their country of nationality.

I had been in Washington only a few months, filing petitions and working on Argentine cases, when I learned firsthand of the political pitfalls that face the IACHR. Through diplomatic pressure, the IACHR had been forced to accept the appointment of the son of an Argentine general as a staff attorney who would be privy to investigations of thousands of cases of atrocities and to the identities of persons who brought those abuses to the attention of the IACHR. My Argentine friends and I were concerned that information we submitted could be leaked back to Argentina, and petitioners and perhaps even our families back home could suffer repercussions; even worse was the danger to people like Emilio Mignone, Augusto Conte MacDonnell and the Mothers of Plaza de Mayo, who came to Washington to plead with the IACHR but then returned to Argentina. I tentatively approached Charles Moyer, an American lawyer who was the IACHR's deputy executive secretary. It was the first time we met, and I chose not to confront him on the issue of the attorney's appointment but rather to stress the risks that courageous Argentine human rights leaders were facing in their country. He explained that the IACHR operated so as to maintain confidentiality and avoid harm to petitioners and witnesses. Moyer and I later became good friends and, through frequent interactions in cases, I learned how hard the IACHR worked to honor the confidentiality it promised to petitioners. Over the years, the IACHR has gained control of its staff appointment procedures. Also, although its budget remains inadequate to cope with the enormity of the IACHR's task, today annual budget discussions are at least overtly focused on financial matters and free from political considerations. It is possible, therefore, for a body with a sense of purpose and mission to defend its independence successfully if it stands on principle and is not afraid to discuss those principles openly with occasional adversaries.

Regarding the election of new members, however, the IACHR has no power. If some states want to elect a commissioner with no human rights credentials to act as a custodian of state interest at the IACHR, it falls to civil society and to democratic governments to defeat such a candidate. The record in this regard is mixed. The IACHR always has had some excellent jurists as members, and their intellectual force usually carries the day; in recent years, independent and human rights–minded members have been a majority of the seven members. (Alas, they have never made up the entire body.) But some valuable members have been lost at the time of reelection when some states campaigned against them.

I was nominated by Argentina and elected as a member of the IACHR at the General Assembly of 1999 and began a four-year term on January 1, 2000. I was the commission's vice president in my first two years and, then, between January 1, 2002, and February 15, 2003, I was the president of the IACHR. (The seven members of the IACHR choose a president among themselves for a one-year term.) In 2002, as president, I led the IACHR's only on-site visit to Venezuela in fifty years, just a month after the failed coup attempt against Hugo Chávez in April of that year. Chávez and his acolytes wrongly accused the IACHR and me of supporting the coup, despite the fact that we had moved swiftly to demand Chávez's release during the few hours in which he was held in custody as well as the release of his supporters. In late 2002, we published our report of that on-site visit.[6] The IACHR condemned the coup attempt but also criticized Chávez's heavy-handed treatment of the media and his domination of supposedly independent institutions, such as the judiciary.

The Chávez regime angrily rejected our findings and publicly called for the firing of the IACHR executive secretary, Santiago Canton. Before we left Caracas, Chávez himself told us that we could return any time we wanted, but since 2002, his government has refused to deal with the IACHR or to set a date for its members to return. Despite the support of the Argentine government, in 2003, I failed by one vote to secure reelection to the IACHR, mostly due to an active campaign against me by Venezuela and many English-speaking Caribbean nations. (The latter were unhappy with my position regarding capital punishment.) Several years later, Venezuela also blocked Victor Abramovich, an excellent commissioner and a world-renowned expert on economic and social rights, from a second term.

Because of its oil riches and its relations with Latin America and the Caribbean, Venezuela plays a powerful role in political debates at the OAS. That fact has not prevented the IACHR or the Inter-American Court from issuing stinging reports and case decisions against Venezuela, mostly in matters of freedom of expression and due process of law. But the defiant attitude of the Chávez regime is a bad example. Some other governments reject reports and decisions by the system of protection and use the election of new members to settle those accounts and try to seat more compliant members. So far both institutions continue to exercise independent judgment and to enjoy great legitimacy, but the struggle to keep them independent and effective is never-ending.

In the same span of thirty years, other groups have also improved their effectiveness in the protection and promotion of human rights. The African Commission on Human and Peoples' Rights has now been joined by the new African Court of Justice. This new court has yet to issue any decision on the merits of the cases, so its effectiveness is untested; but the African Commission, despite being under even more powerful pressures than those suffered by its sister organization in the Americas, continues to produce some very effective reports on matters of great import, such as the Sudanese violations in Darfur and the situation of the Endorois indigenous community in Kenya.[7]

The European system of human rights protection operates under the umbrella of the Council of Europe and is the oldest regional system, dating back to 1950. In 1998 it changed from a two-organ mechanism, as in the Americas, to a single court that operates year-round and now also has jurisdiction over countries of the former Soviet bloc and Russia and several countries of the old Soviet Union. In its sixty-year history, the European Court of Human Rights has produced admirable decisions in cases dealing with such diverse matters as the death penalty, freedom of expression, minority rights and religious freedom. The court struggles, however, with a daunting caseload and with the need to monitor compliance with its decisions.

At the UN level, several treaty bodies combine periodic country reports, general commentaries on interpretation of human rights treaties and treatment of case complaints. In response to rising demands from the public, they have increased their workload and continue to make important contributions to the advancement of law, at least in connection with states that have ratified the respective treaty. The so-called special procedures are UN-based mechanisms with jurisdiction over every country in the world, since they are not treaty based; their authority is based on the Charter of the United Nations, and they are set up by the Human Rights Council, a political organ of the UN. They include special rapporteurs and five-member working groups on specific human rights themes, such as torture, disappearances, human rights defenders, housing rights, right to food and the like. Country-specific special rapporteurs are appointed from time to time to deal with particularly problematic country situations. The special procedures do not issue binding decisions, but they do command authority and respect. They and the treaty bodies are a marked improvement over the confidential procedures that were used for years at the now-defunct UN Commission on Human Rights.

Some members of the Human Rights Council, which oversees all of this machinery, still exert political pressures. But the combined action of the treaty bodies and the special procedures has broken the stranglehold of political control that prevented the UN from working on human rights protection in the 1980s. The organization has become independent, creative and serious regarding its purpose, and is backed by increasingly professionalized support from the Office of the High Commissioner for Human Rights, created in 1994.

HUMAN RIGHTS CONCERNS are not only about political murder, disappearances and torture. As the human rights movement has gained recognition and asserted its moral weight, its remit has inevitably expanded. Feminist organizations and advocates for gay and lesbian rights have joined the movement, as have those specializing in race relations and in the plight of vulnerable children. If personal liberty was the dominant legal standard in the early stages of the human rights movement, today the principle of equality plays that role. As a result, human rights organizations worldwide are now richer and more diverse, and their aim is to have an impact on the quality of exercise of democracy by all citizens. I sometimes call these aspects of human rights work the "new horizons" of human rights protection, because they draw their strength from previous successes of the movement, but their complexity requires innovation in strategies and methodologies.

Today the human rights discourse injects itself into public policy, in the United States and around the world. The worldwide debates about immigration policy are now primarily a discussion about the human rights of migrant workers and their families. In race relations, there has been undeniable progress, as the election of an African American to the most powerful elected post in the world attests. That fact alone energizes the work toward true racial equality and offers hope to millions of members of oppressed minorities everywhere. The international human rights movement has embraced the promotion of economic, social and cultural rights as a way to achieve both freedom from want and equality of opportunity.

But these issues are political as well as legal: A truly functioning democracy demands the inclusion of all marginalized peoples, and that in turn requires that every person's vote and opinion count in the formulation of policy. It is clear, then, that inclusion requires effective realization not only of economic, social and cultural rights but also of civil and political rights. Periodic, free and fair elections do not by themselves satisfy the ideal of political participation; we still need to guarantee that such elections are genuine expressions of the will of the people and that every vote is counted fairly. Even in the United States, the electoral system is far from this goal. For example, the clumsy vote counting in Florida in the 2000 presidential election, and particularly the decision to stop counting and decide the winner by judicial fiat, would rightly cause accusations of banana republic practices if it had happened in Latin America or in Africa. Another complication was the recent Supreme Court decision in the *Citizens United* case; under the pretext of freedom of expression, it allows for money to exert a degree of power and influence over electoral outcomes that is essentially inimical to the democratic ideal of equality in political participation.[8] Instead, we need to recognize that freedom of expression is not the prerogative of media conglomerates or of corporate interests; it is urgently needed for the poor and disenfranchised everywhere in the world, in the form of access to the media, but also in the protection of their own way of expressing themselves, through peaceful assembly and demonstrations.

Under various administrations, the United States has promoted democracy in many parts of the world, as I witnessed in the 1990s, as director of the Inter-American Institute of Human Rights (IIHR), which implemented programs of electoral reform in the Americas. Electoral systems are vastly improved in much of the world, including in the poorest countries, and international elections observation has been a key contributor to that result. Although it is now easier to detect fraud, the international community still needs to stand firm and insist that election results be respected, as in Cote d'Ivoire and Haiti in early 2011. In addition to elections, it is important for human rights and democracy proponents to focus on the day-to-day exercise of democracy through political participation, the effectiveness of the rule of law and its institutions and the proper place for independent organizations of civil society.

AS A LAW STUDENT in the 1960s, I worked my way through school by working for the legal advisor in the Mar del Plata city government. I saw many corrupt practices that enabled the rich and powerful to bend city planning rules, and saw many disputes between squatters and the purported owners of the land where they had established their shantytowns. I trembled with indignation when I heard a chronic City Hall "client" demand that the municipal government send the police to evict squatters from a vacant lot. As this man had recently paid the unpaid taxes on the lot, he claimed ownership under the doctrine of adverse possession. My bosses and I were looking for solutions that attended to the social needs of the squatters and not to the "rights" of speculators; the man hinted to us that if the government dragged its feet, he could solve the problem with kerosene and a few matches in the dead of night.

After graduation, I participated with others in efforts to provide legal advice and representation to the poor who inhabited those shantytowns. These services were not well organized, and they may well have dashed the expectations of some of those we wanted to serve. One important reason why is that they were conceived primarily as a political organizing tool and only secondarily as a genuine service.

When independent organizations of civil society did enter Argentine public life in the late 1970s, they did so in response to the brutal violence of repression; human rights entities were set up to defend political prisoners, to search for the disappeared and to stop torture. They became a second stage—and eventually a much more effective one—to the largely solitary and dangerous efforts of my colleagues and myself to link the defense of political prisoners to our political identity as opponents of the regime. The human rights organizations that arose during the worst days of repression in Argentina continue today to offer the best hope to the poor and vulnerable and are highly regarded for their role in the formulation of public policy; they have succeeded in that endeavor precisely because they defended their integrity and independence throughout the quarter century of democracy the country has enjoyed since the fall of the military junta.

I am especially fond of the Centro de Estudios Legales y Sociales (CELS), the Buenos Aires–based organization founded in 1979 by Emilio Mignone and Augusto Conte MacDonnell after their children disappeared. At first these men joined an umbrella organization, the Permanent Assembly for Human Rights, but they found the group's decision making slow and cautious. Without breaking with the assembly, Emilio and Augusto founded CELS to engage in litigation, documentation and analysis in a more agile, dynamic way. They and other colleagues were successful beyond their expectations in bringing legal challenges at home and abroad to the practices of arbitrary detention, torture and disappearances. In 1982, they were briefly apprehended and accused before federal courts; fortunately, by then they were so well known that the international outcry forced the military to back down.

At the newly created HRW, I concentrated on the most egregious violations of civil and political rights, conducting fact finding and reporting on massacres, imprisonment, torture and disappearances in the Central American wars. Even then, an important part of the HRW mission became the defense and protection of colleague human rights activists in the Central American countries and of the right of their organizations to exist and to work even in the most hazardous circumstances. The defense of civil society organizations turned later to a deeper analysis of their proper role in the new democracies that began to emerge in Latin America in the 1980s and early 1990s. Some of these organizations made the difficult transition to a very different place in a very different political climate, and their contributions to the quality of democracy are evident.

I had occasion to put this knowledge of the role of independent organizations of civil society to practical use in the late 1990s, when I left HRW to become the executive director of the IIHR. The IIHR offers training and capacity building to civil society organizations and to public sector institutions, particularly in the area of election monitoring but also regarding best practices of election organization and delivery. It trains civil society organization members in using domestic institutions to pursue human rights policies, and it trains public institutions, such as the ombudsman or people's defenders,[9] judges and prosecutors, and police, military and corrections officers, in being responsive to societal claims.

At the IIHR, I worked to expand freedom of expression, bringing together journalists, media enterprises and judges to devise more modern protections for free speech, freedom of information and public access to the media. Earlier on, while still at HRW, I represented Horacio Verbitsky, Argentina's best-known investigative journalist, in challenging a conviction for *desacato* (criminal contempt) arising out of an article he wrote about a supreme court justice. I brought the case to the IACHR where it was settled, with the conviction vacated and expunged and the law that allowed it repealed. As part of the friendly settlement, the government and Verbitsky jointly urged the commission to produce a study of desacato laws and their inconsistency with international treaties, as well as a strategy for their abolition. The commission produced that report in the 1990s and has promoted repeal of desacato laws where they still exist.[10]

Starting in 2000 as a member of the IACHR, I worked to abolish criminal statutes for defamation or libel and to promote the adoption of criteria in international law known as actual malice. The actual malice doctrine says that the standards for defamation are different when the aggrieved party is not a private person but someone acting in the public sphere, such as a government official, politician or public commentator. Defamation of a public person occurs not only if the substance of the information published is proven to be wrong; the alleged perpetrator must be found to have acted with actual malice regarding its truth or falsehood. "Actual malice" means proffering the allegation, knowing it to be false or in "reckless disregard" for whether it is true or false. The reason for this doctrine is that democracy requires a very active debate and an informed public; those who willingly enter the public arena must allow for information to reach wide sectors without fear of suppression. This standard, for instance, applies in U.S. law as a result of the Supreme Court decision in *New York Times v. Sullivan*.[11] It also has been adopted by the European and inter-American judicial systems, albeit with slight variations.[12] The IACHR greatly aided these efforts to expand free expression in the Americas in the late 1990s by creating the position of a Special Rapporteur on Freedom of Expression.

My years at IIHR and later at the IACHR gave me the opportunity to work on a wider variety of human rights challenges and to witness the efforts of newer civil society organizations to generate interest in the plight of indigenous peoples and African descendants in the whole Western Hemisphere. The Inter-American Court has produced landmark decisions favoring indigenous communities in *Awas Tingni v. Nicaragua, Moiwana v. Suriname* and other cases.[13] These cases deal with collective reparations for violence *(Moiwana)* but also with the rights of indigenous collectives to the use of land and natural resources and to be consulted by the government in decisions regarding economic development that can have an impact on their cultures and ways of life. In *Awas Tigni,* for example, the Inter-American Court found that Nicaragua had violated agreements with the Sumu indigenous minority by granting a foreign logging concern a concession to cut down forests in lands that the state had recognized as ancestral Sumu lands. The court reasoned that the very existence of the indigenous culture depended on its special relationship with land and that the state should recognize a special form of collective title to it by the community. Nicaragua was ordered to demarcate the land in order to make that official recognition effective and to consult with the community on any future development project. Since then, the Inter-

American Court has issued equally important decisions on indigenous rights in several other Latin American countries.

The struggle for economic, social and cultural rights, beyond the question of equality of treatment, is very much in its infancy, particularly when it comes to practical ways of making those rights justiciable—that is, subject to enforceable court determination. Public benefits granted in ways that discriminate on the basis of race, religion, national origin, gender, sexual preference or other prohibited grounds are brought up and resolved fairly easily in the domestic jurisdiction. But denial of access to benefits where there is no discriminatory intent or impact is a very different matter. While a commissioner at IACHR, I had the opportunity to test the possibility of making the right to health care justiciable in the case of *Odir Miranda v. El Salvador*, in my capacity as rapporteur for that country. Miranda and another twenty-five or so Salvadorans were patients in terminal stages of AIDS and were being denied antiretroviral treatment as it was simply unavailable in public hospitals. At my insistence, the IACHR ordered precautionary measures instructing the state to provide treatment to the named petitioners who otherwise would die. At first, the government protested, but when the measures were about to expire and the IACHR faced having to decide whether to ask the court to issue its own provisional measures, El Salvador announced that it had borrowed the medicines from Costa Rica and would comply with the order. A year later, during a hearing on the merits of the case, the health minister of El Salvador proudly announced to the IACHR that the government was now in a position to test all AIDS patients to determine if antiretroviral treatment was indicated and to offer it to all those found eligible.[14]

Through my HRW research and advocacy, and through the cases brought before the inter-American system of protection, I have seen how the human rights canon can be adapted to confront endemic problems of our societies—abuses that are not the product of political turmoil but which surface in democratic times and challenge the state institutions and the very quality of democracy as lived by ordinary citizens. One example is rural violence in the struggle for land and the use of "private armies" to solve conflicts with landless peasants, often with the complicity of state agents or due to the neglect of officials or the weakness of institutions. In extreme cases, such people are forced into slavery or indentured labor. Included here also are problems of domestic violence that have, until recently, been considered outside the realm of both the law and international protection. That changed, for the Western Hemisphere at least, in 1994 with the passage of the Convention of Belem do Para—the Inter-American Convention on the Prevention, Punishment and Eradication of Violence against Women.

Feminist organizations persuaded the OAS and member states that a treaty was needed to force national institutions to take seriously the epidemic nature of domestic violence against women and to provide adequate sanctions and effective protection of women by courts and police. In Brazil, for example, until recently, some courts even entertained the theory of "legitimate defense of honor" to excuse murder of women by men who felt betrayed. In custodial settings, police and corrections officials often get away with the sexual assault and rape of women in prison. Under the new treaty, state parties assume responsibility to protect women from violence, even in the domestic setting, and to prosecute and punish abusers. This treaty blurs the traditional thick line between the private and the public spheres (wherein the former was not the concern of human rights law), although the emphasis is still very much on states' responsibilities to apply due diligence to protect women from violence. As a member of the IACHR, I had the opportunity to vote on the first case in which the treaty was applied. We ruled on a case in which Brazilian courts had had ample notice of an abusive husband's threats and previous acts of violence and had allowed him to attempt to murder his wife, leaving her paralyzed for life.[15] We ruled in favor of Maria da Penha and the Brazilian government fully accepted our recommendations. In fact, the law that was passed in Brazil at our behest, criminalizing domestic violence, is now called the "Maria da Penha law."

I HAVE NOT KEPT UP with the law in Argentina and would not be able to practice if I returned there now. But my interest in judicial and police reform, in my homeland and other countries, through the constitutional review of laws and practices—especially the role of courts in protecting citizens—has continued. I try to maintain contact with human rights developments in the domestic law of several countries. I also have been in touch with many young lawyers who come from abroad to study human rights in the United States; it is gratifying to see so much talent and serious academic attention being turned toward human rights activism. Even with progressive legislation, the law is insufficient to protect all victims of all human rights violations; that is why I am convinced that the struggle for human rights requires multidisciplinary approaches and the coordinated efforts of many people with different talents and skills. But I am also persuaded that the law and lawyers must continue to play a decisive role at the center of that struggle.

CHAPTER SEVEN

WAR

In the 1970s and 1980s, human rights organizations dealt only with violations of international standards in peacetime or under states of emergency. War, including internal conflict, was considered outside their scope. One reason was the difficulty of conducting fact finding in conflict-ridden areas. Another was that invariably in such situations, there was another group, usually a guerrilla force, that was not a state actor and therefore was not bound by human rights law. Some human rights activists thought that reporting on all sides would dilute the special stigma that governments deserved if they violated human rights and would somehow offer them an excuse because of the violence of their adversaries. And some activists did not want to report on insurgents because they sympathized with their causes; needless to say, that was the worst possible reason to ignore abuses committed by insurgents. Ultimately, human rights organizations were hesitant to report on wars because they felt that war was by definition the absence of law, and no clear rules were applicable to the conduct of forces on the ground.

In the early 1980s, when my colleagues and I were conducting fact-finding missions on the Central American wars, Human Rights Watch (HRW) began to treat the abuses committed by all sides of a conflict in a methodical manner. The decision to apply norms systematically to all parties to a conflict changed the way human rights work is conducted everywhere.

At the time, the Reagan administration was intent on supporting the armed forces of El Salvador and Guatemala, no matter how undemocratic or how criminal their practices of massacres, extrajudicial killings, disappearances and torture. With U.S. support, the militaries of those countries were fighting against leftist rebel groups. There and also in Peru and Colombia, very serious atrocities were committed by paramilitary groups not formally linked to the official security forces but doing their dirty work. Determining the extent to which paramilitary atrocities were the state's responsibility created another challenge for human rights monitoring and reporting.

The U.S. government at that time was also supporting the contras in Nicaragua, a right-wing rebel force that wanted to topple the leftist Sandinista government that in 1979 had ousted long-term dictator Anastasio Somoza. The record of the forces supported by the United States was so terrible that, inevitably, when a human rights group tried to report on the atrocities, the preferred tactic of the Reagan administration and its allies was, in essence, to shoot the messenger. Organizations that monitored and reported on violations by governments were accused of being silent on the crimes committed by insurgents in El Salvador and Guatemala. Those that reported on abuses by the contras were charged with being shills for the Sandinistas. In the first instance, the human rights groups defended themselves by arguing that multilateral treaties applied only to states, not to nonstate actors. This was, of course, correct from a legal point of view, but to the general public, it sounded like a lame excuse for ignoring abuses by the rebels. As for those who criticized the contras, U.S.-based organizations argued that they were interested mostly in informing the public about abuses committed by forces that received economic and military support paid by American taxpayers; rebels in El Salvador and Guatemala and the Sandinista government in Nicaragua were not supported by the United States and therefore their conduct did not affect U.S. policy. This argument was unpersuasive because it seemed to ignore the fact that the wars' generalized violence caused widespread suffering; those who invoked this argument sounded as if they were concerned about some victims but not others.

At HRW, our fact finding on the ground put us in touch with victims of abuse by all sides. We did not want to be in the awkward position of telling some victims that their plight did not interest us, while others, who were experiencing the same losses and suffering, were squarely within our mandate. It was for this reason that we reported on all violations and applied the same standards to all violent actors, regardless of their affiliations. Eventually this local decision was adopted as an HRW policy. Before putting it in practice, however, we needed to sort out a number of obstacles.

In the first place, we needed to be sure that our decision could not be used against our sister organizations that chose not to report on nonstate actors. This was particularly important in relation to human rights groups working in their own countries. Colleagues in Washington and in Europe argued that by reporting on all sides we would be putting our sister organizations in a difficult and even dangerous situation, as the governments in their countries would compare them to us and accuse them of shielding rebel forces from criticism while denouncing official abuses. In fact, we found that our decision, which we discussed with many groups before adopting, was met with interest, not with hostility. Many organizations wanted to know more about the body of law that we would apply, known as the law of armed conflict, and how it could be applied in their own setting.

In the armed conflicts that came later, most notably in Peru, the local human rights groups made the decision from the start to report systematically on both state and nonstate agents. They gained great legitimacy in public opinion because of this choice, but it was by no means a risk-free decision; the Sendero Luminoso (Shining Path) insurgency openly attacked and threatened human rights defenders as "bourgeois" protectors of a legal order that should be destroyed, not upheld. Peruvian government, military and police forces also rejected the findings of the human rights movement, and some defenders paid dearly for their courage to denounce abuses by all sides.

When HRW announced its decision to report on all sides, we made it clear that we respected the decision of other organizations that reported only on governments. That stand, with which we respectfully disagreed, had a long trajectory in the human rights movement and support in international human rights law, and we considered it a legitimate choice.

The second challenge was to apply an objective standard that would be easily understood by our interlocutors and by the public at large. International human rights treaties contain obligations addressed only to states, not to private actors. Even if a state has not ratified those treaties, some provisions apply to it simply because of its membership in a community of states. Nonstate actors are not subject to those obligations; when they break the law, they can and should be criminally prosecuted. But nonstate actors that are organized and operate under a central command are indeed covered by international law—albeit by a different branch of law—particularly if they aspire to replace the government. Their actions must comply with applicable rules in the law of armed conflict, largely codified in the four Geneva Conventions of 1949 and in the two Additional Protocols approved in 1977. Robert K. Goldman, a member of the advisory board of Americas Watch (a predecessor organization to HRW) and an expert in both human rights and the laws of war, was the first to urge us to apply the Geneva Conventions to the conflicts in Central America. He and Theodor Meron, another active member of HRW boards, explained that those treaties covered even internal conflicts and civil wars, but it was crucial to understand which specific aspects of those treaties were applicable to the kinds of conflict we were covering.

International wars are covered by international humanitarian law, or the laws of war, codified in all four Geneva Conventions, Additional Protocol I of 1977, the several Hague Conventions of the early twentieth century and several rules that are widely accepted as having acquired the status of customary international law and thus are applicable to states that have not ratified these multilateral treaties. Broadly speaking, "Hague law" applies to weapons and methods of warfare, while "Geneva law" defines combatants and their rights and protects civilians and those not actively participating in hostilities. A conflict is of an international character when two or more nations—at least one of which is a party to the Conventions—are fighting each other with their armies and under their flags.

Conflicts not of an international character are governed by Protocol II of 1977, which prohibits attacks on civilian populations, bans orders not to take prisoners and condemns both the killing of adversaries who have surrendered and outrages against the personal dignity of prisoners, among other rules. It is a very detailed code of conduct for all sides in a conflict, but it has a very demanding threshold of applicability: The state where the conflict is occurring has to be a party to the Protocol, and the conflict must be of such regularity and intensity that the insurgents are in a position to implement the Protocol. Essentially, this requires the insurgents to be able to act as a quasi-government in at least part of the country—to be able to control population and territory for a relatively sustained period of time. It follows that conflicts in which rebels engage in urban or rural guerrilla warfare but without controlling the population are not covered by Protocol II. Rebels who do not control a population or territory are, however, covered by Article 3 common to all four Geneva Conventions, as long as they operate under a unified command and engage in hostilities that are sustained over a certain period of time. "Common Article 3" as it is generally called, provides the absolute minimum rules applicable to the humane treatment of enemy and civilian populations in conflicts not of an international character. Sporadic or spontaneous public disturbances, even if very violent, are not covered by international humanitarian law. Significantly, insurgents in an internal conflict are not protected by combatant status and, upon apprehension, are not treated as prisoners of war; the state has a right to prosecute them under the criminal law of the nation for the crime of rebellion or sedition, even if otherwise they have fought without violating the laws of war.

At HRW, we first established the facts of each internal conflict in Central America as generally agreed on, then proceeded to pinpoint which ones constituted violations of the laws of war and to attribute responsibility to one or the other side of the conflict. Any ideological, political or even economic support from third-party countries did not change the character of the conflict. For example, Honduras allowed the contras to use Honduran territory to launch attacks on Nicaragua, and the United States offered moral, political and funding support and some military training, but the actual fighting was conducted exclusively by Nicaraguans. The Sandinista government, meanwhile, enjoyed political support from Cuba. The contras never controlled any part of the Nicaraguan territory, nor did they exercise control over any significant population. We were criticized for stating that the contras were legally responsible for the abuses they committed. Supporters of the contras flatly denied the veracity of the facts we uncovered; leftist critics of U.S. policy wanted us to make the U.S. government responsible for every atrocity committed by the forces it supported. We did point out the moral and political dimension of that support, but as a matter of legal responsibility, the contras and their leaders were responsible for violations of the laws of war. Our analysis was later validated by the International Court of Justice (ICJ) in the case brought by Nicaragua against the United States. The ICJ found against the United States on several violations of international law but did not make the United States legally responsible for law of war abuses committed by the contras.[1]

Our third challenge was to maintain our credibility as an organization that was independent of the political factions at war with each other. We were certainly not impartial when it came to mass atrocities, but we needed to distinguish political objectives from the actual behavior in the field of battle. The laws of war were very helpful in this regard because they clearly address what is known as *jus in bello* (the law applicable to conduct in war) as opposed to *jus ad bellum* (the law applicable to the conditions under which resort to force is legitimate). Since 1945, international law prohibits jus ad bellum except in self-defense or when ordered by the Security Council of the United Nations. The question of when there is a right to rebellion or whether killing a tyrant is legitimate is no longer a legal issue; it is a moral and philosophical matter. For that reason, our reports chose to stay silent on the matter of jus ad bellum and did not question the right of each state to impose law and order. Instead, we held rebels and state agents to their respective obligations under jus in bello—the laws of armed conflict.

It is important to explain why we would uphold norms of behavior in war instead of advocating for peace. Some felt that our position legitimized the use of force and that, if we really wanted human rights to be observed, we should focus our energies instead on seeking peaceful resolution of disputes. The laws of war do not in any way legitimize war, even though, of course, peace is always more conducive to human rights than conflict. The laws of war simply state that, regardless of the motive that drives persons to war, once they decide to fight, they are obliged to follow rules that tend to avoid suffering by those not taking an active part in the conflict. It is also important to note that HRW did not consider itself a pacifist organization but one that tried to protect individuals from human rights violations, whether those violations occurred in peacetime or in war. Nevertheless, our attitude toward peace initiatives was not indifferent: Whenever possible, we favored negotiated solutions as long as we found that they would, in fact, uphold human rights standards.

In these activities, we were not alone. In El Salvador, Monsignor Arturo Rivera y Damas, the archbishop of San Salvador, called on all sides to "humanize the war," meaning that all parties should exercise restraint in the way they fought, and that they should respect and protect civilians and spare the lives of surrendered adversaries. Like the church organizations in El Salvador, we described horrible acts of violence, applied the laws of war to them and rigorously determined institutional responsibilities.

Monitoring and reporting, at home and abroad, gradually affected the conduct of the warring factions. In practice, we found that efforts to humanize the war in Central America not only saved many lives but actually contributed to building mutual trust among the parties to the conflict and among the public at large, and eventually created the conditions for a lasting peace that was finally obtained in El Salvador in 1992, and in Guatemala in 1996.

Some who argued for reporting only on human rights violations by government agents believed that applying the laws of war afforded rebels a status in international law that they neither enjoyed nor deserved, given their behavior. Governments that were fighting insurgents in the 1980s accused us of this intention. Common Article 3 and Protocol II explicitly state that their application does not confer any status on nonstate actors, and we were careful to spell that fact out. Nevertheless, those rebel groups that were interested in some kind of standing in the international community did engage with us on our complaints about human rights abuses and tried to show that they were doing something about them. That allowed us to comment, for example, on the rudimentary judicial practices that they claimed to use in the areas under their control. Our reporting resulted in some positive changes on practices on the ground.

Our final challenge was methodological. We knew where to find victims of government abuse, especially after years of contacts with local organizations whose good faith and professionalism we could count on. In contrast, victims of actions by insurgents generally were brought to our attention by governments or their allies, and there was always the risk of false or grossly exaggerated information. Since we were already under scrutiny in Washington over everything we said or wrote, we had to develop careful protocols about contacts on the ground. We would arrange for our own transportation to war-torn areas and would never accept security escorts, lodging or any assistance from any party to the conflict. Over time, I and a colleague, Jemera Rone, who had opened an HRW office in San Salvador and covered the Central American wars from there, were able to uncover vital information on incidents that had happened only hours before and were able to find the right locations and times to talk to victims and witnesses, free of outside influence. We also developed ways of corroborating what we heard with separate evidence or by visual inspection of the sites.

Leftist sympathizers of the Sandinista government accused my HRW colleagues and me of not allowing for the "context" to explain away the violations committed by the Nicaraguan government. That context, of course, was that a tiny country recently liberated from the Somoza dictatorship was fighting an armed attack inspired and assisted by the world's most powerful nation. Jemera once responded to these critics by providing very detailed information about the testimony of a peasant woman who had been harassed, detained and abused in custody for being suspected—with no serious evidence—of contra sympathies. She then asked, "How much 'context' can justify these violations?"

In the course of one of my missions, I interviewed a man in his fifties who farmed with his family near a small village in the northern mountains of Nicaragua. As an independent farmer—rather than a member of a government-sponsored cooperative—he was an unlikely target for the contras. But he had sons, and a rampaging contra detachment must have suspected them of ties to the Sandinistas. He showed me a scar near his ear where a bullet had grazed him as he was shot point blank while turning his head. He said he woke up to find his twenty-year-old son lying dead by his side. Without crying, he told me that dogs were lapping up parts of his son's brain. Neither he nor his son was armed or participating in the war in any way. The case was typical of the thousands of senseless murders of civilians that the contras perpetrated; we documented many instances of their contingents firing indiscriminately at civilians on farm cooperatives or traveling in trucks on the roads. One of the better-known cases had a young American as a victim: Benjamin Linder was an engineer who was working on a dam to bring water to the Nicaraguan village where he lived. The contras attacked the village and killed him and two others—Sergio Hernandez and Pablo Rosales. In a rare case in which an investigation of some seriousness took place, a forensic examination determined that he had been shot in the head as he was kneeling.

As the U.S. government's campaign to unseat the Sandinistas gathered steam in the late 1980s, contra supporters in Congress, in U.S. civil society and in some parts of the media attacked HRW bitterly because we insisted that the true behavior of U.S.-supported troops on the ground should be known and discussed. At a hearing in the House of Representatives, Robert Lagomarsino (R-CA), a member of the Subcommittee on Western Hemisphere Affairs, purported to show that we criticized right-wing but not left-wing insurgents and claimed to have found evidence of that alleged bias in our reporting on other conflicts. Aryeh Neier, executive director of Human Rights Watch, was able to point out that, in fact, our decision to cover violations by all sides in countries undergoing armed conflict was first applied in El Salvador regarding the Frente Farabundo Martí para la Liberación Nacional (FMLN) before we ever applied it to the Nicaraguan contras.

In El Salvador, one dispute was about the Salvadoran army and air force's practice of attacking civilians in areas dominated by the FMLN guerrillas. The government claimed that the villages were FMLN strongholds and took no precautions to minimize harm to civilians. In many cases, government forces directed their attacks against clearly civilian targets. For example, often they attacked columns of people moving toward safer zones. Typically, hundreds of women, children and the elderly would walk under the guidance of a few armed FMLN soldiers who were not participating in hostilities. Under the laws of war, those FMLN combatants were indeed legitimate military targets; but attacking them by firing on the whole contingent of civilians trying to escape violated the obligations to distinguish between military and civilian targets and to minimize harm to civilians even in the course of a legitimate attack. In a 1985 case closely documented by María Julia Hernández, director of the Office of Legal Protection of the Archdiocese of San Salvador, air and land troops had attacked a large number of women, children and the elderly who were fleeing toward Honduras to seek refuge. There were easily three hundred civilians, guided by perhaps two or three FMLN soldiers. The attack, near the Lempa River, had left dozens dead and wounded.

Defending the legality of the attack, Salvadoran and American leaders claimed that the presence of armed FMLN combatants made the group a legitimate military target. They also maintained that persons who lived in areas controlled by the FMLN were what the guerrillas called *masas*. Because they were relatives and former neighbors of the rebels, they were also their natural rearguard. Since the masas chose to live in that area, they were legitimate military targets, according to Salvadoran and U.S. officials.

Needless to say, this interpretation made a mockery of the cardinal rule of the laws of war that establishes a distinction between civilians and combatants. In international humanitarian law, civilians are all persons who are not making an effective contribution to the military operations of one of the parties to the conflict. Attacks targeting civilians and attacks that do not discriminate between civilians and combatants are serious war crimes.

In other cases, the Reagan administration simply ignored human rights violations that stood in the way of its support for the Salvadoran armed forces. The main example occurred early on in the American involvement in Central America with the massacre of hundreds of peasants in the village of El Mozote in December 1981. It was perpetrated by the Atlacatl Battalion, the first Salvadoran army unit trained by the U.S. military. The State Department initially denied that the massacre had happened. The debate about El Mozote was the subject of the first hearings I attended in Congress for my job with HRW. At one of those hearings, in February 1982, Thomas Enders and Elliott Abrams, respectively assistant secretaries of state for Western Hemisphere affairs and human rights, told Congress that U.S. Embassy investigations on the ground proved that the massacre had not happened. They claimed that there could not have been hundreds of casualties as the population of El Mozote was only about two hundred, disregarding press reports of victims being brought to El Mozote from six neighboring villages.[2]

More than ten years later, as the war in El Salvador came to an end, the Truth Commission set up by the United Nations as part of the peace agreements confirmed the story as originally reported, thanks to the testimony of the lone survivor, Rufina Amaya. She had been a refugee in Honduras for the whole of the war, and her toddler daughter had been taken by the army and sent to the United States as an unidentified orphan. A meticulous study of the crime scene and exhumations conducted for the UN by U.S. and Argentine forensic anthropology experts corroborated the story that Abrams and Enders had tried to discredit. In one burial site alone, next to the school in El Mozote, the Argentine team found 147 bodies, 131 of them children. All had been killed with ammunition used by the Atlacatl Battalion. Incidentally, the same U.S.-trained unit ended its tragic participation in the war in November 1989 (it was disbanded when peace finally arrived) by murdering six Jesuit priests, their housekeeper and her fifteen-year-old daughter at their residence on the campus of the Central American University in San Salvador.

THE LAWS OF WAR operate on a few general principles. One is the principle of distinction, which, as mentioned before, mandates that attackers must differentiate between legitimate military targets and prohibited civilian ones and must distinguish themselves and their troops from the enemy and from civilians. This is done generally by the use of uniforms and emblems or by carrying weapons in plain view; importantly, what can never be allowed is to mingle with civilians in order to hide among them or to use them as shields. Another is the rule of proportionality: If an attack is going to result in civilian casualties ("collateral damage" to an otherwise legitimate attack), the officer in charge must weigh that damage against the relative military advantage to be gained by the attack. If the cost in civilian dead and wounded outweighs that military advantage, the attack must be halted.

The principle of humanity forbids killing enemy soldiers who have been rendered *hors de combat*—out of combat—by their wounds or by surrender. It is likewise a war crime to impart an order to take no prisoners. Even giving officers the benefit of the doubt and recognizing that the fog of war can cloud split-second decision making on the ground, these principles are not difficult to apply. Finally, an important duty is contained in Articles 85–89 of Protocol I to the Geneva Conventions that very clearly establish the obligation to investigate, prosecute and punish "grave breaches" of their provisions. There is ample consensus that an affirmative obligation to punish war crimes exists; as we will see in the next chapter, that rule has offered formidable support in the pursuit of accountability for mass atrocities.

With HRW board member Ken Anderson, I also applied the laws of war to an analysis of civilian casualties during the U.S. invasion of Panama in 1989, which was launched to capture strongman Manuel Noriega. Our report questioned the military tactics that resulted in the burning down of the poor neighborhood of El Chorrillo in the capital city and the supposedly "surgical" operation that resulted in six times the number of civilians killed as Panamanian soldiers and ten civilians dead for each American soldier killed. We also debunked some of the exaggerated numbers of civilians killed that had been reported by organizations and individuals who criticized the invasion on political grounds or as a violation of Panama's sovereignty. To do so, we looked for records kept at hospitals and morgues and interviewed officers in charge of those facilities; we also asked detailed questions about weapons and tactics used and queried high-ranking officers as to why Panamanian civilians had not been warned of an attack on a densely populated area of the capital, although Americans living in the nearby Panama Canal Zone, then under U.S. control, were given a few hours' notice. We proved that no evidence supported attempts to blame the burning of the El Chorrillo slum on Noriega's defense forces.[3]

I later had occasion to apply these rules to the conflict in Somalia, which I visited in early 1993, a few weeks after international troops were deployed to protect famine relief deliveries. My visit was months before the disastrous decisions that resulted in the death of American soldiers (depicted in the book *Black Hawk Down*) and eventually the withdrawal of international forces and two decades of anarchy.[4] In the capital city of Mogadishu and in Baidoa, I interviewed persons displaced by the war waged on civilians because of their tribal affiliation. International forces had stabilized the country and were providing support for the delivery of services.

The famine that had resulted from the interethnic war was quickly being reversed, but one could still see heartbreaking scenes of malnourished children. Guns were everywhere, and it was impossible to distinguish between security guards protecting buildings or families from members of a militia who might attack at any time. International forces kept the uneasy peace, but otherwise the state had disappeared, and with it all services. The efforts of some individuals to keep schools running, or even just to direct traffic, were heroic. There was virtually no economic activity: At a market downtown, all one could buy were pieces of copper piping torn from abandoned houses.

The international forces led by the United States had daily skirmishes with militias; we criticized the fact that they would report on the number of casualties in each encounter without bothering to identify and deliver corpses to families for decent burial, violating their Geneva Conventions obligation to "search and collect the wounded and sick," to "ensure that burial or cremation . . . is preceded by a careful examination" and that "the dead are honorably interred according to the rites of the religion to which they belonged."[5] Undoubtedly, disregard for these obligations only fueled more resentment and emboldened militias. International forces were increasingly the targets of attacks by gunmen shielding themselves with demonstrators, often women. The tactic of "shielding" used by combatants intermingling with civilians is itself a war crime.[6] Eventually, an illfated decision to try to capture Mohamed Aidid, the most notorious of the Somalian warlords, resulted in the death of more than twenty U.S. soldiers and in President Clinton's decision to withdraw later in the year. Soon thereafter all international forces left, and humanitarian assistance to Somali civilians became very hazardous and therefore sharply limited. The wrong lesson was drawn from the Somalia experience, and in 1994, the United States did not deploy forces that could have prevented the genocide in Rwanda.

HRW and other human rights organizations later applied the laws of war to conflicts between states, mostly concentrating on weapons and tactics to determine if civilian casualties could have been avoided. The first report on a major international conflict was on the first Gulf War in the early 1990s. The research occurred after the Iraqi takeover of Kuwait had been reversed, sanctioned by the UN Security Council and large parts of Iraq had been invaded. At the time, the largest controversy was about the use of "smart bombs" that supposedly target so well that they minimize harm to civilians. Unfortunately, only a very small percentage of the ordnance dropped on Iraq was smart bombs; the overwhelming majority consisted of ordinary bombs dropped from ten thousand feet in the air. In addition, there were some well-known attacks with penetrating smart bombs, particularly one that perforated an armored building and killed hundreds of civilians who had taken shelter there. The HRW report was titled *Needless Deaths in the Gulf War*.[7] As we expected, the Pentagon originally dismissed or ignored the report, but its careful analysis did attract comment from specialists and from persons with military background and experience. Eventually some of them joined HRW and other human rights organizations; as a result, the factual and legal analysis of violations of the laws of war has become increasingly sophisticated.

After 1994, I was the general counsel at HRW, and my responsibilities included vetting all our reports for correct application and interpretation of international law. Many countries were contributing forces to international peacekeeping in different parts of the world, and we recommended full respect by those troops of their international humanitarian law obligations and an active and aggressive assumption of responsibility by each member state for investigating any allegation of violations. There have been some encouraging judicial developments by Canada (regarding torture and killing of suspects in Somalia) and the United Kingdom (regarding torture of prisoners in Iraq and Afghanistan). In 2010, the Conservative government of the United Kingdom launched a formal judicial inquiry into mistreatment of detainees in Iraq, entrusted to a distinguished jurist, Sir Peter Gibson. In February 2011, as the inquiry was being launched, I participated in an encounter between the Gibson Commission and civil society organizations in my capacity as UN Special Rapporteur on Torture.

By 1996 I had left HRW, but my colleagues monitored the bombing of Serbia in 1998 during the NATO operation to prevent a Serbian invasion of Kosovo. The principal incidents were the bombing of the Chinese embassy and the central radio and TV building, both in Belgrade. As to the former, the United States apologized and said that the building had been used, several years before, as an intelligence agency headquarters. The destruction of the radio and TV building, in which some technicians died, was justified as a legitimate military target because its broadcasts could carry coded messages and because it engaged in war propaganda. In both cases, the explanations seemed wrong on the law and much more should have been expected in terms of a serious investigation of who was responsible. Otherwise, the bombing that lasted four months was accurate and directed at military targets.[8]

Nonetheless, the U.S. military was unwilling to investigate its own actions and to be transparent with the public about the outcome of whatever inquiries it had conducted. It was a bad example for the rest of the world. In its reaction to the intifada uprisings in Palestine and the attacks on Lebanon and the Gaza Strip, Israel displayed a similar disregard for demands that civilian casualties be accounted for. The Israel Defense Forces attack on a Turkish merchant ship resulting in the death of nine civilians was defended as legitimate by an inquiry concluded in early 2011. The inquiries that did take place on the incidents in Gaza were conducted under procedures that did not allow for victim participation and were largely closed to public scrutiny. No one was punished for any wrongdoing, save for a few low-ranking soldiers who were scapegoated. The effect of such inquiries has been to preserve impunity. In fact, the reaction to the recent UN Factfinding mission on the Gaza Conflict,[9] directed by South African judge Richard Goldstone, on violations of the laws of war in Gaza was met with vitriolic attacks on Goldstone's character and with precious little in the way of accountability. If a highly sophisticated military like the Israel Defense Forces will not conduct serious investigations into possible war crimes, how can we expect less developed states to live up to their obligations under the Geneva Conventions?

In the United States, the Pentagon's behavior has gone from bad to worse. There have been many reports of military actions in Iraq and Afghanistan that resulted in civilian deaths. The wedding parties that have been bombed "by mistake" now count in the dozens. The pattern has been for commanders on the ground to announce an investigation in response to media inquiries and public concern after victims are clearly identified as women and children. Those investigations are conducted without respect for internationally recognized standards of impartiality and independence, and a few days later, it is announced that no charges will be filed because the civilian casualties were incidental to a legitimate military operation. By then, public outcry about that particular incident has faded as the world's attention has been shaken by new revelations. All of these incidents merit a serious, unbiased, transparent inquiry by independent investigators to determine if courts-martial are in order.

The Bush administration used the "war on terror" to attempt to redefine the laws of war. It thought the United States could erase rules developed over five hundred years to humanize conflict and protect civilians merely because it believed those rules were an obstacle to fighting terrorism. The United States felt it was powerful enough to override existing practice and rewrite international law. In testimony before Congress, White House legal advisor and later attorney general Alberto González said that the norms in the Geneva Conventions were "quaint."[10] David Rivkin, legal advisor to President Bush, likewise argued that the Geneva Conventions did not allow the United States to treat captured terrorists the same way as it treats its own soldiers during training. This disingenuous rhetorical device hides a very sinister purpose: to allow for the mistreatment of enemy combatants and to disregard obligations solemnly acquired by the United States when it ratified treaties that are the most widely accepted standards in international law.

Central to this debate is the question of whether anyone captured in the context of the war on terror is entitled to prisoner-of-war (POW) status. The laws of war offer an easy answer: Enemy soldiers captured in combat are entitled to that status. They can also forfeit that status if they fight in violation of their own obligation as soldiers to openly wear uniforms or distinguishing emblems and openly display their weapons. If they act with perfidy—by using disguises or otherwise leading their enemy to believe they are protected persons—they can be denied POW status and become "unlawful enemy combatants." Even so, unlawful or unprivileged combatants are entitled to some, but not to all, rights and protections attaching to POWs—particularly to humane treatment while in captivity. The Geneva Conventions make it clear that a determination of POW or other status has to be made on a case-by-case basis, according to the behavior of each individual, and by an independent adjudicator; in the absence of such an impartial adjudication, all captured enemies are presumed to be POWs.

The Bush administration purported to declare, by fiat, that *all* persons captured in the context of what it defined as the global war on terror were by definition unlawful enemy combatants; the president himself stated this.[11] The term was used to describe anyone captured in combat, whether they had violated their obligations as soldiers or not, as well as anyone captured outside of combat in a law enforcement operation. Certainly, the label "unlawful combatant" may be appropriate for a fighter disguised as a medic and captured in the battlefield while attacking U.S. forces, for example, as long as the facts are ascertained by an independent and impartial body. But, for example, the Department of Defense applied that label to persons apprehended in Bosnia and kidnapped by U.S. agents after their release by the local authorities.[12] Initially the government did not allow any judicial challenge to these practices. It should be noted that, from the start of the war on terror, many U.S. military officers, including high-ranking military lawyers, objected to these distortions. To the credit of military traditions in the United States and elsewhere, these officers, retired as well as on active duty, spoke out against the mistreatment of detainees in Guantanamo, in Abu Ghraib in Iraq and in Bagram Prison in Afghanistan.

During my term as president of the Inter-American Commission on Human Rights (IACHR) of the Organization of American States (OAS), in 2002, my fellow commissioners dealt with these important human rights questions raised by the so-called war on terror. We issued precautionary measures on Guantanamo at the request of the American Civil Liberties Union and the Center for Constitutional Rights. We urged the U.S. government to allow judicial bodies to determine the status of each inmate at Guantanamo, as the rights they could enjoy in prison would flow from such a status determination. The U.S. government participated in our deliberations but ultimately announced that it did not feel bound to comply with our precautionary measures. The IACHR reiterated its order of precautionary measures several times. Although the OAS has no power to enforce these judgments, they built pressure on the Bush administration through public opinion and became an effective advocacy tool.[13] Eventually, U.S. federal courts came to conclusions similar to those reached by the IACHR in 2002.

For example, the U.S. Supreme Court ruled against the Pentagon's interpretation of the laws of war in *Rasul v. Bush,* affirming that the status of detainees could not be categorically decided by the president and instead had to be ascertained on a case-by-case basis by an impartial adjudicator. In *Boumedienne,* it ruled that detainees held in Guantanamo could apply for habeas corpus relief to federal courts.

And in *Hamdan v. Rumsfeld,* the Supreme Court struck down the military commissions created by the executive branch to try some of these prisoners.[14] The majority vote by Justice John Paul Stevens ruled that military commissions created at the discretion of the executive branch violated Common Article 3 of the Geneva Conventions, which calls for punishment of war crimes by regularly constituted courts that afford the fair trial and due process guarantees recognized by all civilized nations. The Bush military commissions did not meet that standard because they would have allowed conviction of prisoners on the basis of evidence that they were not allowed to see. Even in the admittedly new situation created by the September 11, 2001, attacks, the United States must abide by the laws of war.[15]

In 2002, when I was the president of the Inter-American Commission, we embarked, on our own initiative, on a long-term study of human rights in the context of the struggle against terrorism. We held hearings and invited independent experts from different ends of the ideological spectrum to testify. Eventually we approved a report on the subject that is a comprehensive, rigorous assessment of international law standards governing human rights in the event of armed conflict, applicable to the struggle against terrorism.[16] Since that time there have been other similar reports, notably one by the International Bar Association and another by the International Commission of Jurists.[17] In 2009–10, the International Bar Association asked me to participate with Richard Goldstone and others in a task force to prepare an updated report on terrorism and human rights (it was published in February 2011).[18] These reports reflect a growing consensus that an attempt to fight terrorism with dirty war tactics and by circumventing well-established principles of humanity and due process of law is illegal as a matter of international law. Of course, those tactics are not only illegal but immoral: They betray the principles that we hold dear regarding how we want our societies to run. And beyond legality and morality, ignoring deeply rooted principles ultimately is counterproductive in the war on terror. Every detainee who is tortured, held in prolonged arbitrary detention or convicted in an unfair trial becomes a symbol that facilitates the recruitment of many more terrorists bent on destroying our way of life.

To be sure, the worst examples of this contempt for the laws of war happened during the George W. Bush administration, and many were reversed as soon as President Obama took office. Military operations by external forces in Iraq have officially ended, but it has been revealed that U.S. and British forces have for years transferred detainees to Iraqi authorities, knowing that they would be tortured. Since early 2011, the American presence in Afghanistan has been more careful to prevent civilian casualties, in part because such incidents adversely affect U.S. strategic objectives. On March 1, 2011, U.S. helicopters killed nine Afghan boys who were collecting firewood for their families. General David Petraeus, the U.S. commanding officer in Afghanistan, issued an apology.[19] But we are still seeing little in the way of serious investigations when acts of this sort do occur.

CHAPTER EIGHT

ACCOUNTABILITY

When I joined the human rights movement in the late 1970s, its efforts were directed at releasing political prisoners, stopping torture and preventing press censorship. As soon as situations improved, the human rights community shifted its attention to the next trouble spot. In fact, the orthodoxy of that time held that it was not the job of human rights organizations to press for the punishment of individuals responsible for human rights violations. The focus was on the state and particularly on getting states to treat their citizens more humanely. It is a measure of the maturity, growth and sophistication of the human rights movement that nowadays its objectives have changed. Now advocacy focuses on the many new ways to protect and promote human rights, including finding the appropriate institutional response when human rights abuses do occur.

When it comes to mass atrocities, the appropriate response has to be the investigation, prosecution and punishment of those responsible. Mass atrocities are characterized in international law as crimes against humanity or war crimes, depending on the context in which they occur. Crimes against humanity include abuses such as genocide, torture, murder, massacres, forced disappearances, forcible displacement of populations and prolonged arbitrary arrest that are committed on a massive scale or pursuant to a systematic plan. War crimes are serious breaches of the laws of armed conflict, such as targeting civilians, torturing or murdering enemies who have surrendered, pillaging, destroying civilian property or causing catastrophic damage to the environment. The consensus that the appropriate response to any of these violations is criminal prosecution has been with us since the terms were coined at the Nuremberg trials after World War II. The obligation to prosecute and punish these crimes applies first to the state where the crimes were committed or whose nationals were the perpetrators but also to the international community if the state is unwilling or unable to do so.

War crimes and crimes against humanity were committed extensively in the decades after 1945, with little effort to redress them appropriately.[1] The situation began to change as Latin American countries began their transitions from dictatorship to democracy in the 1980s. The military regimes did not suddenly relinquish power but tried in all cases to protect themselves and their legacies by conditioning those transitions. In particular, they enacted "self-amnesties," or extracted amnesty laws from the fledgling new democracies (almost literally at the point of a gun).

But unwilling to let their suffering be forgotten, civil society organizations and relatives of victims insisted on seeking criminal prosecutions in domestic courts. As these efforts proved futile or were truncated by political expediency, they petitioned the organs of international human rights protection—the Inter-American Commission on Human Rights (IACHR) and Court of Human Rights—to overturn the amnesties and other obstacles to prosecution inconsistent with the state's obligations under human rights treaties. As a result, since the late 1980s, a robust body of law declares such amnesties unlawful as a matter of international law and requires states to investigate, prosecute and punish mass atrocities. Similar rulings have been obtained in the European Court of Human Rights with respect to torture and disappearances in Turkey and by the various treaty bodies and special procedures of the United Nations commenting on impunity for serious human rights crimes in many parts of the world.[2]

In 1983, Argentina was the first Latin American country to experiment with a transition from military dictatorship to democracy in the region's "wave of democratization" during the 1980s and 1990s and beyond. Raúl Alfonsín was a surprise winner in the presidential election that year, after campaigning chiefly on the promise that disappearances and other human rights violations would be investigated. He created the first of many truth commissions that have been created around the world to deal with legacies of mass atrocities. In the case of Argentina it was called the National Commission on the Disappearance of Persons (CONADEP). Alfonsín also ordered the prosecution of members of the military juntas that had misgoverned the country between 1976 and 1983 as well as some well-known insurgency leaders. The CONADEP inquiry was extraordinary. It was chaired by the writer Ernesto Sabato; all other commission members were highly respected and well-known personalities from the judiciary, journalism, science and the arts. More important, many members of human rights organizations joined the staff of the commission.

All of the organizations put their own files and records at the disposal of CONADEP. The most important information came from thousands of relatives of the disappeared who literally lined up for hours in order to render their testimonies and provide leads in the hope of learning the fate of their loved ones. CONADEP representatives were able to locate and visit secret detention centers in many parts of the country. Although the commission did not have subpoena powers, it could apply for search warrants from the courts in order to fulfill its mission. Survivors of disappearances who were living abroad were allowed to testify at Argentine consulates. The commission members and its staff also did substantial research and detective work following documentary leads at governmental offices, although the military and security forces refused to provide any assistance.

On my very first trip to Argentina to end my exile, in December 1983, I visited with CONADEP members and staff and witnessed the incessant parade of visitors both offering and seeking information. Inevitably some suspicious characters offered leads that would take the investigations into wild goose chase territory, but I was impressed with how quickly the staff was able to discern good information from bad. Human Rights Watch was a small organization at the time, and, with so many other hot spots in the Americas demanding our attention, we made an early decision that, since Argentina was now under the rule of law, we would not comment on what the new government should do about the recent past.

The developments in Argentina, however, were fascinating to all of us. Aryeh Neier had visited Buenos Aires for Alfonsín's inauguration on Human Rights Day, December 10, 1983. Mass mobilizations in favor of human rights in Argentina had also impressed our specialist on Chile, Cynthia Brown; what she saw made her think that justice was possible for Pinochet's Chile as well. From Argentina, Emilio Mignone and Augusto Conte MacDonnell relayed details about the release of prisoners, repeal of the military's last-minute self-amnesty law and orders to prosecute, and opinions about whether military courts should have jurisdiction over those cases and so on. Things were happening so quickly that soon HRW decided to allow me to continue to report on Argentina.

In July 1984, CONADEP presented a prime-time television show broadcast to the whole of Argentina, the same week in which I was conducting a fact-finding mission for HRW there. It consisted of perhaps twenty relatives of the disappeared sitting on a bare stage, with the spotlight moving from one to the other as they described the circumstances under which their loved one was taken. They also added poignant details about the person's life, dreams of a better future or decision to engage in political activities for social and political change. Each relative also described in some detail what he or she had done to find the *desaparecido* and how those inquiries were treated in government offices, courthouses, police detachments and military quarters under the dictatorship. The two-hour program had a large viewership and great repercussions in Argentine society, perhaps more so because of the format chosen—it avoided the more typical interview or talk-show style and let the relatives speak by themselves—and the quiet dignity of each speaker: No one cried or sobbed; each person described their tragic loss succinctly, with no added dramatics.

The night the show was presented, Argentina was rife with rumors that army tanks from a suburban military unit were marching toward Buenos Aires. It might have been only a vague threat, but everyone was struck with how fragile Argentinean democracy was. The morning after the show aired, I spoke to Graciela Fernández Meijide, the mother of a disappeared teenage son. She had been one of the most active and savvy of the founders of the Mothers of Plaza de Mayo. I had met her during her trips to Washington, DC, and now she was the head of the team drafting CONADEP's report, which was due in three months. Her husband had been one of those speaking on the TV program. When we discussed the possibility that a coup d'etat might have occurred, she said to me, "If this is how they react to the truth, imagine what they will do when we get to justice."

For me, those words suggested that, in Argentina at least, truth telling was not conceived as a substitute for justice. The trials of the junta commanders had not begun yet, but Alfonsín had given orders that trials would take place. The CONADEP investigations were expected to help build evidence that could be used in prosecutions. When I returned to Washington and relayed that conversation to Aryeh, we agreed that truth and justice were the bases of what we were referring to as "accountability" for past human rights crimes.

The full CONADEP report was issued in September 1984, after an investigation lasting about ten months.[3] It describes the practice of disappearances in detail, identifies 340 clandestine detention centers in Argentina and signals institutional deficiencies that allowed for such a system to operate. It also gave excerpts of some testimony from relatives and from survivors and listed 8,960 persons who were still counted among the disappeared at that time. At the last minute, the Alfonsín administration persuaded the members of CONADEP to leave out the names of more than three hundred officers who were identified as torturers or kidnappers. The list was leaked, however, and two weeks later, it was circulating widely in Argentina.

The episode gave rise to an important debate as to whether truth commissions should name names. The Chilean Truth and Reconciliation Commission (TRC), working several years later, decided not to publish names it received from witnesses but instead to transmit them to appropriate judicial authorities for criminal investigation if warranted. The Salvadoran Truth Commission, sponsored by the United Nations, did include names of alleged perpetrators in its report, although their guilt or innocence was still to be determined by the courts of the country. The commission even went so far as to recommend some sanctions for the alleged perpetrators: specifically that they should be disqualified from any public office. This commission was criticized for naming names of alleged perpetrators. It only revealed names it received in testimony and corroborated. Since it had operated for only six months, the list was inevitably incomplete and perhaps even imbalanced since many other perpetrators had simply not come to the commission's attention. The issue of naming names continues to be a central part of discussions about the role of truth-seeking and truth-telling bodies.

It is true that truth commissions should not usurp judicial functions. But that does not mean that they should never, under any circumstance, name names. If there is to be a justice phase following the truth telling, it is best for names to be revealed only in the context of proper criminal prosecutions, when those named have the opportunity to be heard under due process. If, however, the truth telling is the only measure of accountability contemplated—that is, if prosecutions are explicitly eschewed—then not naming names would mean that the truth told would be incomplete. In those cases, names should be supplied, but some basic due process rules should apply: Although the standard for including the names cannot be that of guilt beyond a reasonable doubt, truth commissions have a duty to do a thorough investigation in good faith to discover all those who have committed crimes and should give each person an opportunity to be heard before their names are publicized.

In general, truth commissions have been useful in establishing accountability in many settings. Recent examples include Sierra Leone, Peru, Timor Leste and Morocco. In some cases, the effort has been misguided from the start and has resulted in failed exercises, as in Haiti in the 1990s, Indonesia and most recently Liberia. Even when the truth telling has been exemplary, in some cases prosecutions have not followed or have been disappointingly centered on scapegoats, as in El Salvador, Guatemala and South Africa. Truth commissions that are created deliberately as substitutes for prosecution of even those responsible for mass atrocities tend to leave in their wake a sense of frustration and of "justice light."

The trial of the junta members in Argentina took place in 1985. Nine commanders in chief of the three armed forces were brought to trial. General Jorge Rafael Videla and Admiral Emilio Massera, members of the first junta—during whose term most of the worst crimes were committed—were convicted of about forty-four murders and sentenced to life in prison. General Roberto Viola, who replaced Videla as army commander and then as president, was sentenced to seventeen years in prison. Admiral Lambruschini was also convicted, but the other four commanders were acquitted (although General Galtieri, the third president of the military dictatorship, and others still faced prosecution in other courts for crimes committed while occupying other posts earlier).

The trial was held in public for five months, with the defendants present and witnesses heard orally and cross-examined by defense counsel. The public was glued to the proceedings for the whole time, and the daily newspaper that printed them almost verbatim became an instant best-seller. The decision, issued in December 1985 and confirmed by the supreme court exactly a year later, was exemplary: The Federal Court of Appeals for Buenos Aires used a very rigorous standard of evidence and accepted charges of murder only if a body had been found. Consequently, the much more numerous disappearances generally were treated as abductions and torture as "illegal pressure," both with comparably benign penalties. Nevertheless, the decision convincingly established the defendants' criminal responsibility as the men behind the acts—as committing the murders without firing a shot through the actions of their subordinates. Significantly, the appeals court extracted evidence pointing to other culprits and submitted it to different courts with territorial jurisdiction over the crimes. Thus, the stage was set for prosecution of a second echelon of generals and other officers who had played key roles in repression.

However, military pressures, including four attempted uprisings, forced the Alfonsín government to retreat from this principled position and enact two pseudoamnesty laws in 1987. One, called Punto Final (full stop), ordered courts to drop all charges not filed within two months of the law's promulgation; it resulted in a race to the courthouse and frantic activity by prosecutors and judges who did not want to be saddled with the responsibility for allowing impunity to reign. The second, called Obediencia Debida (due obedience), was passed after the first uprising, during Easter of 1987. It established that all those officers who were occupying positions below a certain high level would benefit from an irrefutable presumption that they had been acting under mistaken belief about the legality of the orders they had received. The cycle of impunity was completed in 1989 and 1990, when Alfonsín's successor, Carlos Menem, pardoned convicted junta members as well as another twenty-five or so generals who were still being prosecuted because they were not covered by the amnesty laws.

Human rights activists in Argentina fought hard against the passage of these laws and then tried to have them declared unconstitutional by Argentine courts. When those strategies failed, they approached the IACHR to have them declared contrary to international law. Robert K. Goldman and I served as their copetitioners. In a parallel case, we were joined by Uruguayan activists who were similarly attacking the legality of the Ley de Caducidad,[4] as the Uruguayan pseudoamnesty was called. Representatives of both newly democratic governments were our adversaries in the proceedings, and they defended the amnesties as necessary for the stability of democracy and "national reconciliation" after bloody conflicts. We insisted that victims of grave atrocities, such as torture, murder, disappearance and prolonged arbitrary detention, deserved more than being told to forgive and forget and to look forward, not backward. They and their relatives had a right to a remedy under international law, and that remedy had to be proportional to the seriousness of the crimes committed against them. When it came to crimes against humanity, the remedy had to include a right to see justice done through criminal prosecutions. Since the pseudoamnesty laws and presidential pardons effectively barred that right to justice, they were contrary to the states' obligations under international law. These debates with democratic governments that succeeded dictatorships sharpened our understanding about the challenges of dealing with legacies of mass atrocities. Although we argued on legal grounds, we did not neglect the political or moral dimensions of the problem. Impunity could not be the basis of a newly democratic arrangement that aspired to establish the rule of law.

As a result of these two cases, HRW created a mandate to demand criminal accountability for gross and systematic violations of human rights.[5] We developed it at the time President Patricio Aylwin, Chile's first democratically elected leader, delivered the report of the Chilean TRC and apologized to the victims of the Pinochet regime in the name of the nation. That mandate was applied in reports and advocacy on Chile and later in El Salvador and Guatemala, where the United Nations was called on to facilitate the resolution of the armed conflicts and insisted on "truth and justice" through specific mechanisms. Eventually, HRW, Amnesty International and other human rights organizations will apply those principles in each country with a legacy of mass atrocities as it emerges from conflict, as well as in international wars. The human rights movement unanimously has demanded truth and justice in Cambodia, in the Balkan wars, in Sudan's two major conflicts (Darfur and the north–south war) and most recently in the violence caused by electoral fraud in Kenya in 2009.

In 1987, right after the enactment of the due obedience law, I wrote a report for HRW called "Truth and Partial Justice in Argentina." [6] We thought at the time that the cycle of accountability was closed. Still, Argentine defenders of human rights continued to insist on truth and justice, so we issued an updated report in 1991.[7] The challenges to overcome impunity continued to raise important issues beyond Argentina, and my country's experiences with accountability—both positive and negative—elicited broad interest elsewhere. The report was published in Spanish and circulated in many Latin American countries. In 2001, it was published in Serbo-Croatian by Samizdat B92 in Belgrade, and two years later, I was invited to speak in that city by the preeminent human rights organization in the Balkans, the Humanitarian Law Center, whose director, Nataša Kandić, is the region's major proponent of truth telling. She also promotes and monitors domestic prosecutions and disseminates and generates support for the rulings of the International Criminal Tribunal for the Former Yugoslavia.

Eventually, our efforts before the inter-American system of protection bore fruit. In *Velásquez Rodríguez v. Honduras*, mentioned in chapter 6, the issue of amnesty had not arisen; the impunity in

Honduras was all de facto. Nevertheless, in the July 1988 decision, we secured a very strong pronouncement by the court to the effect that:

1. Disappearances are crimes against humanity.
2. With respect to disappearances, the state is obliged to investigate, prosecute and punish perpetrators and to disclose to the families and to society all that can be established about the circumstances.
3. Those obligations to justice and to truth remain in effect for as long as there is any doubt about what actually happened.
4. The state must exercise due diligence and place all the apparatus of state power at the disposal of these objectives.
5. The victims' families are indirect victims themselves and are entitled to reparations.

Armed with these groundbreaking principles, we urged the IACHR to rule on the validity of the pseudoamnesty laws in Argentina and Uruguay. It did so in landmark reports in January 1992. In summary, it decided that since the laws of Caducidad in Uruguay and Punto Final and Due Obedience in Argentina were obstacles to the government fulfilling its obligations, they were contrary to both the spirit and the letter of the American Convention on Human Rights, a treaty binding on both Uruguay and Argentina. Since that time, the IACHR has had occasion to rule on other amnesties and de facto impunity. It has expanded on this legal argument to decide that:

- Impunity for major crimes is a breakdown of the whole rule of law.
- Impunity deprives victims of the "right to a remedy" that is at the heart of all human rights treaties.
- Refusal to prosecute major crimes is impermissible because it amounts to validating a suspension of rights that can never be suspended, not even in times of emergency.

The Inter-American Court of Human Rights (the judicial body of the Organization of American States that sits in San José, Costa Rica) eventually pronounced judgments along the same lines in cases dealing with amnesties and their effect in El Salvador (in the cases of the murder of the Jesuit priests, their landlady and her daughter in 1989 and of Archbishop Oscar A. Romero in 1980), in Chile and most recently in Brazil.[8]

In 2001, I had occasion to appear before the Inter-American Court in the case called Barrios Altos (*Chumbipuma Aguirre et al. v. Peru*).[9] It related to a particularly gruesome massacre in downtown Lima, in which members of a secret branch of the armed forces called Grupo Colina shot and killed seventeen street vendors and their families who had migrated from Ayacucho, the Andean city where Sendero Luminoso was strong.[10] The vendors were having a cookout at a home, presumably to raise funds to organize themselves and petition authorities to obtain street vendor permits; members of the Colina group had infiltrated and thought they were raising funds for Sendero Luminoso. A masked Colina contingent entered the house, ordered everyone against a wall and shot them at nearly point blank range, killing many, including an eight-year-old boy. The survivors were left for dead. A journalistic investigation uncovered the existence of the Grupo Colina and its responsibility for this incident as well as for the disappearance and later execution of ten students and a professor from a technological university near Lima popularly known as La Cantuta. Some of the Grupo Colina members were arrested, and the initial judicial investigation pointed to a direct relationship between them and the government's official intelligence service.

In 1995, the Peruvian congress, dominated by supporters of President Alberto Fujimori, passed an amnesty law protecting the Colina defendants, but Judge Antonia Saquicuray decided to continue investigating the Barrios Altos cases to determine if they were indeed covered by the amnesty. A few days later, parliament passed another law—the public jokingly called it the Saquicuray law—clarifying that the previous law was unreviewable by courts; Judge Saquicuray was threatened with prosecution and eventually fired. All the accused members of Grupo Colina were released. In 2000, the IACHR sent the case of

Barrios Altos to the Inter-American Court in Costa Rica, and a hearing was held at which I appeared as a member of the Inter-American Commission. By then, Fujimori had fallen from power after a failed attempt at fraudulent elections and had fled the country. The new democratic government of Peru wanted to restore justice. The court issued its decision[11] and set an important precedent. As it had stated before in other cases, it reaffirmed that amnesties that have the effect of preventing investigations into crimes against humanity are contrary to the American Convention on Human Rights. This time, however, it went further and stated that Peru was under an obligation to deprive those amnesty laws of any legal effect in the domestic jurisdiction. The government of Peru went back to Lima with this ruling; a few days later, the supreme court established that Peru was obliged to comply with the Inter-American Court decision and ordered the Barrios Altos criminal case reopened. Some of the previously identified defendants were rearrested while others absconded. Many years later, Fujimori was extradited from Chile on this case and other charges; after a trial that was exemplary in its fairness, he was convicted for his role in the massacre and its cover-up. He is currently serving a twenty-five-year sentence in a prison near Lima. The Inter-American Court has since reaffirmed its jurisprudence on the matter in several cases involving amnesties and other obstacles to truth and justice such as statutes of limitations and fraudulent double jeopardy. In 2007, in *Almonacid-Arellano v. Chile,* the court reiterated this jurisprudence and said that Pinochet's self-amnesty law of 1978 could not remain in the books even though the Chilean courts had not invoked it for several years.

THE STRUGGLE OF ARGENTINE civil society to overcome impunity eventually resulted in an astounding reversal: Following international law precedent (including but not limited to the Inter-American system's decisions just mentioned), in 2005, the supreme court declared the amnesties and pardons unconstitutional, and trials have resumed against about 600 defendants. Some notorious killers have been convicted and are serving long sentences. In December 2010, for example, General Videla received another life sentence for his command responsibility for murders and tortures committed in 1976 in the notorious Unit 1 federal prison in Córdoba, Argentina. In November 2010, after a public trial, the federal court of appeals for La Plata convicted prison warden Dupuy, who was chief of Unit 9 when I was held there, for several crimes, including the torture or murder of my fellow inmates Dardo Cabo, Roberto Rufino Pirles, Horacio Rappaport and Ángel Georgiadis. Several of my friends testified.

In late 2010, judicial proceedings also were headline news in my hometown of Mar del Plata. Federal prosecutors there filed charges against several members of the right-wing death squad Concentración Nacional Universitaria (CNU) who were accused of being responsible for the deaths of Silvia Filler and many others. Prosecutors have persuaded the courts that murders committed by the group in 1975 (during the government of Isabel Perón) are also crimes against humanity because CNU members were acting, for all intents and purposes, as agents of the government by kidnapping and murdering its enemies.

Most notably, charges were filed against a prominent local lawyer, Gustavo Demarchi, who had been a federal prosecutor in 1975 and 1976 and is accused of refusing to investigate any of the crimes committed by CNU against left-wing students and professors. Among the crimes of which they are accused are the murders of Enrique "Pacho" Elizagaray, who had led the peaceful student occupation of the law school when I was arrested. Pacho was killed at a house where he was hiding; his uncle and two young cousins were taken away, and their bullet-riddled bodies were later found in the outskirts of town. CNU members also are accused of the gruesome murder, a few days later, of my friend Daniel Gasparri, who had been arrested with me as we were leaving the law school building.

By the early 1990s, the international community had borrowed a page from the human rights struggles of Latin America. After the fall of the Berlin Wall in 1989, stark comparisons were made between the Latin American experiments and the emerging democracies of the former communist bloc, which were dealing with their own legacies of human rights violations. In those countries, liberals and progressives—who for the most part had led the resistance against communist abuses—now wanted only to look forward and forget about the past.

Right-wing opportunists were (and in Poland continue to be) the ones digging up stories about an adversary's alleged complicity in human rights abuses, usually in order to eliminate him or her from the political arena.

Obviously, these attitudes regarding how to reckon with the recent past do not reflect prevailing views in Latin America. What explains the difference? Under the communist regimes, people were used to pervasive systems of surveillance and violations of privacy, and serious elections had been prohibited. Freedom of expression and of association were completely suppressed. It may well be that institutionalized systematic violations of that sort do not lend themselves to criminal prosecutions, which require the assignment of individual responsibility for acts that are criminal when they are committed. In contrast, Latin American dictatorships did not control all of the population in such oppressive ways; rather, they focused their repressive actions on a large but distinct portion of society, the members of which were denied all rights, including the right to life, freedom and personal security. In 1993, during a conference in Cape Town, South Africa, I had the opportunity to engage with Polish pro-democracy activist Adam Michnik on this issue. He argued that in the former Soviet bloc states, moral and legal responsibility for what went on under communism was so widespread that justice could not be served without a far-reaching witch hunt. When I asked him if he would let the killers of Father Jerzy Popeliuzko, an activist Polish priest assassinated by the communists, go free, he said that "murder is murder" and no, he would not object to their prosecution and punishment.

Murder on a grand, massive scale is precisely what needed to be prosecuted in Latin America. There were plenty of dictatorship cheerleaders, sycophants and opportunistic supporters in Latin America and civilians who joined the military governments, although not in repressive functions. Some of those now feign horror at past atrocities revealed at the trials. Their responsibilities are moral and political; there is no point in using the criminal justice system against them. Because the military regimes established whole machineries of extermination, trials in Latin America have to be numerous and against many perpetrators; but they are not and will not be witch hunts, nor will they be directed against persons whose only crime was moral cowardice. The discussion with Michnik illuminated for me a crucial difference, not between the two sets of newly democratic regimes but between the legacies of abuse they confronted. Tina Rosenberg, a *New York Times* writer who was also at the conference in Cape Town, summarized the issue very intelligently: Latin American dictatorships were "regimes of criminals," whereas communist dictatorships were "criminal regimes."[12]

Nevertheless, in Eastern Europe, a few countries have bravely upheld the rule of law, even for crimes that occurred in the past. In Hungary, Estonia and elsewhere, there have been trials for those accused of Nazi and Stalinist war crimes, including deportations to Siberia. Poland is insisting on Russian accountability for the Katyn massacre of close to twenty thousand Poles during World War II, one that for years the Kremlin had blamed on the Nazis.

Nevertheless, the overall eastern European experience with transitioning to democracy has given justice a bad name. Several governments have enacted what they call "lustration" laws, which are imposed on persons simply because their names appear in files of the old security agencies. A person under lustration is prohibited from holding a public job, teaching or engaging in journalism. These measures are applied without hearings or trials or any opportunity to defend one's reputation. Justice does demand that perpetrators of abuse should be excluded from some public offices, but that punishment should come as a result of proceedings that include some modicum of due process and fair trial guarantees. In November 2010, I visited Budapest and Warsaw to talk about justice and peace. I learned that twenty years after the return of democracy, right-wing forces in eastern Europe still resort to lustration—even passing new and tougher laws—to get rid of their political adversaries.

The differences between the Latin American and eastern European experiences in dealing with the aftermath of human rights abuses have been debated in many forums. Nowhere were they debated as intensely and as rigorously as in South Africa after the end of the apartheid regime. In the early 1990s, the long struggle for a multiracial South Africa had finally led to negotiations to release

Nelson Mandela after twenty-seven years of imprisonment and to allow for the return of exiled leaders of the African National Congress (ANC). As a condition of those talks, the apartheid leaders and the military demanded an amnesty that the ANC was forced to accept in order to obtain Mandela's release and the return of exiled leaders so that a permanent peace could be established. In response to the indignity of racial segregation, and with all avenues of political participation denied to them, South African majorities had fought against the regime with organized violence as well as through peaceful means. The regime had waged a brutal counterinsurgency war that resulted in multiple murders, state-sponsored terror and pervasive torture and inhumane conditions of detention. These tactics and the human suffering they caused were open wounds in the fabric of society that could not be ignored.

With the negotiated end to apartheid, on February 11, 1990, an amnesty was inserted in an interim constitution, although the details and mechanics of its implementation were left to be determined by Parliament after free and fair elections. South Africans had the opportunity to try a new tack about how to confront that painful legacy. To their credit, they analyzed all existing models and adapted the experiences of others to their own situation. After Mandela's historic presidential election, in 1994 a definitive constitution was adopted, but the country still was saddled with an amnesty for horrendous crimes. The ANC government honored the promise it made during the negotiations but instituted a process of accountability that explored the truth wherever it might lead and made indemnity from prosecution conditional on the beneficiary contributing to the nation's healing. The resulting TRC was charged with investigating and revealing the truth about atrocities by all sides, and it was empowered to grant amnesty in exchange for confessions and truth telling. It was clear that those who refused to come forward, or whose statements were untruthful, would expect to face prosecution or would not be released if they were already serving time. The establishment of the commission was widely seen as a reflection of Mandela's generosity of spirit and desire for reconciliation in a multiracial society. Undoubtedly, Mandela inspired the best in the South African process, but he also must be credited with the idea that amnesty would not be unconditional: It would be granted to those who came forward and only on the condition that their statements were full and truthful. If they preferred not to confess, they could be tried in court.

The South African process was admirable for its truth telling and particularly for its process of public hearings in which victims for the first time were heard by the whole nation and the world. It also resulted in a groundbreaking five-volume report[13] published in 1998 that left no doubt about the gravity of the crimes of the apartheid regime. The report did not benefit much from the information revealed by the culprits who came forward and requested amnesty, although there were some spectacular findings. In fact, most of the worst perpetrators refused to seek amnesty, safe in the knowledge that the prosecutors and judges, inherited from the previous regime, would not investigate them. The most sensational trial—against General Magnus Malan and others alleged to have organized clandestine operations against ANC supporters resulting in many murders—collapsed because of the misbehavior of one such prosecutor and the defendants were acquitted.

The ANC government was not anxious for prosecutions either; the TRC had found that some ANC practices during the insurgency also amounted to war crimes. In addition, the ANC was focused on making an ambitious experiment in multiracial coexistence work, and its leaders probably felt that prosecution of apartheid crimes might lead to massive flight by South African whites and serious economic disruption. There have been a few successful prosecutions, and the constitutional court has opened the way for some other cases to be tried. The most important result of the South African process is the example in truth telling that it set for the world. In a separate process, South Africa has conducted very encouraging reform of its security bodies; but in terms of reparations and justice, the results have been discouraging to victims and to civil society at large.

Although many truth commissions have been created since the mid-1990s, nowhere has there been an attempt to replicate the South African experience in this offer of amnesty in exchange for truth. Part of the reason for this is that some of the amnesty decisions issued by the TRC are not valid under international law.[14] Although they enjoy legal force within South Africa, the rest of the international community, operating under legitimate forms of jurisdiction, is not required to accept them.

The TRC statute itself was not contrary to international law, but as applied in specific cases, it did not pass international law muster. For example, amnesty was granted to members of an extreme anti-white group who shot at churchgoers only because they were white. Indiscriminate attacks against civilians and, in addition, with a racist intent, are crimes against humanity that may not be excused even if perpetrators confess. The fact that the South African amnesty was not blanket or unconditional still leaves some room for compliance with international law, but the most disappointing aspect of the process is that there have been precious few prosecutions against those who defied it and did not come forward with their statements. The statute may have been consistent with international law in 1994, but the rapid evolution of its principles since that time make a similar scheme contrary to current human rights law. The law is unlikely to be tested by an international tribunal with jurisdiction over South Africa, in any event; but the fact that no other country has replicated the truth-for-amnesty idea is evidence of the evolution in international standards. Societies that want to confront legacies of mass abuse in good faith and with proper regard for the rights of victims thus continue to strive for solutions that combine truth and justice.

IN ADDITION TO THE CONTRIBUTIONS of the Inter-American Court and Commission, other international human rights institutions have added to the body of emerging law about what states owe to the victims of mass atrocities. Together, these principles are termed "transitional justice," and they are based on the prohibition of suspension of certain rights even in times of emergency. If such rights are so precious that they can never be suspended, they also cannot be the subject of an ex post facto suspension in the form of amnesties or pardons. Under transitional justice, these negative obligations become affirmative ones. The state is obliged to:

1. Investigate, prosecute and punish mass atrocities (justice).
2. Find out and disclose all the circumstances of their commission (truth).
3. Offer appropriate compensation to the victims (reparations).
4. Conduct an overhaul of state institutions that have been the vehicle of those violations in the recent past (institutional reform).

These objectives can be achieved in a variety of ways. Societies are encouraged to use the practices and institutions that make most sense in their own cultures while respecting the overall principles. In addition, a state is compliant with these obligations if it does all that is within its power to do, with due diligence and in good faith, even if not all guilty parties are punished and aspects of the truth are never known.

As the Special Advisor to UN Secretary-General Kofi Annan on the prevention of genocide, I insisted on accountability for the crimes that had been committed in Darfur in 2003 and early 2004, when the government of Sudan suppressed an insurgency by way of a genocidal campaign of murder of civilians, destruction of villages and massive forced displacement. That campaign cost at least 200,000 lives in less than one year. My job was to offer suggestions to prevent further crimes. I insisted on accountability not only because of the need to uphold transitional justice principles; I felt that it also was essential to the resolution of the conflict and to the international community's efforts to protect the millions of Darfurians who are, even today, at the mercy of the Khartoum regime and the Janjaweed militias formed from other ethnic groups. In 2005, the UN Security Council referred the case of Darfur to the International Criminal Court (ICC), and in 2008, the prosecutor obtained an arrest warrant against Sudan's president, Omar al-Bashir. The Khartoum regime and its allies in Africa and the Arab world have denounced this decision and amplified their outrage by an active diplomatic campaign as well as by thinly veiled blackmail: Unless the warrant is revoked, Khartoum will not cooperate with peace initiatives or with relief and protection measures. The International Criminal Court has refused to be blackmailed and, as of 2011, the warrant against a sitting head of state, for genocide, war crimes and crimes against humanity, is outstanding. Bashir is isolated, but the prospects of arresting him and bringing him to justice are uncertain. I have spoken out about the need to make justice and peace reinforce each other and have joined many colleagues in supporting a groundswell of African civil society pressure for accountability for mass crimes.

The struggle for accountability regarding human rights abuses around the world by the turn of the century had resulted in the acceptance of "emerging standards" in international law and with them a defined field of practice among human rights defenders. In many countries, those who had been on the front lines of resisting torture, massacres and disappearances have adapted their agendas and strategies to the need to reckon with those abuses in times of transition from dictatorship to democracy or from conflict to peace. They have been assisted enormously by emerging rules of international law that oblige governments to ensure that mass atrocities do not go unpunished. As a lawyer for the victims, I participated actively in the judicial cases that gave shape to these rules, starting with the landmark decision *Velásquez Rodriguez v. Honduras* on July 29, 1988. During my term as HRW general counsel in the mid-1990s, HRW became an innovator and leader in this area by systematically following or documenting transitions and advocating measures to achieve truth and justice. National groups had been at the forefront of these endeavors in their own countries on their own initiatives and we amplified their voices.

In order for truth, justice and reparations to result in the healing of a country after human rights abuses, there must also be institutional reform. Those institutions that were the instruments of repression must be thoroughly reformed so that they cannot be used in the same way in the future. What is needed first is a fair process for vetting all those who can be identified reliably as having participated in illegal repression. The key distinction between "vetting" and "lustration" is the process: Vetting includes fair opportunities for those who may be disqualified to be heard; lustration does not. In cases where the violations have had an ethnic, racial or religious dimension, the four transitional justice objectives must be complemented with specific mechanisms of reconciliation between communities in the form of inter-communal conversations about restoration of property, rights to land, water and grazing fields, and return to homelands. Each country must come up with the proper mix of judicial and nonjudicial mechanisms that makes the most sense in its context and culture; the preceding norms are only a legal framework that leaves room for implementation and innovation. A good-faith effort at realizing each of these objectives not only heals the wounds but also offers the best chance to achieve post-conflict reconstruction and prevention of future mass atrocities.

Transitional justice sometimes has been confused with "soft justice" by which a country promotes reconciliation by laying out the truth of what happened but largely forgoes any attempt to prosecute and punish perpetrators. Transitional justice is different in a number of ways. In the first place, "reconciliation" is not valid if it is used as a code word for impunity, as was often the case in Latin America. While reconciliation should be the ultimate objective of a policy of transitional justice, true reconciliation can come about only as a result of justice, meaning criminal prosecution of at least those bearing the highest responsibility for the crimes. This does not rule out clemency for humanitarian reasons but requires first that the process of justice take place. It also follows that victims have a right to see justice done. They cannot impose their will on the institutions of justice by insisting on a certain kind of punishment or on the prosecution of a particular individual. But they have a right to a process that allows them a proper way to participate in the proceedings.

Earlier on in the Latin American process of transitioning to democracies, well-meaning colleagues told us that because the democracies were fragile, efforts at justice (and even at truth and reparations) should be abandoned. The choice of democracy over justice was supposed to prevent regressions into dictatorship and consequently more and worse violations. This is a false dilemma. Today it is fair to say that democracies in Latin America are more stable than they ever have been precisely because they engaged in an honest effort to deal with the past. At other times, some commentators insisted that there should be "truth, not trials."[15] A misreading of the South African experience led some people to think that truth would produce reconciliation automatically, while trials were inherently vindictive or reflected a logic of confrontation, of prolonging the war by other means. With most human rights scholars and practitioners, I emphatically reject the notion that using the institutions of the state to dispense justice can be equated with war.

More recently, the dilemmas have been about peace versus justice. In many cases, this is not a false dilemma; insurgents will *not* lay down their arms if all they can expect is to go to jail. We must realize that the perpetrators are engaging in blackmail. They demand amnesty (and often more than that: a house by the lake, a cabinet appointment) in exchange for giving up their weapons and not committing further atrocities. Still, the reality of the dilemma does not justify always promoting peace over justice. In fact, recent history is full of examples of bad deals that resulted in neither justice nor peace; the "peace" that was created did not last precisely because it was unfair. The trick is to make peace and justice strengthen and nurture each other, and to strive for better peace arrangements, even if the process takes a little longer. Peace negotiations are definitely made more difficult in those cases; but they also force all of us to come up with better, more just and more lasting solutions. An example of a "bad" agreement is the Lomé peace accord of 1999 to end the civil war in Sierra Leone. It contained a blanket amnesty for criminals like Foday Sankoh, who six months later was fighting and committing atrocities again. From this perspective, a "good" peace agreement is the Dayton accord, which put an end to the war in the former Yugoslavia without lifting the arrest warrants against the actual spoilers of a peace process, like Radovan Karadžić and Ratko Mladić. Their absence from the Dayton talks probably made peace possible.

Justice must be an integral part of transitions, both from dictatorship to democracy and from conflict to peace. This does not mean that it is the only ingredient, or that it has to happen all at once. It also does not mean that various forms of clemency, including some limited amnesties, cannot be included in a fair peace negotiation. Some amnesties clearly are contrary to international law, but not all are. Amnesties for the purpose of allowing insurgents who have not committed atrocities to give up their weapons and join the political process are not only permissible but encouraged by international law. The same can be said of amnesties for comparatively minor violations committed by state agents, or in exchange for providing evidence leading to the conviction of more seriously involved persons.

In 2000, the Ford Foundation opened a new field of human rights practice by creating the International Center for Transitional Justice (ICTJ). In 2004, I was asked to become president of ICTJ, by then a well-established international human rights organization. It was growing fast when I took the helm, but in the next five years, it went from about 31 permanent staff members to 140 and from an annual budget of $6 million to $22 million. From one office in New York in 2004, ICTJ in 2009 had a presence in twenty countries. ICTJ develops partnerships in the thirty-plus countries where it conducts programs— with state officials, civil society organizations and international actors. It provided advice in the design and operation of truth commissions in Peru, Morocco, Timor Leste and Liberia; assisted prosecutors in Colombia, Argentina and Lebanon; consulted with governments and civil societies on reparations in Indonesia, Nepal and Fiji; and assisted in the reform of security forces in Burundi, the Democratic Republic of Congo and Bosnia. It insists on consultation with victims, transparency in decision making and an approach where reconciliation, truth telling and reparations are not offered under the condition of the provision of amnesty to the perpetrators. Over time, the field of transitional justice has become deeply connected not only with efforts at redressing abuses but also with fostering post-conflict reconstruction and sensible, long-term approaches to peace making, peace building and prevention of future human tragedies.

The principles of transitional justice do not apply only in situations of failed states coming out of protracted conflict or deeply repressive regimes. "Transitional" is not meant to qualify the kind of justice to which victims are entitled; it merely signifies the particular complexities of trying to achieve justice in moments of change, when democracy is the aspiration but other urgent issues can take precedence over the need to establish the rule of law. And yet it is a rule of international law that victims of abuse deserve something from the state.

It is with this in mind that ICTJ conducted operations in Canada to assist in efforts to come to grips with historic injustices committed against its indigenous population ("First Nations" in Canada) through the system of residential schools. In that system, children were taken away from their families and communities under the premise of "integration" into the wider society and severely mistreated in what amounted to orphanages or reformatories. The Assembly of First Nations (AFN) had sued the federal government for these historic injustices and obtained an unprecedented settlement in May 2006. In addition to reparations, the plaintiffs insisted on a nationwide truth-telling experiment and localized hearings within the territories of indigenous communities. At the request of both the AFN and the government of Canada, ICTJ provided advice on truth seeking and dissemination.

The principles of transitional justice are very much part of the debate about what should be done regarding abuses committed by the U.S. government in the global war on terror. My ICTJ colleagues and I have joined American organizations in calling for an honest reckoning of this legacy, which has both damaged the reputation of the United States around the world and resulted in less security, not more, for its citizens. Many organizations and individuals have tried to persuade the Obama administration to create a commission of inquiry to conduct a serious, complete investigation into the various illegal and immoral acts committed in the war on terror, such as torture, prolonged arbitrary imprisonment, denial of fair trial, use of secret detention centers and "extraordinary renditions." In December 2010, a group of non-governmental organizations announced the creation of a citizens' committee to conduct such an inquiry, given the administration's reluctance to do so.

In the two theaters of war in which U.S. armed forces are engaged as of 2011, there is much to investigate and disclose about attacks in which civilians have died, about inadequate offers of compensation, about detention and interrogation practices and about collusion with repressive actions of our allies. The United States always has demanded accountability and transparency from other governments in dealing with the past and has encouraged them to face the legacies of abuse honestly and with compassion. Above all, it always has stood for the need to restore justice where serious human rights violations have occurred. In this new era of respect for multilateralism and hands extended in friendship to the rest of the world, the only way the United States can regain its position as a moral leader in the fight for human rights is if it is ready to confront its own mistakes and wrongdoings and to show that they are, indeed, in the past.

CHAPTER NINE

JUSTICE

The human rights movement has witnessed remarkable growth in the pursuit of justice since the 1980s when local activists insisted on accountability. Today there is the possibility of bringing to trial individual perpetrators of the most serious crimes, and this change has transformed the goals and practices of the men and women fighting to end atrocities in a very positive way. The potential for international criminal prosecution also has engaged international decision-making groups and public opinion, thereby magnifying the possibilities for human rights activists who campaign for justice for victims, the cessation of violations and the prevention of future wrongs. Even the most powerful organ in the United Nations (UN), the Security Council, is heavily engaged in decisions to create these courts of criminal justice and to submit cases to them.

International criminal justice also has been pivotal in attracting large numbers of highly professional, dedicated individuals with diverse backgrounds—judicial, prosecutorial, law enforcement, criminal investigations and forensics—to the human rights movement. Obviously, this comes with the added burden for practitioners to be more precise and rigorous with evidence, since the information gathered for human rights trials has to stand up to the highest level of scrutiny if it is to be used in court against the accused, whose innocence is presumed, just as in any other criminal case. Human rights work has risen to this challenge in the last decade and has become more professional, rigorous and unassailable than ever before. For a movement that depends so heavily on credibility, that is a very welcome development.

The possibilities of international justice should not obscure the fact that justice in the national court of a country where mass atrocities happened is still paramount. It was the extraordinary movement, especially in Latin America, of countries insisting on reckoning with legacies of past human rights violations that inspired the international community to create these new organs of justice in the first place. The experience of Argentina and Chile in transitioning from dictatorship to democracy gave new meaning to the concept of "crimes against humanity" and its legal ramifications. In those nations, civil society was responsible for the notion that some crimes are so egregious that they cannot be left unpunished. Since justice was the best way to set these fledgling democracies on a more certain footing, it became clear to the international community that justice is an essential element for effective reconstruction.

At times, the human rights movement rushes to participate in international justice mechanisms, assuming too quickly that national justice is unavailable and not placing sufficient emphasis on national institutions living up to their obligations. International criminal justice courts are necessary only when national courts do not do their jobs well. This is not a negative; it means that the ultimate purpose of international courts is to allow states to regain their legitimacy as agencies of justice.

Today human rights violations in one country can be addressed in a variety of ways. The most visible is the International Criminal Court (ICC), which came into being in July 2002, when enough states ratified the Rome Statute of 1998 that founded it. As of 2011, 113 states participate in the court. It is prosecuting perpetrators of genocide, war crimes and crimes against humanity in six countries and conducting preliminary investigations in several others. The ICC also can act on situations referred to it by the Security Council, even if the relevant state has not ratified the Rome Statute. A second means to ensure international criminal accountability is the creation of ad hoc courts by the Security Council in exercise of its duties to ensure the peace and security of nations. Before the creation of the ICC, the Security Council installed the International Criminal Tribunal for the Former Yugoslavia (ICTY) in 1993 and the International Criminal Tribunal for Rwanda (ICTR) in late 1994. A third way in which the UN has participated in helping countries overcome impunity, beginning in the late 1990s, is through *mixed courts* that are part of the national jurisdiction of the relevant state but operate with considerable international assistance, including judges and prosecutors contributed by the international community. Examples of mixed courts (sometimes called hybrid courts) are the special tribunals set up for Sierra Leone and Cambodia and the incorporation of foreign judges and prosecutors in Kosovo, Timor Leste and Guatemala. Finally, it is possible to bring perpetrators to justice in the courts of other countries under the principle of universal jurisdiction. Under this principle, a state authorizes its courts to hear cases even if the crime was not committed in its territory and did not affect victims who are nationals of the forum state, and the accused are also nonnationals. The best-known attempt to use universal jurisdiction to prosecute mass atrocities was the arrest of General Augusto Pinochet, the former dictator of Chile, in England, pursuant to an arrest warrant issued by a Spanish court.

In 1994, after I became general counsel of Human Rights Watch (HRW), one of my first responsibilities was to engage with the newly emerging international criminal courts. At that time, the Security Council already had taken the unprecedented step of creating the ICTY in response to the ongoing atrocities resulting from the breakup of the former Yugoslavia and the ensuing interethnic wars among Serbia, Croatia and Bosnia-Herzegovina, as well as within Bosnia between Bosnian Serbs and its majority Muslim population. Armed contingents fought those wars by targeting civilian populations on a large scale for the purpose of displacing hundreds of thousands of persons in the phenomenon that, since then, has come to be known as ethnic cleansing. Although the international community did attempt to intervene militarily to protect innocent civilians, the savagery of the attacks and the international community's failure to bring the warring parties to a negotiated solution convinced the Security Council that impunity for genocide, war crimes and crimes against humanity should not be tolerated. Those international crimes were well documented as having occurred in the Prejidor detention camp and the cruel siege of Sarajevo; they culminated in the genocidal murder of eight thousand unarmed men in Srebrenica in July 1995. Although all sides committed atrocities, the major culprits were supported by Serbia's president, Slobodan Milošević through units of the former Army of the Republic of Yugoslavia. Milošević's main allies acted under the banner of a Republica Srpska that they wanted to carve out of Bosnia for Bosnian Serbs, and they were commanded by Dr. Radovan Karadžić and General Ratko Mladić.

Some in the human rights movement thought that the Security Council's decision to institute a court was a poor substitute for more robust action by the outside world to protect ethnic and religious minorities from genocide and other international crimes. Others thought that not much could be expected of a tribunal that would take years to get up and running, with no assurances that it would have the ability to enforce its arrest warrants or conduct investigations, given the hostility to the court in most of the former Yugoslavia at that time. In spite of these and other disadvantages, we at HRW understood that the creation of the ICTY would for the first time bring human rights squarely into the center of international conflict resolution. It also would signal that impunity itself was a factor of instability that actively fueled the crisis. For our part, we believed that the ICTY vindicated our desire to stand with the victims and gave us an unprecedented opportunity to expand our advocacy on their behalf to larger decision-making circles.

We did have one important advantage: the extensive and rigorous fact finding that the Europe Division of HRW (formerly known as Helsinki Watch) had been conducting on the mass atrocities since the breakup of Yugoslavia and the outbreak of war.

Our colleagues knew what was going on in the Balkans and could offer sharp and focused analysis; that knowledge, in turn, lent credibility and sophistication to our advocacy for human rights–based solutions. My job was to understand how international law, human rights standards, the laws of war, and criminal law and procedure could work together to effect change in the region. My experience with mechanisms of state responsibility for human rights violations, such as the European Court, Inter-American Court and the UN treaty bodies and special procedures, was of some value, but those procedures were set up to determine whether a state has violated its human rights obligations against the rights of its citizens. The ICTY would be the first international tribunal since Nuremberg to try individuals for their criminal responsibility. For that reason, the rules of due process and fair trial guarantees had to be different. Procedural standards are obviously stricter when the outcome can result in long prison terms for those who are convicted. To add to the complexity, the ICTY was the first international criminal court, and its experimental nature meant it would have to solve problems as they came up. And at each step, the international court had to establish and defend its legitimacy.

The enterprise could have failed miserably, but the UN selected excellent leaders of high integrity and unsurpassed subject matter knowledge to lead the ICTY. The first president of the court was the Italian professor Antonio Cassese, and its first prosecutor was Richard Goldstone of South Africa. Cassese is a professor of international law at the University of Florence and a former president of the Council of Europe's Committee for the Prevention of Torture. In 2005, he was asked by the Security Council to lead a commission of inquiry that produced the most extensive report on atrocities in Darfur. Goldstone had been a judge in his country; the inquiry he had led into violations by the apartheid regime had become a model for what serious, independent, impartial investigations should be. In recent years, Goldstone has produced an influential report on the legality of the military actions of NATO to prevent Serbian atrocities in Kosovo and a UN investigation into crimes committed by all sides in the incidents in the Gaza Strip in late 2008 and early 2009.[1]

Political pressures were not absent, especially at the time of the Dayton negotiations to put an end to the conflict in the former Yugoslavia in 1995. Some of the five permanent members of the Security Council wanted the ICTY to grant amnesty to Karadžić, Mladić and Milošević, ostensibly so that they could participate in peace talks but obviously yielding to what could only be understood as blackmail: Karadžić and Mladić were threatening to continue to attack civilians if they were not given a seat at the table. Cassese and Goldstone resisted those pressures by insisting on their independence. The Security Council had created the ICTY and could close it down, but the judges and prosecutors were appointed specifically to avoid injecting political considerations into the process, and they were not there to accept instructions from any political masters.

Contrary to some predictions, Goldstone's and Cassese's principled positions did not derail the Dayton peace process. The ICTY was allowed to continue its work on all cases, and its arrest warrants against Karadžić and Mladić remained in effect. As a result, neither man was allowed to travel to Dayton, Ohio, so the Republika Serpska was represented by Milošević, the president of Serbia and Montenegro. This was, of course, a victory for justice; Karadžić and Mladić were not allowed to blackmail the international community into letting them get away with egregious crimes. But it was also a triumph for peace: Dayton illustrates that sometimes peace processes can proceed only if spoilers are removed. In this case, the peace that did come to the former Yugoslavia did not require justice to be abandoned.

There were, however, objections to the composition of the Dayton talks from voices demanding justice. They argued that allowing Milošević to participate in the process amounted to an amnesty for him, a more egregious denial of justice because he was seen as the most powerful figure of the three. The same critics also expressed skepticism that Karadžić and Mladić would ever be captured. But when political fortunes changed in Belgrade, Milošević was indeed indicted and remanded to The Hague to be tried by the ICTY. He managed to manipulate the process for four years and then died before being convicted. The ICTY's credibility as an effective justice mechanism faltered, but the outcome should not cloud the fact that Milošević actually was brought to justice and given a fair trial. Surprisingly, it was a decade later that Karadžić was apprehended (in Serbia in 2008) and delivered to The Hague, where his trial is proceeding. Mladić was finally arrested near Belgrade and arrived in The Hague on May 31, 2011, to be tried for his crimes.

In 1994, I began to work on advocacy strategy regarding the unfolding genocide in Rwanda with Alison Des Forges, an HRW consultant and one of the world's leading experts on the history and politics of the region.[2] Ethnic violence between the Hutu majority and the Tutsi minority had given rise to periodic massacres since independence from Belgium in 1960. An insurgent force of mostly Tutsis was waging war from neighboring Uganda, and the Hutu-dominated government of Juvénal Habyarimana was increasingly repressive and paranoid. Alison had written reports on the human rights situation for HRW and, together with other authoritative voices, was concerned about the possibility of mass killings.[3]

The calls for preventive action went unheeded, however, and in April 1994, a plane carrying Habyarimana and other leaders was shot down in the capital, Kigali. Ten Belgian soldiers of a contingent deployed in Rwanda on a UN peacekeeping mission were killed in retaliation, and Belgium ordered the rest of its troops home. In reaction to the death of the president, armed militias called Interahamwe, organized and instigated by parties in the governing coalition, unleashed a wave of killings of Tutsis all over the country. The genocide lasted one hundred days and may have resulted in 800,000 deaths.

The international community was paralyzed. In fact, instead of protecting vulnerable populations, the UN ordered the evacuation of the few international troops that were in Rwanda when the killing started. Like many others, we at HRW struggled with how to pressure major powers and the UN to act in defense of the innocent victims. At the time, there were hard questions as to what, given the limitations of international law, HRW should advocate: Should we propose jamming the radio station Milles Collines, which was spewing hate speech and directing the Interahamwe to places where they could find targets among the Tutsi and their sympathizers?

A few months before the genocide had started, Habyarimana had sued HRW for slander in a French court based on a report written by Alison and published by HRW; the case was dropped after his death and the beginning of the genocide. Using Alison's contacts, even before the genocide ended, we filed a civil case for damages in New York under the Alien Tort Claims Act against Jean-Bosco Barayagwiza, an owner of Radio Mille Collines and a leader in a party allied to the Habyarimana government; Barayagwiza had come to meetings at the

UN but had no diplomatic immunity. The case was mostly symbolic, as it would not result in the defendant's detention; but it served to raise awareness in the United States about the magnitude of the crimes and to start identifying some culprits for future criminal action.

In mid-1994, the genocidal government collapsed, and its rival, the Rwandan Patriotic Front (RPF), invaded from Uganda and set up a new government. Paul Kagame initially acted as vice president and minister of defence, with Augustin Bizimungu as president. There were serious questions at the time about how to deal with tens of thousands of alleged *genocidaires* (perpetrators of genocide) who had not fled into the Democratic Republic of Congo (DRC); how to denounce what appeared to be French protection of fleeing genocidaires and Radio Mille Collines, which was still broadcasting from areas not yet under RPF control; and whether the UN should set up a tribunal similar to that for the former Yugoslavia. HRW, at Alison's direction, was supportive of measures the new government wanted to take to redress the genocide but maintained a healthy distance from Kagame and his team in order to be credible when and if their actions called for criticism.

In contrast, other noted human rights professionals took a decidedly pro-RPF position. Rakiya Omaar and Alex de Waal, who had worked with us at HRW until 1992, now led a London-based organization called African Rights, which published reports documenting atrocities by the deposed regime. Omaar and de Waal collected and published important information, but they did so by traveling with RPF forces without distinguishing themselves from them. They also criticized the international community, taking the same stance as the Kagame government: that the RPF was the only force that had actually lived up to the obligation to prevent genocide. I admire much of their work in Rwanda, but I believe they hurt their own case by working too closely with the new government.

In the years since 1994, the Kagame government has done many important things to prevent new ethnic strife in Rwanda. It also has played an important role in other African trouble spots, such as Darfur, where Rwanda supplies all of the protective forces for UNAMID, the joint African Union–UN peacekeeping force. But Kagame also has exhibited an authoritarian streak in many internal decisions, and African Rights has diminished credibility in either critiquing or being silent about those decisions. Alison never refrained from criticizing actions contrary to human rights, no matter which side perpetrated them, but she never allowed her comments to be used by those who would rewrite history and pretend that the genocide was actually "fighting as usual" between rival forces or that the RPF was equally genocidal. Although Alison incurred the wrath of the new Rwandan government for her stance, her human rights reporting was never affected. She was one of the first to promote *gacaca*—a traditional form of community justice—when questions arose about how to deal with 130,000 detained persons accused of taking part in the genocide. We agreed that international law did not prohibit community-based justice, but we insisted on the highest standards of due process if the defendants were going to receive harsh prison sentences.

The gacaca courts eventually were put in place. As I witnessed during a visit to Kigali in 2005, they did not live up to international standards of due process, whatever their other benefits might have been. Community participation was indeed a positive feature, as it contributed to healing by allowing people to tell their tragic stories and to identify and locate key witnesses. But community pressures could and did result in unfair trials. Most important, community leaders with no training in law were allowed to hand down prison sentences of up to thirty years on the basis of unreliable evidence and without an adequate opportunity for the accused to defend themselves and offer exculpatory evidence.

At HRW and as early as 1994, we advocated for the creation of an international criminal court to try Rwandan genocidaires. By then, most of the leaders of the genocide were in exile, and some had been apprehended in other countries. Large contingents of perpetrators of the genocide were in the eastern part of the DRC and, according to the Kagame regime, were organized militarily to return to Rwanda. They were living in camps with about fifty thousand refugees. Rwanda protested that the international community was not just hosting refugees but also protecting a fighting force. Eventually this situation gave rise to the bloody massacres of the late 1990s in eastern DRC, where hundreds of thousands—perhaps millions—of Rwandese and Congolese civilians perished at the hands of militias supported by the DRC, Rwanda and Uganda.

We at HRW urged the new Rwandan government to prosecute and try genocidaires but with full respect for due process of law. The government wanted other states to extradite suspects back to Rwanda but was not willing to renounce the death penalty, so we could not support its request. The Kagame government wanted to be able to execute those most responsible for the genocide within their own jurisdiction. International law does not prohibit the death penalty, although it encourages its abolition and, for countries that retain it, demands the highest standard of fair trials. Years earlier, HRW had made its position clear: As a matter of principle, we oppose the death penalty under any circumstance and advocate its abolition. The UN and several regional organizations had adopted similar stances with regard to capital punishment, so Rwanda could not expect the international community to support its demands for extradition or for judicial assistance of any type unless it gave up executions. In late 1994, the Security Council created the International Criminal Tribunal for Rwanda, at first operating as an offshoot of the ICTY (sharing the same prosecutor and the same appellate panel).

In 1995 and 1996, HRW and a number of other nongovernmental organizations (NGOs) participated in discussions at the UN about creating the first permanent international criminal court. The International Law Commission had produced a draft statute, and a number of UN member states periodically participated in these detailed discussions. Early on, U.S. representatives kept saying that the United States had no position on whether an ICC was desirable, but they participated in the talks nonetheless. Such preface to each U.S. intervention in the discussions obviously colored their generally negative remarks and influenced the position of other state actors. HRW colleagues and I inquired at the White House to see if that noncommittal position could be reversed. Mort Halperin, who had worked closely with HRW during earlier positions at the American

Civil Liberties Union, was then at the National Security Council, and he took on our request. We provided him with comments on how the draft under discussion at the UN actually addressed any concern the United States could have about the risks of supporting an international tribunal to prosecute genocide, war crimes and crimes against humanity, particularly the principle of complementarity, which prevented such a court from acting as long as the country involved was willing and able to investigate in good faith. A few weeks later, President Clinton announced that he supported the creation of an ICC under certain conditions. From then on, U.S. input in the discussions had a more positive tone, and the prospect of obtaining strong majorities for an ICC improved considerably.

Before leaving office, Clinton signed the Rome Treaty but did not submit it to the Senate for ratification. In an unprecedented move, the George W. Bush administration "unsigned" the treaty by publicly announcing to the UN that it was withdrawing its signature, and declared its hostility to the whole concept of an international criminal court. With Republican majorities, the U.S. Congress passed the American Service-Members' Protection Act in August 2002 which contained provisions prohibiting U.S. officials from even talking to the ICC. It also included more damaging provisions, such as a threat to cut off military aid to countries that dare sign on to the ICC treaty.

Later the Bush administration's hostile attitude proved self-defeating: In 2005, when Washington wanted to punish those responsible for the genocide in Darfur, it was forced to realize that the only realistic option was to allow the Security Council to refer the situation of Darfur to the ICC under its prerogatives to protect the peace and security of nations and issue measures that are binding on every country. As stated, referral by the Security Council is contemplated in the Statute of Rome and is one of the ways in which the ICC acquires jurisdiction over a case. On March 31, 2005, the Security Council adopted a resolution referring the situation in Darfur to the ICC. The United States abstained, thereby not exercising a veto and making it possible for warrants of arrest eventually to be issued against Sudanese president Omar al-Bashir and others. In March 2011, the Security Council issued its second referral to the ICC regarding the situation in Libya.

This time the United States did not abstain but voted favorably (the vote on the referral was unanimous).

The United States dropped its threat to cut off military aid to friendly countries that supported the ICC, as it was not preventing small countries from signing and only complicating U.S. relations with allied military forces everywhere. All of this hostility to international justice and to multilateralism contributed to the United States' low standing in world affairs toward the end of the Bush administration. The Obama administration has since established a relationship of "engagement" with the ICC through the office of the ambassador for war crimes, but because treaties have to be ratified by a two-thirds vote in the Senate, the United States will not become a party to the international community's most effective tool against human rights abuses anytime soon.

I left HRW in September 1996 to become the executive director of the Inter-American Institute of Human Rights (IIHR). At the time, Latin American NGOs were expressing growing interest in the possibility of a permanent international court to judge perpetrators of mass atrocities and overcome the problems with impunity that the courts of their countries had faced. Before the final UN-sponsored conference in Rome in 1998, the IIHR contributed to Latin American efforts to support an ICC and to prepare its diplomats for the highly technical conversations leading to it. As executive director, I asked Chilean lawyer Francisco "Pancho" Cox to organize a seminar in Guatemala to train Latin American diplomats and civil society activists on the key legal issues to be decided in Rome. Delegates and civil society representatives were able to consider in depth, for example, the provisions to ensure that the ICC is effectively subsidiary to the national courts and the mechanisms that would trigger its jurisdiction as well as the safeguards against the possibility of a rogue prosecutor exceeding his or her powers. In the draft statute, these provisions were highly technical, and our conference participants welcomed the opportunity for discussions within a shared legal culture.

Some states, such as Mexico, actually changed their initially negative positions toward the ICC after sustained civil society lobbying, and delegation members credited our Guatemala meeting with the final push in favor of that change. Latin America ended up presenting a very strong common position in favor of an ICC and of the more progressive provisions in the draft. Eventually it became the area of the world that most consistently ratified the statute.

In July 1998, I was privileged to witness the last two days of the Rome Conference that produced the treaty known as the Rome Statute for an International Criminal Court. It was a huge victory for the NGO community and for the group of like-minded states that for years had held fast to the strongest parts of the draft. In particular, the Rome Statute made an excellent contribution to international law by providing a formal definition—now agreed on by a large number of participants—of "crimes against humanity"; prior to this time, the term's definition was vague and not enshrined in a treaty. The statute reaffirmed that obedience to orders is not a defense in these types of crimes and succeeded in creating a truly independent tribunal and an equally independent office of the prosecutor. Proposals to make either of them subordinate to the decisions of political organs of the international community were firmly rejected. In particular, the NGOs obtained a provision that allowed the prosecutor to initiate investigations *proprio motu,* or by receiving complaints from the public. The prosecutor now needs to seek authorization from the trial chamber only after deciding that there is a reasonable basis to proceed with an investigation. In 2009, Prosecutor Luis Moreno Ocampo exercised this power for the first time to take the initiative with respect to Kenya. He subsequently obtained the green light from the pretrial chamber, and in late 2010, he filed charges against Kenyan principals for their responsibility in the massacres that took place in connection with the fraudulent elections of 2008.

The Rome Statute of 1998 has become a turning point in human rights advocacy. The existence of a permanent court is itself a powerful instrument for victims to obtain redress when a state is unwilling or unable to afford it to them. In addition, the statute represents a very broad agreement by the international community on the meaning and scope of important terms that have been around since Nuremberg—such as war crimes and crimes against humanity—but for which precision was lacking. Also, the states that sign on to the statute (there are now about 160 signatures and 113 ratifications) recognize that impunity for mass atrocities cannot be allowed and pledge to provide accountability and to cooperate with each other to stamp out impunity for these crimes. The Rome Statute has created a new paradigm for resolving violent conflicts; now peace negotiations cannot countenance impunity for international crimes.

From the perspective of the human rights movement, the year 1998 was perhaps not so much a turning point as a tipping point, or a moment at which changes that were already beginning to happen accelerated to produce a complete change. Over the last decade, the character of human rights monitoring and advocacy has changed dramatically. Now the movement has instruments of justice and can effectively advocate their use against major perpetrators. The movement itself has been enriched with the entry onto its scene of many more professionals and activists with a broad variety of skills and backgrounds. And the movement's weight in the formulation of public policies has increased with this injection of professionalism and scientific certainty to its findings of fact.

There is another way in which human rights activists can fight impunity, especially in those countries that are not under the ICC's jurisdiction. It is the possibility of using the courts of another nation to prosecute crimes committed extraterritorially under the universal jurisdiction principle. Discussions leading to the Genocide Convention of 1948, and then to all the major human rights treaties, dabbled with the idea of treaty norms that would mandate states to allow their courts to hear criminal cases even if the offenses had happened in the territory of another country, were committed by non-nationals and against non-nationals of the forum state. But that affirmative obligation was never approved, not even in more recent treaties, such as the UN Conventions on Torture (1987) and on Disappearances (2006).

References to universal jurisdiction have been vague enough that most countries have treated them as permissive rather than obligatory. The United States is a party to both the genocide and the torture conventions. In legislation adopted by Congress to implement those treaties, the United States does afford the possibility of prosecuting crimes committed elsewhere. But the United States takes a limited view of this provision: For genocide, the United States will prosecute acts committed outside the country only if the perpetrator is a U.S. citizen. For torture, the United States does allow for prosecution of foreign nationals. A unit at the Department of Justice is available to analyze claims against individuals accused of such crimes if the suspect is in U.S. territory and to recommend prosecution if warranted. So far, this criminal statute has been used only once: against "Chuckie" Taylor, the U.S.-born son of dictator Charles Taylor, for crimes committed against Liberian nationals as his father's chief of intelligence in Liberia. He was convicted and is serving a life sentence in a U.S. prison. In other cases—such as suspected Nazi war criminals—the Justice Department prefers to extradite or to deport suspects to countries where the crimes were committed, as long as the territorial state requests their extradition and will give them a fair trial.

Several accused Latin American war criminals who were discovered in the United States have been removed through immigration proceedings, including Argentine task force members Ernesto Barreiro and Juan Miguel Méndez (no relation to this author) and Peruvian suspects Telmo Hurtado and Manuel Rivera Rondón. Barreiro is said to have been a principal figure in clandestine detention, torture and extermination centers in Córdoba, Argentina. I provided detailed background information to federal investigators, and in the end, Barreiro abandoned his claim for asylum in the United States and departed voluntarily. He is in custody and on trial in Argentina. In the case of Juan Miguel Méndez, Robert Goldman testified as an expert witness on conditions in Argentina and, in December 2010, Méndez was sent back there, where he will be tried on charges that he was a member of the task force that ran three clandestine centers in the greater Buenos Aires area: Atlético, Banco and Olimpo. Eduardo González, my colleague at ICTJ, who had previously been a staff member of Peru's Truth and Reconciliation Commission, gave expert testimony on the cases of the Peruvian army officers. Both men had been identified as alleged perpetrators of the infamous massacre of sixty-nine peasants in Accomarca and the disappearance and murder of the man who had led their patrol to the Andean village.

In contrast to the limited scope of universal jurisdiction in the United States, several countries have broad statutes allowing for criminal prosecution of crimes committed elsewhere. Those statutes generally have been used to prosecute Nazi-era war crimes. However, the whole picture changed when former Chilean dictator Augusto Pinochet was suddenly and surprisingly arrested in London in 1998, while being treated at a hospital, pursuant to a warrant of arrest issued by Spanish judge Baltazar Garzón. A close friend of former prime minister Margaret Thatcher, Pinochet had been in the United Kingdom many times before and never expected to face any problem there. Garzón was able to issue the warrant for crimes committed under Plan Cóndor, a program that Pinochet himself had proposed and helped implement and that consisted of covert cooperation between the security forces of several South American dictatorships to apprehend and "render" suspects to each other. Many victims were tortured and made to disappear under Plan Cóndor in the late 1970s. Garzón and other Spanish judges had been hearing complaints against South American officers for crimes committed in Argentina, Chile, Uruguay and Paraguay, and, while they did not have anyone in custody, they gathered evidence against several South American criminals, including Pinochet.

Invoking a European extradition treaty, Garzón asked the British authorities to detain Pinochet and bring him to Garzón's jurisdiction in Madrid. Pinochet spent eighteen months under house arrest in the United Kingdom, riveting the attention of the entire world. The Law Lords, a part of the House of Lords acting as Britain's highest court, issued landmark decisions. Upholding the universal jurisdiction invoked by Spain, a panel of the Law Lords confirmed that it could be used even against a former head of state and authorized Pinochet's extradition for several cases of torture. Eventually, and before extradition actually took place, the British government allowed Pinochet to return to Chile on humanitarian grounds, when his health seemed to deteriorate. Upon arrival in Santiago, Pinochet proceeded to make a mockery of that decision by appearing quite healthy at the airport. The most important result of the Pinochet case was that Chileans engaged in a long and rich discussion about what should be done in their country about his crimes. The debate accelerated the shift toward the active prosecution and trial of all those involved in war crimes and crimes against humanity. Pinochet himself was stripped of the immunity he enjoyed as the self-appointed senator for life, and his trial in Chile was under way before it was interrupted by his death.

The Pinochet case created a surge in interest in using universal jurisdiction statutes in Spain and elsewhere in Europe. Many human rights activists joined the bandwagon and dedicated themselves to bringing such cases, each more sensational than the previous one, before European judges. Rwandan participants in the genocide were prosecuted and punished in Belgium, where they had fled after the collapse of the genocidal regime. Germany, Denmark and other countries opened their courts to prosecute criminals from the Balkan wars, although in most of these cases the charges were dismissed and the defendants transferred to the jurisdiction of the ICTY.

Prime Minister Ariel Sharon, of Israel, was accused in Belgium of ordering Israeli troops temporarily in Lebanon to allow allied local militias to murder hundreds of Palestinian refugees in the Sabra and Shatila camps in September 1982. A French judge summoned Henry Kissinger as a witness in an investigation of crimes committed by the Pinochet regime, but he declined to appear. U.S. General Tommy Franks also was accused in Belgium for alleged crimes in the war in Iraq. Soon Secretary of Defense Donald Rumsfeld, the president of China and others were the subjects of similar complaints before the courts of Belgium, France and Spain. A backlash occurred almost immediately. Rumsfeld threatened to move NATO out of Brussels if the case proceeded, and diplomatic pressures were brought to bear, both secretly and overtly. In time, Belgium and Spain amended their universal jurisdiction statutes to make them less "user-friendly" to NGOs and members of the public and to allow for political considerations to rule on whether to proceed.

More recently, Rwandan exiles have filed charges against Paul Kagame and his ministers before French courts in a thinly disguised effort at genocide revisionism. In solidarity with Rwanda, African leaders accused European countries of engaging in "judicial colonialism" by arrogantly deciding who should be prosecuted for human rights crimes.

In turn, some used this wave of recrimination cynically against the ICC, even though thirty-seven African states have voluntarily joined it and the first cases were self-referred to the ICC by African nations. President Bashir of Sudan contributed to this false accusation against the ICC in order to delegitimize the warrant for his own arrest on charges of genocide. This and similar irresponsible uses of universal jurisdiction have hurt the potential effectiveness of the ICC. Even the venerable International Court of Justice—the judicial organ of the UN that hears state-versus-state claims under general international law and issues advisory opinions at the request of UN political organs—has been affected by the backlash. For example, Israel boycotted its proceedings on an advisory opinion regarding the legality of separation barriers built by Israel in the occupied Palestinian territories.[4]

Universal jurisdiction could have yielded much more favorable results for human rights protection if, instead of a rush to the courts, a more careful selection process had taken place. Quality control is impossible, however, because human rights lawyers and NGOs cannot put themselves in the position of gatekeepers to decide which cases should be brought; in principle, any person can apply for a case under universal prosecution. Prosecutors and courts eventually play that necessary screening role and decline far-fetched petitions, but by the time they exercise their power the political damage has been done. In the meantime, cases that should have proceeded to a serious trial have stalled, such as the case of Hissène Habré, the former dictator of Chad who is responsible for the death of some forty thousand persons, which languished first in Belgium and more recently in Senegal. The African Union asked Senegal to judge him because he is living there and because Senegal's laws allow for universal jurisdiction. However, the courts there have been reluctant to go forward, and the president of Senegal, Abdoulaye Wade wants to get rid of the case rather than break the cycle of impunity for crimes committed in another country.

This expansion of the human rights field is not without controversy, although of course the human rights movement has never tried to escape controversy; mostly it relishes it. When push comes to shove, politics as usual between states prevails over consideration of justice, no matter how meritorious some cases may be. Less cynically, some voices complain that human rights get in the way of other important values, such as peace making, peace building and post-conflict reconstruction. It is suggested that insistence on criminal punishment only complicates the search for solutions to meet the need for humanitarian assistance and even to prevent future violations. A recent example of these debates is the arrest warrant against a sitting head of state, Omar al-Bashir of Sudan, who has been accused by the ICC's prosecutor of genocide, war crimes and crimes against humanity. The trial chamber issued the warrant in early 2009, and, after appeal, the warrant now includes genocide. Sudan has refused to cooperate with the ICC and hints that any future cooperation with the international community on matters as important as protection of Sudan's civilian population, peace talks and humanitarian relief is conditional on revocation of the arrest warrants. (In addition to the warrant against Bashir, there are outstanding warrants against one of his ministers and a Janjaweed leader.) Bashir has tried to stir African opposition to the ICC and has in part succeeded. The African Union has formally asked the Security Council to suspend the case of Darfur at the ICC under Article 16 of the Rome Statute; the Security Council can do this if, in its judgment, suspension of ICC operations for one year at a time is necessary in the interests of preserving the peace and security of nations. So far the Security Council has not acted on that request, and to their credit, several African leaders have renewed their support for the ICC. The warrants for crimes committed in Darfur are outstanding and "live," even if no effort is made to execute them. Bashir has been embarrassed by announcements by South Africa and other states that, if he were to visit, they would have to arrest him. But his partial diplomatic victory at the African Union has indeed undermined the authority and legitimacy of the ICC in the eyes of some Africans.

The international community, including the United States, has done very little to support the ICC in this conflict or to generate conditions under which Bashir eventually could be brought to justice. On the contrary, it seems willing to make concessions for him in exchange for his "cooperation" with humanitarian relief in Darfur and with a referendum in Southern Sudan.

Similarly, when Uganda and the Lord's Resistance Army (LRA) announced that they would negotiate an end to a twenty-one-year war in the north of the country, the fact that the LRA leaders had pending arrest warrants by the ICC was used as an obstacle to peace. Obviously, LRA chief Joseph Kony wanted to blackmail international public opinion by refusing to negotiate until the arrest warrants were revoked; however, some well-meaning leaders of the Acholi people of northern Uganda who were not complicit in LRA atrocities also took that position. In the end, the arrest warrants were not withdrawn, and the talks did start in 2006 and a ceasefire was reached that year. Unfortunately, it did not result in peace because Kony withdrew in 2008, which proves that he was never serious about peace and had agreed to meet only to see if he could get the warrants quashed.

I was the president of ICTJ when these talks were starting, and we produced two rigorous opinion surveys of the people of northern Uganda that helped dispel myths about the Acholi and other Ugandans only wanting peace, or being more interested in traditional forms of conflict resolution more than in justice.[5] A much more nuanced picture of the attitudes of Northern Ugandans emerged from these surveys: Although their most urgent needs were to return home, to feed their children and to have peace, they were also interested in seeing justice done for the crimes they had suffered and placed their hopes for that squarely on the ICC.

The surveys also helped a great deal in bringing information about the ICC to northern Ugandans. One positive result of the talks that did take place during the peace negotiations in Juba, Southern Sudan, was that the leaders of civil society and the paramount tribal leaders from northern Uganda began to talk to one another and were heard for the first time by the LRA and the government of Uganda. All parties accepted that the matter of accountability for crimes committed in Uganda was a national responsibility and that the ICC could not be turned on and off according to political necessity. Since then Uganda has created a national court and procedures to deal with crimes within its national jurisdiction. The ICC is no longer under pressure to abandon the Ugandan victims; if the ICC ever becomes unnecessary in this context, it will be because the Ugandans are doing what they have to do.

The mere possibility of being brought before the ICC or other international tribunals has had the beneficial effect of helping peace and justice begin to coexist and nurture each other in a variety of places. When Colombian leaders were designing a "justice and peace law" to demobilize paramilitary groups, they were conscious of the need not to be too lenient with punishment for mass atrocities lest the ICC decide to bring the perpetrators under its jurisdiction. The fact that the ICC prosecutor has had Colombia "under investigation" since 2007 has motivated the Colombian prosecutors and courts to keep focused on each case to ensure that they are adhering to international standards. In Cote d'Ivoire, the possibility that hate-mongers could be brought before the ICC has been a factor in preventing ethnic tensions from igniting at crucial moments.

Israel is not a party to the Rome Statute (it has signed but not ratified it), but the Palestinian Authority has requested an opinion from the ICC prosecutor on whether the Rome Statute is open to signature by an entity like it. (Palestine is not a state, so its ability to join a multilateral treaty raises interesting legal issues.) If the Palestinian Authority is allowed to become a signatory, and if events like the armed conflict in Gaza in 2008–2009 should happen again, the ICC would have jurisdiction to prosecute both Israeli and Palestinian fighters who violate the laws of war. Burma also is not a party to the Rome Statute, so the atrocities that its repressive government commits against the Karen and other ethnic minorities could come before the ICC only through a Security Council referral, as happened with Darfur and Libya. The Security Council has been called on to refer the Burma case, but the threat of veto by China has so far rendered such a referral impossible. Nevertheless, the mere legal possibility of referral gives China great leverage with the Burmese dictatorship and probably helps to check the worst aspects of Burma's behavior.

As UN Special Advisor to the Secretary General on the Prevention of Genocide from 2004 to 2007, I saw firsthand how justice can contribute to the prevention of atrocities and protect populations at risk. This was especially the case in Darfur, where in briefings to the Security Council, I joined others in calling for measures to break the cycle of impunity for the crimes already committed against Darfurians. In this case and others, however, justice should not be promoted only for its utilitarian value in persuading warring parties to behave better; conceived in such a manner, justice mechanisms tend to be turned on and off when convenient. The result can discredit the independence and impartiality of the courts. Justice should be pursued for its own sake. When it is, justice generally works to make peace more possible rather than less, and it certainly makes peace ultimately more lasting and sustainable. In this respect, in the last fifteen years, there has been a veritable paradigm shift in international relations when it comes to peace making.

If in the past the conventional wisdom was that justice and human rights should always take a backseat to peace, even if peace obtained at any cost was little more than the momentary silencing of the guns, now the existence of the ICC and the emerging norms of international law against impunity make it necessary for mediators and peace makers to pay attention both to the legitimate desires for peace and to the equally legitimate interest in justice.

CHAPTER TEN

GENOCIDE

The word "genocide" attracts attention, and often that is a good thing. Like the word "torture," however, it can be used unsystematically and sometimes in harmful ways, because if everything is genocide, nothing really is. And given the consequences of an actual genocide, it is important not to use this word in vain. The international community spends far too much time debating whether some event amounts to genocide and not enough time deciding how to deal effectively with ongoing events or, more important, preventing genocide in the first place. As a result, the international community failed miserably to prevent genocide in the twentieth century, and its prospects of being able to do so in the twenty-first century are not promising.

The history of the twentieth century is undoubtedly a history of genocide. In 1905, the German colonial forces committed genocide against the Herero ethnic minority in what is today the African country of Namibia. Ten years later, the Ottoman Empire, under the rule of the extreme nationalistic faction of the Young Turks, commenced a series of actions against Armenians living in what is today eastern Turkey, including mass deportations to areas in the Middle East. The Turkish/Ottoman government was aligned with Germany during World War I, and it accused Armenians of siding with Russia against it. Actually, hostility against Armenians had begun years before the war began, as evidenced by the policy of forced assimilation of all minorities to a common language, religion and culture. In the sense that the primary motivation for assimilation was ideological, based on Turkish nationalism, the Armenians' case is the first instance of genocide as we came to know it in the twentieth century. Western powers protested, but the decimation of Armenians continued through murder, deportation and famine. Historian Arnold Toynbee estimated that 1 million Armenians perished out of a pre-1915 population of 1.6 million.[1]

Soviet leader Joseph Stalin's campaign against the peasantry, to eliminate the *kulaks* (rural money lenders), to abolish private ownership and to impose collectivism also should qualify as genocide. Beginning in 1929 and lasting until the beginning of World War II, it resulted in countless deaths through famine, deportation to the Arctic and murder of anyone who was perceived as resisting. Although this campaign may not qualify as genocide by today's standards because the victims were not identified as belonging to a religious, racial, ethnic or national group (except perhaps for the exceptional cruelty suffered by Ukrainians), the Stalinist crimes certainly fit a broad definition, perhaps colloquial if not legal, that would include what is called "politicide": the murder and destruction of communities identified by political affiliation or ideology.

The signal moment in this tragic history is the Nazi policy of the "final solution" by which Adolf Hitler tried to eliminate all Jews in Europe. His campaign also included the destruction of other minorities, such as the Roma (Gypsies) and the disabled and infirm of any race or religion. The Holocaust, or *Shoah*, resulted in the murder of at least 6 million Jews; an estimated half a million Roma were killed as well.[2] Although most of the murders happened during World War II, extreme measures had begun well before the war broke out in 1939, at least against German Jews. A few years before 1939, the Jewish population of Germany and Austria had been cut almost in half by a combination of flight and murder. The principal motive for murdering the Jews was also ideological, and it originated in theories of racial superiority. The main methods used are sadly well known: deportations to forced labor camps and gas chambers.

The international community, stunned at the scope of the horror, vowed that "never again" would crimes of this magnitude be allowed to happen. At Nuremberg after the war, the Allies prosecuted war crimes and also "crimes against humanity," a category that allowed the tribunal to judge perpetrators of persecution against Jews. But even that new category of crimes was insufficient to capture the essence of genocide, and the newly created United Nations set about to codify the crime and to apply the word created for it by Raphael Lemkin.[3] The result was the Convention to Prevent and Punish the Crime of Genocide, approved by the General Assembly on December 9, 1948 (one day before the Universal Declaration of Human Rights). It was believed that a strong commitment to making genocide an international crime would serve as a deterrent in the future.

The Genocide Convention may well have had some deterrent effect, but it certainly did not operate efficiently either to prevent or to punish crimes of genocide. There can be no doubt that genocide and genocide-like atrocities happened again in the second half of the past century, and that by and large they have gone unpunished.

Consider these examples. In 1971, Pakistani forces committed genocide in a futile attempt to prevent Bangladesh from seceding. The Cambodian policy by the Khmer Rouge to push people back to the countryside and eliminate professional and merchant classes is another such atrocity. It was executed by the Pol Pot regime between 1975 and 1979; the regime murdered or starved to death 1.7 million of the country's 8 million inhabitants.[4] Indonesia enforced the annexation of Timor Leste in 1975 through aerial bombing, massive destruction of crops and fields, forced starvation, mass arrests, torture and murder of Timorese opponents. In the 1980s, famines in Africa originated in natural catastrophes but also in policies of governments and insurgents to subdue ethnic minorities by using food as a weapon, as in Ethiopia and Somalia. Even today, indigenous populations in the Americas may be at risk of extinction because of "development" policies that push them off their ancestral lands and take advantage of their extreme vulnerability.

In the 1990s, the trend to use genocidal tactics as part of war or as counterinsurgency accelerated, particularly in the extreme examples of the Balkan wars and the Rwandan genocide of 1994. As mentioned, "ethnic cleansing" (a term with no definition in law) was the official, stated policy of the Serbs to displace Croatians and Bosnians from regions they wanted to occupy and govern. The mass deportations and killings that were used for that purpose demonstrate that ethnic cleansing may well be a euphemism for genocide. In 1993, eight thousand Bosnian men and boys under the protection of international forces were murdered by a Bosnian Serb armed contingent under the command of General Ratko Mladić in Srebrenica, Eastern Bosnia. This was the only case that the International Criminal Tribunal for the Former Yugoslavia categorized as genocide, but the mass murder has to be considered in the larger context of the many crimes committed in that war. The Rwandan genocide started in April 1994 and lasted one hundred days; at the end, about 800,000 Tutsis and their Hutu relatives or friends were killed. Never before had genocide happened so quickly, although that does not mean that it came without warning. As explained in chapter 9, interethnic tensions and bloody episodes had happened many times before, and the preparations of the ruling government for the slaughter had been the subject of warnings to the international community at least a year in advance.

What Rwanda and Srebrenica had in common was precisely the inability or unwillingness of the international community to make good on its 1948 promise of "never again." In both places, international troops were on the ground; they should have been ready and able to protect innocent civilians from attack. In Srebrenica, NATO forces were paralyzed by a byzantine debate about their "mandate." The international community had sent them there to protect humanitarian assistance operations and to protect those who were receiving assistance; the troops were under orders *not* to fight against any of the factions in the war and at any rate would have been outgunned by Mladić's forces. NATO commanders made no effort to reinforce them, and they stood by as the disarmed internal refugees they were supposed to protect were systematically murdered. In Rwanda, most of the international forces were withdrawn by their governments at the outset of the genocide; the few that remained were not reinforced despite desperate calls by Canadian general Roméo Dallaire, their commander.

It does no good, however, to put all the blame on the United Nations, the Security Council or the governments of the large and powerful countries of the world. Without minimizing their obvious responsibilities, we must also recognize that the rest of the world is not prepared to react to genocide in a preventive way—and that includes the human rights movement.

Although the network of human rights institutions has crafted a relatively successful approach to responding to human rights violations once they have taken place, preventing them from happening in the first place is a challenge we are all struggling to meet. The international community understands how to monitor and report on atrocities and follows sophisticated rules about redress and remedies. Thanks to such progress, advocacy for remedies to ongoing abuses is now widely shared by many institutions, including courts, working groups, special rapporteurships and nongovernmental organizations (NGOs), and there exist international criminal mechanisms to punish the worst offenders. But experience shows that prevention requires much more than that and is hampered, at different stages, by the difficulty in mustering enough political will to adopt the hard decisions needed to protect defenseless people from extensive loss of life.

IN JULY 2004, KOFI ANNAN appointed me as the first Special Advisor to the Secretary-General on the Prevention of Genocide, a post created as part of an action plan designed to fill the gaps in the UN architecture that had been identified after Rwanda. In the 1970s and 1980s, the UN Commission on Human Rights had created a Special Rapporteur on Genocide, a post occupied by highly regarded specialists on the issue. They produced several reports designed to strengthen the provisions of the Genocide Convention and to raise awareness of the possibility that genocide could happen again. As independent experts reporting to a commission that had no role in political affairs, their reports were intellectually influential but did not affect policy making. The post of Special Rapporteur on Genocide had been abolished well before the events of Srebrenica and Rwanda. My role was to bring to the Security Council's attention situations that, if left unattended, could lead to genocide, to create a system of early warning of such situations, and to offer recommendations about what early action could be adopted to prevent such occurrences.

Although the Secretariat would never censor me, I was instructed to speak out "without undue publicity." This new human rights mandate was therefore very promising, at least in comparison with the special procedures (rapporteurs and working groups) established under the old Commission on Human Rights and inherited by the Human Rights Council, given that those mandates have no access to the secretary-general or the Security Council.

Creating an effective early warning system for genocide demanded that we be aware of situations around the globe, and my assistants and I struggled to keep well informed. The United Nations produces a large stream of information every day, coming to New York from a variety of departments and agencies, including the United Nations Children's Fund (UNICEF), the United Nations Development Programme (UNDP), the High Commissioner for Refugees and the department of peacekeeping operations. Unfortunately, a great deal of this information is restricted or else not particularly organized around prevention of atrocities, so my colleagues and I had to invent our own system of data collection. The secretary-general encouraged me to look for information outside the UN as well, and through Amnesty International, Human Rights Watch and the International Crisis Group, we were able to obtain information and analysis that was more focused on human rights.

There was also the question of what information to collect in order to prevent genocide. The convention's definition of genocide includes killing members of a group, causing serious mental or bodily harm, creating conditions of life calculated to bring about their destruction, preventing births and forcibly transferring children from one population group to another. Those actions have to be taken "with intent to destroy, in whole or in part, a national, ethnical [sic], racial or religious group, as such."[5] This specific intent can be found in the facts themselves, as the International Criminal Tribunal for Rwanda successfully did in the *Akayesu* case, for example. Hutu leaders were found responsible for genocide because of their instructions to the actual killers, their organizational efforts and their speeches and other utterances that left no doubt about their specific intent not just to kill but to destroy the Tutsi as a community, in whole or in part.[6]

We were urged to stay focused on events clearly pointing toward genocide, since human rights violations more generally were the purview of the High Commissioner for Human Rights. Yet we could not wait until all the elements of the crime of genocide were in place, because by then it would be too late. For the purpose of convicting someone of genocide, a court may not need the smoking gun of a public statement of the defendant's intent to destroy a population group. But for purpose of prevention, proving the specific intent of a group to commit genocide—before that genocide actually happens—is impossible. When I made initial inquiries about troubling situations, at first I received exactly that reaction, even from well-meaning colleagues within the Secretariat. Nepal? "That's not genocide." Cote d'Ivoire? "That's not genocide." Fortunately, I was able to state my interest in a certain conflict without necessarily having to characterize what was happening as genocide. Since my task was prevention, I needed to act before all the aspects of genocide were in place, because otherwise I would be judging, not preventing. As soon as I explained that I was trying to apply early warning and wanted to look into the facts before the situation degenerated into genocide, my colleagues at the UN understood.

Among representatives of member states, the reaction varied. Countries that were supportive of the Office of the Special Advisor on the Prevention of Genocide (OSAPG) readily agreed with my approach to early warning, but countries that were interested in a certain conflict and did not want the word "genocide" applied to it reacted negatively. They not only assumed that a UN official whose title included the word "genocide" was already making a characterization; they also argued that such involvement would only complicate matters.

Being able to comment on worldwide troublesome conflicts without defining them explicitly did allow us to take an interest in many situations that were clearly not genocidal yet. But it was essential to narrow down the scope of our concerns, not only to avoid turf battles with other agencies but also to limit the sphere of situations to a size that we could realistically follow. Although at first we wanted to avoid a rigid list of criteria that could become a straitjacket, early on we discovered the usefulness of establishing a set of such criteria, or "indicators," as it let our NGO partners know what kind of information would be most helpful if they wanted us to act.

We were, of course, still bound by the conventional definition: For an act to be genocidal, it had to be directed against "a national, ethnical, racial or religious group, as such." This excludes killings or massive torture and disappearances against a group designated by political or ideological identity, which was the case in most of Latin America.[7] Even the killing of close to a million persons in Cambodia in the late 1970s might not be properly genocide under international law, because—except for a tiny fraction of victims who were members of ethnic minorities—most had been killed because of class and profession; they were indistinguishable from their victimizers in terms of race, ethnicity, national origin, religion or other cultural traits. The fact that this "politicide"—genocide for political or ideological reasons—is not included in the definition is purely historical: The drafts originally submitted to the Genocide Convention did include "political groups" among those to be protected from genocide, but reference to them was dropped during the debate in 1948.

Some jurists have argued that the definition has evolved in the intervening years; for example, in approving a request for the extradition of Augusto Pinochet in 1998, Spain adopted a definition that included political groups as targets. There are also some in Argentina who want the courts that are trying the crimes of the dirty war to consider it a genocide. Not only do the facts in Argentina not meet the definition in the convention, the courts also have rightly characterized the actions as "crimes against humanity," which allows them to refuse to apply amnesties, pardons or a statute of limitations and to judge them despite the passage of time. There is no hierarchical ranking among genocide, crimes against humanity and war crimes.[8] In addition, the moral and legal obligation of the international community to prevent or to prosecute and punish such acts after the fact exists for all three categories of crimes. Unfortunately, the weakness in the preventive instruments also is the same for all three categories. A journalist once asked if I did not need to qualify the crime as genocide in order to trigger a response by the international community; I answered that the international community had an ethical and a legal responsibility to prevent the crime, whether it was genocide or a war crime or a crime against humanity. In 2005, the General Assembly, with more than one hundred heads of state physically present in New York, adopted the "Responsibility to Protect" doctrine that clarifies that such a responsibility applies to all international crimes.[9]

At the OSAPG, we began with "populations at risk," defined by ethnicity, national origin, race or religion. Those categories are notoriously difficult, as they are quite subjective. During my first visit to Darfur in September 2004, a local authority defied us to say who among his advisors (all present before us) belonged to the so-called Arab tribes and who to the African tribes. They were all racially African, all Muslim and all dressed alike. Nevertheless, distinctions among Massalit, Fur and Zaghawa and the so-called Arab tribes did make sense in their own cultural setting: Everyone in Darfur knows who belongs to what group. More important, the human rights violations going on at that time were clearly directed at groups based on their identity as Fur, Massalit or Zaghawa, even if some members of those communities were welcome in government ranks. Belonging to those communities was unmistakably an "ethnic" categorization, and it certainly carried risks for their members. At the time, Sudan and its allies were saying that the violence in Darfur was related strictly to insurgency and counterinsurgency operations; however, even if there will never be a "pure" genocidal intent, the fact that other motives might be present does not necessarily exclude the possibility of genocide. As Darfur demonstrates, even if the conflict—at its origin or under its most recent incarnation—has a variety of causes, the fact that an ethnic group is vulnerable to violence is sufficient reason to view the group as being at risk for genocide.

To be defined as potentially threatened by genocide, however, it is important that a group be at risk of the actions also enumerated in the convention: killings, serious bodily or mental harm, conditions of life calculated to bring about their destruction, prevention of births and forcible transfer of children. Some argue that early warning makes sense only if it occurs so early that it prompts action to protect minority groups from discrimination, because in many cases genocide results from an escalation of the conflict over generations. This kind of early-early warning is advocated by, among others, the UN Committee on the Elimination of Racial Discrimination, a treaty body that has established its own early warning system. I did not disagree that such early-early warning is useful; given the constraints of OSAPG's mandate and resources, however, we advocated for international action when it appeared that only the intervention of UN political organs could prevent a tragic outcome.

OUR WORK IN PREDICTING GENOCIDE as early as possible benefited from the paradigms developed over the years by genocide scholars. Their study of many historical genocides and political mass murder all over the world in the last few decades yields a trove of experiences that show certain patterns.[10] For example, harsh censorship of expression over a long period of time does generate violence; the presence of militias and armed groups is an immediate risk factor; and impunity for past and recent abuses can generate a spiral of violence. These scholars also have classified accelerating and retardant factors that not only help predict the immediate future but also identify possible measures that can curb the dangers. Undoubtedly, one also has to look at these cases with flexibility and adaptability, because what works in one situation can be very ineffective or, worse, dangerous, in another. Sometimes these lists of indicators smack of a mathematical model that may help predict some outcomes but fail to predict others. That is why all these formulas have to be applied with a high degree of country- and conflict-specific analysis.

Eventually, institutional turf battles with the larger line units of the Secretariat (i.e., departments like peace keeping, political affairs, humanitarian affairs, the office of the high commissioner for human rights, etc.) emerged, and cooperation from the larger institutions of the UN family (UNDP, UNICEF, UN High Commissioner for Refugees) never materialized. The difficulties were never personal nor the objections mean-spirited; they arose because of institutional problems in the UN's makeup. My job was difficult because the task of preventing genocide is highly complex and even thankless. No one will ever know if genocide has been prevented; even if some clear disaster is avoided, it is difficult to attribute that effect to a single cause, much less one related to effective action by the international community. In contrast, the genocide that we fail to prevent is widely known and shames the international community for decades. Effective prevention requires early warning, which often is delivered at a time when no one wants to hear it. It also depends on political will for early action. The later that such action is adopted, the harder it is to overcome political and diplomatic obstacles. Prevention is also difficult because it requires coordination of several kinds of measures in response to threats, and the exact mix of those measures that is most effective is highly contingent on circumstances—cultural background, conflict history, interests of external powers with a voice in the Security Council and the relative amenability of rogue regimes and insurgent forces to engage with the international community in a meaningful dialogue.

After following the conflict in Darfur closely, I advocated for simultaneous and coordinated action in four areas: protection of civilians, humanitarian assistance, accountability for the abuses that have already occurred and negotiations to resolve the underlying conflict.

Protection often requires the deployment of armed contingents, preferably with the consent of the territorial government. Obtaining such consent is not as hard as it sounds; obviously governments see the presence of foreign troops as an affront to their sovereignty, but by the time it is needed, the situation of law and order is well beyond the governments' capabilities to control. Consensual deployment does require the flexing of considerable diplomatic muscle, however, and it is important for the principal actors in the international community to stand together. Unfortunately, among the permanent five (P–5) members of the Security Council—Russia, China, France, the United Kingdom and the United States—there is almost always one or more state with an interest in protecting or shielding a client state from too much outside intervention.

That was certainly the case with Darfur: Serious action by the Security Council—as opposed to half measures—was never formally discussed (although there certainly was a lot of back-channel negotiation) because China and Russia were expected to veto any measures robust enough to be likely to succeed: China because of its interest in Sudanese oil, Russia as the main seller of weapons to the Khartoum regime. Consent from Sudan for some actions was obtained: first for delivery of humanitarian relief, then for deployment by the African Union (AU) and later by a combined AU-UN force of troops from only African nations. Eventually Sudan also agreed to participate in UN-sponsored peace talks with the Darfur rebels. At each step, however, options for stronger measures, such as sanctions and the deployment of larger contingents with fewer limitations in terms of mandate, freedom of movement and contributing nations, were entertained but never adopted. In time, the regime in Khartoum learned to manipulate the international community by consenting to some actions and then undermining them with its practices on the ground. For that reason, even when consent by the territorial state is obtained, it is crucial to set the specifics of the mandate of peace-keeping forces right from the start. These forces have to be able to protect the civilian population from harm, either in their villages or in displaced persons camps, and there should be no ambiguity as to their permission to do so.

Peace keeping with a mandate to protect civilians may require reasonable troop levels with some mobility as well as adequate equipment and provisions. Ambiguities in the mandate of the Darfur peacekeepers allowed Khartoum to play games with its consent; sometimes it would ground the peacekeepers simply by cutting off delivery of jet fuel to their aircraft. Khartoum also delayed the issuance of visas to foreign troops, denied customs permits to armored personnel carriers donated by Canada and denied military trainers from non-African countries access to train the African forces in how to use such materiel. Such bad-faith actions are to be expected from a regime like the one headed by Omar al-Bashir. This government has a history of brutality against its people and of reneging on its promises to adversaries and to foreign powers; what is inexcusable is that, at every turn, the international community allowed him to get away with such deception.

Armed intervention in cases where consent has not been granted should always be subject to the first-do-no-harm test. In the Darfur case, nonconsensual use of force was not considered, since the United States and its allies were otherwise engaged in Iraq and Afghanistan, and no other force was available. But I am persuaded that, even if available, nonconsensual armed intervention in Darfur would have done more harm than good. Bashir would have depicted any such force as an anti-Arab and anti-Muslim ploy by Western powers and gained support from the Sudanese and citizens from other countries; the fighting and ensuing ethnic tension would have resembled the deadly conflicts in Iraq after Bush declared "mission accomplished." Of course, Iraq was not an example of nonconsensual use of force for purposes of preventing atrocities. Of course, Iraq was not an example of nonconsensual use of force for purposes of preventing atrocities. However, we did see that nonconsensual deployment in the Balkans failed to prevent genocide, and we can conclude that it will not necessarily prevent it in the future because the international community cannot be relied upon to act militarily and to do so firmly and with dedication and grit. Even when a decision is made, it is in the expectation that foreign military presence will end sooner rather than later. Genocidaires know this and act accordingly.

Humanitarian aid is important to curb hunger and disease and reverse the dire circumstances in which people have been placed. Aid also offers a measure of protection by bringing international witnesses to the scene. Here again, consent by the territorial state is always needed, and many times it is granted only after very forceful diplomatic and public pressure. At the same time, humanitarian aid must be allowed to be delivered under well-established principles of neutrality and impartiality. Those NGOs that have specialized in relief operations have honed their procedures and cooperate with each other very effectively. For example, in Somalia, a famine that had caused 300,000 deaths in a few months was reversed in a matter of weeks once humanitarian NGOs were on the ground. Initially they were protected by international troops, but they stayed after the withdrawal of those forces despite serious security risks.

Conditions in Somalia have not improved in almost twenty years of lawlessness; but today famine and disease are not part of the equation. In Darfur, the initial death toll in the camps of displaced persons rose to 10,000 per month from disease; the deployment of humanitarian NGOs likewise cut that rate to equal Sudan's normal mortality rate in a matter of weeks. Territorial states must not be allowed to threaten these NGOs or to direct their actions, much less to retaliate against them, as the Sudanese government did, for example, after the International Criminal Court (ICC) issued its warrants of arrest.

Impunity for massacres that have taken place must cease, because impunity invites a new round of violence and encourages perpetrators to commit ever more serious atrocities. From the perspective of the victims, impunity encourages them to take matters into their own hands; if that is not within their power, it prevents them from making decisions in their own interest and from participating in the solutions.

It was clear on my first visit to Darfur in September 2004 that impunity for the more than 200,000 murders and deaths due to forced displacement that had taken place in 2003 and early 2004 was the main cause of instability and that it prevented the success of peace-making and humanitarian efforts by the international community. We asked Sudanese prosecutors and judges what deaths were being investigated for prosecution or tried in court; our questions were met with only quizzical looks. We briefed the Security Council in October and stressed the need for accountability. That same month the Security Council instituted a commission of inquiry that, after a thorough investigation, issued a damning report in February 2005, recommending referral to the ICC.[11] Simultaneously, I and others within and outside the UN were also advocating referral, which happened on March 31, 2005. Despite Khartoum's blatant refusal to cooperate, the Office of the Prosecutor of the ICC conducted investigations among the Darfur diaspora and was able to file charges against a high-ranking government official, a Janjaweed leader, President Bashir and three rebel leaders. The rebel leaders have voluntarily appeared in The Hague, and their cases are under consideration. Bashir and his two accomplices remain at large and in Sudan, but warrants for their arrest are outstanding. This limited result does not negate the overall impact that ICC actions have had in isolating Bashir and the others and in putting pressure on Sudan to act constructively in the other aspects of the crisis.

It is important to remember that in every case of actual or potential genocide there is an underlying conflict—sometimes generations old—that needs to be resolved satisfactorily if any solution is going to be lasting. If peace negotiations are not taking place, it is imperative that the international community urge the parties to the conflict to initiate them. Without a serious effort to redress old grievances and settle old scores, interim measures on protection, assistance and accountability will be short-lived and ineffective, and the affected population will continue to be dependent on an international community whose attention will soon be directed elsewhere. The Abuja process in regard to Darfur was the appropriate forum for these negotiations, and some very able mediators and advisors participated in it.

Beginning in 2004, the UN and the AU insisted on peace talks on Darfur and succeeded in bringing Khartoum and the various rebel forces to prolonged sessions held in Abuja, Nigeria. The lack of more concentrated and forceful interest by the international community, however, allowed Sudan to manipulate the process and eventually to obtain a very flawed agreement in May 2006. In this agreement, only one faction of one of the Darfur insurgencies agreed to give up the fight. The Darfur Peace Agreement (DPA) said nothing about the disarmament of the Janjaweed, the need for all parties to cooperate with ICC investigations or proposals to continue talks with the majority of rebels who refused to sign. Even worse, Khartoum acted as if the agreement was a sort of realignment of forces that legitimized a new offensive against the nonsignatory parties. Paradoxically, then, the peace agreement resulted only in renewed combat and new atrocities against the civilian population. The only reason why the Abuja accord did not cause even more harm was because the rebels repelled the attacks and inflicted heavy losses on the government forces. As mentioned in previous chapters, it is very important for UN mediators to ensure that peace talks do not reach agreements that by their own terms violate international law, such as provisions for amnesty for international crimes.

Proposed measures for conflict resolution and abatement of human rights violations need to shift and adapt to changing circumstances as conflicts evolve. More important, mediators must approach them comprehensively and in coordinated fashion: Consent to one measure cannot be conditioned on concessions or advantages on any other, as has been the case in the Darfur conflict for too long. For months leading up to the DPA-Abuja agreement of May 2006, the international community was silent on accountability, acquiescent on Khartoum's manipulation of humanitarian assistance and complacent about allowing the AU peacekeeping force to become ineffective and paralyzed. The reason was merely in order to obtain Sudan's signature on the dotted line of an agreement that never brought any serious peace to Darfur. In late 2010 and early 2011, the same attitude was present because of fear that Khartoum would renege on its promise to allow a referendum in Southern Sudan if too much was said about what still needs to be done in Darfur. With intense international attention, the referendum took place, and voters overwhelmingly chose to secede from the North. Although it is too early to tell if Khartoum will honor its promise to respect the results, it is also quite clear that the international community has decided to push Darfur onto the back burner.

I almost stumbled into a very promising partial success in Cote d'Ivoire in November 2004. After a bloody attempted coup, the armed forces had split and the country was geographically divided: The rebels held the North and the government the South and its most important city, Abidjan. The government and its allies considered the rebels part of large minorities that were non-Ivoirien despite the fact that their families had lived there for generations. International forces had been deployed and were holding a swath of territory that separated the rivals, and the UN had a very active and useful field presence over the whole country. In November, President Laurent Gbagbo fired the head of the national radio and television system, and the new boss allowed a full weekend broadcast of corrosive and hateful speech against the ethnic groups that supported Gbagbo's opposition. Such expressions of racial hatred had a dangerous effect on gangs, such as the Young Patriots, that roamed the cities and on armed pro-Gbagbo militias in the countryside. Violence against persons and properties occurred often in Abidjan during that weekend, and the UN field operation, led by a very able Swedish diplomat named Pierre Schori, was on high alert. I asked Kofi Annan and the Security Council to issue statements calling for a halt on hate speech—which both did—and simultaneously publicly warned the actors to the conflict that hate speech utterances under conditions of impending violence could result in charges being brought before the ICC as instigation to genocide. Thanks to Schori and his team, my statement got wide coverage in Cote d'Ivoire. The hate speech abated after that very dangerous weekend, and later we learned that my warning was the subject of consultations with government lawyers; they seem to have confirmed that my reading of the Rome Statute was correct.

At the request of the UN staff on the ground and their counterparts in the UN Department of Public Information in New York, my staff and I visited Cote d'Ivoire in 2005 and issued some guidelines about what press behavior might constitute incitement to commit genocide,. We then commissioned a deeper study that resulted in new guidelines on how to recognize incitement to genocide.[12] States need to respect free speech even when it is unpopular or—worse—disrespectful of other people. Hate speech is not protected when it incites to discrimination or hostility against groups or individuals by reason of their race, religion, national origin, gender or sexual preference. And hate speech crosses the line into instigation or incitement to genocide when it takes place under conditions of clear and present danger that it might ignite murderous violence against those groups. My initial guidelines and the subsequent commissioned study presented the applicable legal standards and offered some pointers as to how to recognize when those lines have been crossed.

I have reflected on this experience and believe that it proves that justice—and even the possibility of prosecution—can have an effective preventive effect on decisions that criminals make as they calculate their options. Of course, it is also necessary to consider the special circumstances of the Cote d'Ivoire example, including the sagacity of Pierre Schori as UN representative on the ground, the disposition of the secretary-general and the Security Council to speak out promptly and the ability of the Office of the Prosecutor to express interest at the appropriate times. Effective prevention of genocide ordinarily requires sustained attention and pressure, as the case of Cote d'Ivoire demonstrates.

The conflict continued in the country without tensions peaking again until January 2011, when Gbagbo refused to accept the results of an election he lost to Alassane Ouattara. This time the international community, led by African democratic leaders, was much more united in trying to persuade Gbagbo to leave and prevent massive loss of life. He was finally ousted in April 2011 and Cote d'Ivoire is now rid of a dangerous tyrant.

My efforts to propose meaningful interventions in the Democratic Republic of Congo (DRC), starting in late 2004, were much more frustrating. Even though my office followed events closely and participated in internal discussions at the Secretariat, my many attempts to visit the country were frustrated by UN officials who felt—for various reasons—that a visit by an official with the word "genocide" in his title would negatively affect their precarious relationship with the government and other actors. Because my job required me to respect the decisions of UN colleagues, my ability to help in ongoing situations depended greatly on their attitude toward my office and its potential. I was able to do my work and enjoy cooperation from UN colleagues on the ground in Darfur and in Cote d'Ivoire, but UN officials in Burundi and the DRC generally felt that I would make their lives more difficult. Although I was able to insert the perspective of prevention of genocide into debates about those countries at the UN and at the Security Council with respect to the DRC, my inability to visit the countries severely diminished the impact of what I could offer. That was a huge handicap in the case of the DRC, where millions had been killed in the late 1990s and whole regions of the country were still involved in armed strife and considerable violence against civilians. To this day, the UN is very much engaged in the DRC, and perhaps my suggestions would not have made much difference. But my frustration leads me to think that the OSAPG will function best if other UN units and officials, especially those on the ground, integrate the purposes and possibilities of the office into their own plans and use it creatively and constructively.

The UN has been criticized for deploying so few resources for what would seem the organization's most important mission: to save vulnerable people from genocide. Some critics (notably from the Bush administration) felt that the level of resources reflected the level of commitment to the task. But a start in the right direction is always better than having no mechanism at all, which was the case before 2004. In order to maximize the effectiveness of the office, Kofi Annan instructed me to conceive of it as a focal point of efforts at prevention by multiple other agencies and units of the UN. His personal investment in prevention of genocide made it possible for me to receive cooperation from virtually all my colleagues in the UN—with the notable exceptions already discussed—and attention when I thought I had something to add to policymaking conversations. As both Annan and I viewed my tenure as an experiment, I made a concerted effort to learn from what my assistants and I were doing and to systematize the experience as much as possible. We commissioned studies by outside experts and created an Advisory Committee on the Prevention of Genocide to help me evaluate the first few steps taken by the office. The committee included important personalities, such as Archbishop Desmond Tutu, General Roméo Dallaire and Gareth Evans, then the president of the International Crisis Group. Before I left the post of special advisor, the committee produced a blueprint for the incoming secretary-general, Ban Ki-moon, on how to improve on the mechanism of prevention of genocide. Ban implemented most of those recommendations, which in general addressed the relative paucity of resources available to prevent genocide and to compensate for it by developing a certain ability to have a multiplier effect. At my insistence, the office has now been considerably upgraded.

My tasks at the UN on prevention of genocide were difficult and frustrating, but the challenge itself continues to attract me. I was able to work with very dedicated and intelligent professionals whose support was essential to my ability to discharge my functions; Kofi Annan and some of his most capable officials also assisted in my work. I continue to advocate for the implementation of the responsibility to protect and for the expansion of UN prevention efforts not only on genocide but also of war crimes, crimes against humanity and ethnic cleansing. Since leaving the UN function, I have joined several prominent jurists in efforts to draft a convention on crimes against humanity. Now that I am a full-time law professor, it is encouraging to see that my law students are attracted to the courses on prevention of mass atrocities of all kinds. I am persuaded that there is no more important challenge to our very notion of a common humanity bonding all of us than the need to develop an effective ability to prevent the slaughter of vulnerable people in our time.

CHAPTER ELEVEN

CONCLUSION

My lifelong human rights career has taken me from secret prisons in Argentina during the height of the dirty war, to meetings at the UN General Assembly and international halls of justice. It has taken me from New York to Cape Town, from Bogotá to Darfur—wherever people gather to discuss what is necessary to respond to abuses of any type and to take action. It is a great privilege to have been able to work in the field of human rights in a variety of capacities for my entire adult life. I have been able to conduct fact finding, monitoring, advocacy, litigation, teaching, research and writing in my chosen field. It is also rather astonishing, given my personal history.

During the last forty years, I have witnessed countless situations, first in Argentina and then around the world, that have taught me a great deal about what happens when institutions allow the rule of law to be breached and, rather than insisting on accountability, a country prefers to cover up abuses. I have also been able to witness the positive results when a society confronts its legacies of the recent past with honesty and compassion for the victims and decides that democratic institutions will protect rather than persecute citizens, their rights and their liberties. The lessons of Argentina have always been my touchstone, and ongoing experiences in my native land with police and judicial reform, democratic policies for citizens' security and social and political inclusion of the disenfranchised continue to inspire me prosecutions for past abuses. Of course, not everything has been positive in Argentina in the last quarter century. But the commitment, sophistication and inventiveness of Argentine human rights activists is a continuing example for me. I have had the opportunity to take a close look at the experiences of many other societies, in Latin America and beyond, and from them I draw lessons as well.

DETENTION, TORTURE

It is important to continue to insist that states not deviate from the law when determining when and by whose order a person can lose his or her personal liberty. This issue is covered in the domestic law of every state as well as in international law. Unfortunately, arbitrary detention is rampant in many countries today. In many places, security forces are allowed—if not by law, then certainly by corrupt practices—to conduct warrantless arrests based on mere suspicion. Suspects are arrested for the purpose of investigation, instead of serious criminal investigations leading to legitimate arrests. It follows that those arrests are the occasion for mistreatment and worse. In my current role as UN Special Rapporteur on Torture, I deal on a daily basis with allegations of torture in the context of detentions without warrants. I have learned that it is essential that the human rights movement make courts and magistrates responsible for every arrest, especially for any interrogation and investigation preceding prosecution, because the most numerous and the most cruel abuses tend to happen in those early hours and days of pretrial detention.

The writ of habeas corpus is a centuries-old institution from the British common law that is now part of the domestic law of every country and, significantly, also a key standard in the international law of human rights. It states simply that detainees can have their arrests examined immediately by a judge to determine their lawfulness. The petition can be made by any person as a friend of a detainee. After receiving the petition, the judge must immediately inquire into who ordered the arrest and by what legal authority, for what reason or purpose, in what facility the detainee is being held and under what conditions. This inquiry must be made even during nonworking hours and weekends. If the judge determines that any of those facts of the case violates the law, he or she orders the release of the detainee.

My experience in many countries, however, shows that the writ of habeas corpus has been distorted beyond recognition via a formalistic, formulaic approach to it. We need to campaign to make habeas corpus an important instrument in the hands of judges committed to the protection of the human person. Judges must be encouraged to act quickly, to inspect detention centers without prior warning, to demand prompt answers from the executive branch and—in cases of detention without trial pursuant to emergency situations—to review not only the conditions of detention but also the reasons alleged for the continuation of administrative detention. The longer prisoners are held in indefinite detention, the higher is the burden on the executive to show that it is reasonable under the circumstances. Over the years, I often have thought how different my torture and prison experience in Argentina would have been if the judicial system had lived up to its obligations.

Then and now, governments that resort to arbitrary detention justify their actions by citing the need to arrest persons for "national security" considerations. As we see today in the United States, the Obama administration has continued a policy of prolonged detention without trial of some individuals in the context of counterterrorism. Such detention is not limited to those arrested in armed conflict, where the holding of enemy combatants until the end of hostilities is legitimate. For those caught in law enforcement operations, prolonged arbitrary detention is a very serious human rights violation. We need to make it clear that the unlawful character of such detention is not cured by a rhetorical extension of the meaning of "armed conflict" to a "war on terror" that has no limits in time, geographic scope or even how we identify the enemy.

The Obama administration has incorporated some procedural improvements on long-term detention by adding periodic review of the reasons to continue holding a prisoner. But those safeguards are not enough, especially if the authority of independent judges to assess those reasons is limited and the detainees themselves cannot participate actively in the review as a matter of right. More broadly, the human rights movement must campaign against the use of prolonged arbitrary detention before the practice becomes a standard that other countries will follow. We need to elevate prolonged arbitrary detention to the category of the most serious human rights violations, as it was before the events of September 11, 2001, made it "acceptable."

Another issue that the human rights movement must tackle in the coming years is the fact that the public everywhere has become more accepting of torture as inevitable, if not exactly desirable, in the pursuit of making us feel more protected from terrorism or from crime. It is essential that we in the human rights movement counter the perception that torture is ever justified. The legal arguments are clear, but we need to insist on the moral and practical ones as well. In other words, activists must demonstrate that torture makes us less rather than more secure, because torture becomes an uncontrollable spiral that is very difficult to stop.

Torture becomes the perfect recruitment tool for the enemies of democracy and of law, and it corrupts and poisons the very institutions (police, military, intelligence agencies, prosecutors, judges) that we need to protect us and to build humane and decent societies. In the debate about torture, it is not enough to repeat that international law contains an absolute prohibition on its use under any circumstance, including emergencies. We need to explain the ethical and political dimensions of torture and, most important, address the question of whether torture "works." In addition to debunking the myth of the ticking bomb scenario, we need to show that any short-term gain in intelligence gathered through torture about other enemies is offset by the long-term abandonment of the moral high ground that is essential to success in combating terrorism and crime in general. Human rights activists must contribute to this debate by continuing to tell the stories of horrendous physical and psychological suffering attached to torture; common men and women are less likely to support torture if they see a human face as a victim. We must also highlight the high price societies pay when governments torture. The drama of Egypt that unfolded in February 2011 is our perfect object lesson. It may well result in a truly democratic awakening in the Middle East; but if it does, Egyptians will not have reason to thank Western powers that for thirty years tolerated and even encouraged torture perpetrated under the Mubarak regime.

DISAPPEARANCES

Forced disappearances are an area where the human rights movement has placed some limitations on a dictatorship's arsenal of repressive measures. Massive programs of disappearances, such as the one that took place in Argentina between 1976 and 1983, are no longer as prevalent, and much credit is due to the way the human rights movement has campaigned against disappearances everywhere. Among other things, international law has developed two important treaties banning disappearances: one in the Americas in 1994 and one in the United Nations, which took effect in December 2010. Of course, treaties do not automatically end practices that are themselves denials of law in all its forms. But the treaties represent the will of the international community to proscribe this brutal method of repression and offer effective tools to the human rights practitioner in seeking the "reappearance alive" of each victim or some other form of redress. These multilateral agreements impose obligations on states, such as ensuring the proper registration of all detentions and establishing a clear scope of judicial powers to act to determine the whereabouts of detainees and the conditions of their detention. Local and international organizations have successfully lobbied state institutions to implement those standards, either by legislation or by judicial decision. In addition, treaties on disappearances establish quick-action proceedings that can be brought before international organizations in order to press—early and effectively—for the release of disappeared persons or for the legalization of their arrests. Because disappearances constitute a crime against humanity, these accords give us strong arguments for the need to investigate, prosecute and punish the perpetrators before national as well as international tribunals.

Experience shows that disappearances do not only affect a victim's right to personal freedom; in the majority of cases, the ultimate fate and even the objective sought is extrajudicial execution. Upholding the right to life is, therefore, the first line of defense against disappearances, even if the victim's death cannot be proven. Arbitrary deprivation of life takes many forms in today's world. Unresolved disappearances, assassinations of political opponents and massacres of civilians in remote areas are by no means things of the past. Even if international law does not completely ban capital punishment, when we campaign against arbitrary deprivation of life, we need to look rigorously at capital punishment. International human rights law does require strict scrutiny of each application of the death penalty to ensure: the highest standard of due process for the defendant; that the death penalty is applied only to the most serious crimes; and that it is applied without discrimination on the basis of race, religion or national origin. In addition, international standards prohibit any infliction of cruel, inhuman or degrading treatment or punishment, either through the death row phenomenon or in the manner of execution. The death row phenomenon is the additional suffering experienced by convicts through long periods of appeal of their death sentences, during which they are kept in conditions amounting to solitary confinement and in the uncertainty of when they will lose their lives. Like others who have looked at this issue, I am convinced that capital punishment cannot be applied anywhere without the state committing serious violations of one or more of those rules. In many countries, courts simply are not equipped or trained to apply the most rigorous standards of procedural fairness; nevertheless, those countries still may insist on capital punishment. Similarly, investment in prisons is the lowest priority in those countries, so the time spent on death row is inevitably in conditions of cruel and inhuman treatment. The fact of prolonged detention awaiting execution itself produces psychological harm that is cruel and inhuman. Despite many attempts, humankind has not developed a method of execution that is painless, so the act is surrounded by pain and suffering. Finally, decisions to apply the death penalty, even if pursued in courts offering fair trial guarantees, are never free from the undercurrents of racial and other forms of discrimination present in every society. Despite our best efforts, courts cannot be isolated completely from discrimination. That is why the human rights movement is against the death penalty and campaigns for its abolition. To achieve success in this effort, we must uphold life as a central human rights value and campaign against capital punishment, extrajudicial executions, collective massacres and disappearances as a complete package.

EXILE, IMMIGRATION, REFUGEES

Population movements have become more fluid and more massive in the last thirty years. But immigration laws also have been tightened, and today it is much harder to obtain legal status in a country where an immigrant arrives. What is much more troubling is that societal attitudes toward immigrants also have hardened to the point that principles we used to consider sacred about rights obtained by birth in a specific country are now under serious challenge. Unfortunately, this is true not only in the United States but in virtually all "receiving" countries, including those that have always been generous and receptive to people from different cultures, such as Canada and all of western and northern Europe. In immigration and refugee policy, we are fighting a rear-guard battle.

For the next few years, we probably will be lucky if we can avoid some of the worst regressions in law rather than expecting to win major victories. But defensive tactics are equally important if they protect people from harm. We need to recognize that migrants and their families are, by definition, exploited persons. They have left their societies in search of better opportunities to sustain their families, and they occupy the lower rungs of the employment market, where rules on salaries, protection against unlawful dismissal and working conditions are not enforced. They are exploited not only by unscrupulous employers and middlemen, but also by people smugglers and hucksters who prey on their vulnerability as nonnationals and on their fear of deportation. We must argue that the more that public policy pushes them into clandestineness and illegality, the more that they will be left at the mercy of unscrupulous gangs and organized crime and others who would exploit them—while, at the same time, restrictive immigration policies will not stem the flow.

In every country, immigration lawyers and nonprofit organizations protect migrant workers and their families against abuse and help them integrate into receiving societies by applying national law and administrative procedures. As those laws become more complex and restrictive, the defense of immigrants becomes more local and less international. That fragmentation of the work for human rights is not beneficial either to local or to international activists, and it certainly limits the chances of immigrants themselves to assert their rights. We all need to make an effort to reverse this trend toward fragmentation. One way to avoid fragmentation is to ensure that work at the international level is informed by the changing and challenging ways in which immigrants live their lives and defend their rights in sending, transit and receiving countries.

SOLIDARITY

In each country as well as globally, the human rights movement has become a very well-established part of civil society. But to be effective, human rights organizations need to be independent from states and from political affiliations, even while acting in a highly politicized field. This requirement cannot be enforced, however, because the very nature of human rights practice is that no one can control the gateway to the movement or decide who is a part of it and who is not.

I have had the good fortune to live and work during a phenomenal period of growth for the organizations and institutions that promote and protect fundamental freedoms throughout the world. This "movement" includes officials in democratic governments, staff of intergovernmental agencies charged with monitoring compliance with treaty norms, leaders and professionals in nongovernmental organizations and front-line activists who confront human rights violations, often in dangerous places. The movement also includes those who teach human rights to others, whether in established universities and professional schools or in organizations exclusively dedicated to human rights education. The movement is now highly diversified and encompasses a rich variety of experiences. It offers opportunities to young men and women who are increasingly attracted to its ranks. Professional human rights work has long overcome the narrow confines of "solidarity" and advocacy; it now includes opportunities for professionals from very diverse backgrounds: lawyers, investigators, forensic anthropologists, medical personnel, scientists, journalists, writers, researchers, specialists in military law and strategy, teachers, statisticians, sociologists, anthropologists and many others. The movement is now vital and influential. In issue after issue, it is possible to see how it helps shape public policy, often against very difficult odds. But if the opportunities to intervene have multiplied, the obstacles to obtain redress and justice for the victims of abuse have only become larger and more complex.

The diversity of the movement is reflected in the incorporation, mostly in the last decade or two, of organizations that focus on the rights of groups of people in vulnerable positions in society. Actually, in historical terms, the protection of racial and religious minorities precedes the birth of the human rights movement. But today the principles of minority rights and nondiscrimination have been adopted and expanded by a highly coordinated network of organizations, especially those dedicated to the rights of indigenous peoples.

The women's movement, in particular, joined the human rights struggle in the 1990s and has had a profound effect on the shape of the movement as well as on its approaches to multiple problems. This phenomenon of feminist influences on human rights has ushered in the incorporation of similar organizations dealing with children's rights and the rights of sexual minorities and has added strength to the advocacy against discrimination in all forms. The women's movement also has had a profound influence on the establishment of international criminal justice mechanisms to recognize rape and other forms of sexual violence as war crimes. Today human rights organizations are increasingly better able to deal with economic, social and cultural rights, such as the rights to education, health care, housing, decent conditions of life and a clean and healthy environment. After having created a relatively successful model through which to respond to violations of the rights to life, liberty, physical integrity and freedom of expression, the movement now faces the challenge of developing means to uphold and defend socioeconomic rights. The successful model must be expanded to include these broader challenges.

Detentions, torture and abuses of civil and political rights are addressed through a "violations approach": We react to their occurrence by insisting on their end and on specific forms of redress, such as investigation and punishment of violators and offers of reparations. But that approach is inadequate when applied to rights that the state enforces through large-scale investments. Such expenditures are subject to the limits imposed by the resouces available to a state, a standard known as progressive realization. Rather than force socioeconomic rights into a model that it fits poorly, the movement is developing mechanisms that are better suited to progressive realization, such as demands for popular participation in the distribution of state budgets and the discussion of priorities. In addition, human rights lawyers are experimenting, both at the national level and in international courts, with arguments to make these rights justiciable, in the sense of being susceptible to judicial determination of their content and scope in specific cases. In this manner, it is possible to envision ways in which human rights can contribute to poverty reduction and to the more democratic integration of powerless social groups into the mainstream of society.

Independence, integrity and transparency are conditions of effectiveness of human rights organizations, and entities that have mastered these conditions are, not surprisingly, the most successful in the field. At the same time, those organizations that have allowed politics or ideology to influence their findings and their policy positions have lost their chance to be taken seriously by policymakers.

Of course, the human rights movement is not immune to the rivalries and competition of any human enterprise. I have witnessed ambition and competition for the limelight and have seen how very worthy institutions have been put in peril because of pettiness and refusal to cooperate. But it is essential to cooperate and share in the tasks and responsibilities of the struggle rather than succumb to the temptation of sectarianism and the competition to obtain credit for results that, in my mind, are almost always the fruit of collective efforts.

At present, the human rights movement is still trying to adjust to the loss of the U.S. government as a partner in the pursuit of more effective means of promoting freedoms and protecting the vulnerable. The so-called global war on terror has placed the United States among the nations that choose to see themselves as exceptional and thus exempt from the rules of international behavior (including respect for human rights). The Bush-Cheney years eroded respect for law everywhere while not making the United States more secure. Unilateral decisions to use force and—worse—the pretense that there were human rights–related justifications for the invasion of Iraq have made the world more cynical about civil liberties and the promotion of freedom. It is easy to see how rogue governments can claim that they are only doing what the U.S. government got away with.

The U.S. foreign policy that promoted and protected human rights worldwide beginning in the Jimmy Carter years will be hard to restore, but it is imperative that the U.S. government come back to the fold of democracies that respect human rights. Some steps taken by the Obama administration go in this direction: Especially encouraging were the reinstatement of the Uniform Code of Military Justice, which unequivocally bans torture; the closure of Central Intelligence Agency "black sites"; and the termination of extraordinary renditions. It may be difficult to be certain that violations are no longer happening, given that they were always mired in secrecy; but there is reason to believe that there have been significant changes from the Bush-Cheney years. But much more—especially in accountability for the crimes that were committed—must take place.

The Obama administration has thus far disappointed the human rights movement in key areas, such as its refusal to launch inquiries into torture and extraordinary renditions, its continued use of the detention center in Guantanamo, its reliance on state secrets to deny torture victims redress, its targeted killings whose methods and procedures are not transparent and its decisions to resume trials by military commissions and to continue to hold prisoners without trial. It is especially inconsistent for the United States to ignore its own past violations, claiming to be forward-looking and bipartisan, while its official position on repressive situations elsewhere demands that human rights crimes be investigated, prosecuted and punished in accordance with international law.

Fortunately, the United States has many resources by which it can regain its proper place in the promotion and protection of human rights everywhere. Even while the Bush-Cheney administration surprised the world by abandoning long-held principles of consti-

tutionalism and respect for human dignity, American civil rights organizations erected the first barriers against abuse and effectively curbed
some of the worst excesses. Journalists have been at the forefront of
investigations into the abuses of the war on terror, and, significantly,
retired and active-duty military officers and military lawyers stood up
to criticize the treatment of detainees and the violations of due process
rights. Human Rights Watch, Human Rights First, the Center for Constitutional Rights and the American Civil Liberties Union struggled
hard against torture and war crimes while Bush and Cheney were at
the height of their power. Equally significant is the fact that, with a different administration in power, these organizations have retained their
independence and insisted that the Obama administration do the right
thing, not only by prohibiting the worst practices but also by investigating them fully and allowing the law to take its course.

If there was some expectation that democratic Europe and other
developed nations could take on the mantle of human rights and in-
corporate them into their foreign policies, that has not happened. To
be sure, human rights promotion is a priority of the European Union's
"common" foreign policy, and some European countries continue very
enlightened policies toward peace, justice and accountability in their
dealings with the underdeveloped world. But Europe's capacity to influence policies and practices in Latin America, Africa and elsewhere
around the globe is not equal to the task. Besides, in immigration and
security-related domestic policies, Europe also exhibits serious contradictions that diminish the effectiveness of its human rights initiatives.
The detention of asylum seekers in appalling conditions in several
southern European countries, as documented in a recent case against
Belgium and Greece by the European Court of Human Rights, is just
the most recent example of those contradictions.[1] Greece's announced
intention to build a barrier to halt immigration from Africa, Central
Asia and the Middle East, no matter how desperate the need for border controls, stands as an important symbol of the European shift
away from human rights policy.

It is too early to tell if we ever will witness a truly multilateral approach to human rights protection in which medium-size states incor-
porate human rights concerns into their foreign policies. For now, it is

encouraging that emerging democracies are participating in initiatives to create or strengthen courts and procedures for human rights protection at the United Nations and at regional organizations, such as the Organization of American States. They champion, sign and ratify new treaties, becoming key actors in the creation of such institutions as the International Criminal Court. They also have created enlightened policies on human rights toward neighboring countries on a regional basis. But to a large extent, they are unwilling to speak out on human rights problems if doing so will interfere with their relations with other countries. In the near future, protection of human rights will have to rely less on political and diplomatic pressures and more on the strength and independence of treaty bodies and special procedures at the United Nations and on regional courts and commissions, such as the Council of Europe, the African Union and the Organization of American States. In recognition of these realities, the movement is placing more effort into actively participating in the creation of strong independent procedures for human rights protection and in using them aggressively to realize their full potential.

LAW, ACCOUNTABILITY, JUSTICE

When I was studying law, our role models were the defense attorneys who used their craft to protect the innocent against the overwhelming power of the state to deprive persons of their liberty. Nowadays, a human rights lawyer is more of a prosecutor, charged with defending justice and obtaining redress for victims by prosecuting those who abuse the power of the state and commit atrocities. I am not uncomfortable with that change; it is essential for everyone in the human rights community to insist on accountability for crimes against humanity. Indeed, some prosecutors are human rights defenders in their own right. Many human rights lawyers increasingly use national and international criminal procedures to represent victims and participate in trials as "private prosecutors" acting alongside state attorneys and urging judicial measures, offering evidence and more generally seeking redress for their clients in the context of criminal trials. This has become a very productive way to generate attention regarding rights that have been abused and to obtain comprehensive reparations for that abuse.

Yet I believe that we lose something by pushing defense attorneys into the background of human rights advocacy. In places where human rights are matters of life and death and the state is the enemy, lawyers and other human rights defenders continue to be our first line of defense against abuse. And even in highly sophisticated legal systems, they are absolutely necessary to correct injustices and make institutions live up to their obligations. One such project in recent years that has exemplified this concept is the Innocence Project in the United States, which has an amazing record of acquittals of people wrongfully convicted, some narrowly saved from the death penalty and some released after decades of unjust incarceration. What is exciting about the Innocence Project is that it applies innovative scientific breakthroughs, such as DNA testing, to this task. More than anything, however, its members painstakingly analyze court documents and records and take the time to reinterview witnesses, prosecutors and other judicial actors until they find the evidence that will right the wrong conviction. An equally significant feature of the Innocence Project is that dozens of young people from law schools, from journalism and from science participate in its important mission. It is all the more impressive that those efforts are provided to prisoners whom the system and society have put away and forgotten.

GENOCIDE

In the future, it will be very difficult to prevent mass atrocities by persuading the world's most powerful countries to intervene militarily and unilaterally—or to form "coalitions of the willing"—when vulnerable populations are at risk. The main reason is because these countries will not be able to disassociate truly humanitarian impulses from their other foreign policy and strategic interests. Even when they do act, the resulting inconsistencies will discredit genocide prevention and disrupt the search for a universal method to protect at-risk populations.

Unfortunately, many groups campaigning against genocide today do so by trying to urge powerful states to intervene militarily with-

out regard to legal niceties and with little attention paid to the consequences of deploying foreign forces. Although diplomatic pressure is a
complicated and cumbersome tool, human rights groups need to use it
more effectively and systematically to prevent genocide. Antigenocide
campaigners need to turn their justified moral outrage into detailed
knowledge of specific conflicts and policy options. Policymakers will
listen to them not so much because they recruit the generous support
of celebrities but because they have constructive and realistic solutions
to offer.

That is not to say that military intervention should be ruled out
from the start in diplomatic discussions; doing so would only provide
genocidal regimes with a level of comfort from which they can resist
legitimate pressures more effectively. The international community
must make it very clear that, if all else fails, vulnerable people will
indeed be protected.

The UN continues to be the focal point of efforts to prevent genocide, even if its record in this regard is not exactly stellar. The reason
that the UN is still a focal point is that only the Security Council can
direct the legal and legitimate use of force in international affairs, so
the threat of force in diplomatic negotiations is most credible when
the UN is involved. But more significantly, international law has been
slowly building instruments that can be brought to bear in preventing
mass atrocities. Those instruments include the extensive UN experience in mediation and conflict resolution, in peacekeeping and coordination of humanitarian affairs, postconflict reconstruction and rule
of law initiatives, and incipient capacities for early warning and early
action to prevent mass atrocities. In the future, human rights activists
will need to understand those levers of international diplomacy much
better, and as they do they will be able to advocate their use as more
effective tools than they are today.

In mastering international diplomacy to prevent genocide, there are
several things we need to do. In the first place, we must insist that world
leaders take genocide prevention seriously and work hard at building
consensus toward unified positions. The lack of coordination among
various human rights groups and governments and inconsistent follow-
through are the main reasons why the international community has yet

to deal effectively with the Darfur crisis. The genocidal regime in Khartoum has been able to game the international community by selectively offering the mirage of cooperation to some and self-righteously rejecting the initiatives of others. Justice and accountability as provided by the International Criminal Court are powerful instruments of prevention, as long as they are coupled with measures of protection, relief and peace negotiations. But all these measures have to be backed up by a will to make them work; adopting half measures and then simply hoping for the best is not the solution.

At the same time, we need to continue building the arsenal of instruments to conduct effective prevention. The bottleneck will always be the lack of political will; but efficient new mechanisms that currently do not exist can go a long way to build that political will and to eliminate excuses for not acting. Among those mechanisms are: early warning systems; analytical tools to detect trends toward deterioration of human rights situations affecting populations at risk and to assess the effect of specific measures on those trends; and serious studies of how justice and other measures do indeed prevent crime and under what circumstances. A comprehensive approach to prevention of genocide and mass atrocities has been lacking.

HUMAN RIGHTS WORK is about *change*. The object of our endeavors is change from situations of oppression, whether individual or collective, to ones of enjoyment of freedom. For such change to occur, we need to imagine a world in which every person, especially the disadvantaged and the vulnerable, is able to fulfill all the capabilities of the human spirit. Imagination, therefore, is what inspires us. But the world we imagine has to be realized through passion and courage to overcome obstacles in the conviction that truth and justice are on the side of human rights. Passion and courage have to be accompanied with an attitude of dialogue. I do not mean that we need to dialogue with human rights violators; I am not naive, and I do not believe that perpetrators of heinous crimes can be redeemed or converted merely by talking to them. The dialogue I propose is with broad circles of the public who are indifferent to human rights violations. They are not guilty or complicit in them, but their indifference still conspires against effective implementation of rights for all. We need to expand the circles of supporters of human rights in every society, not only to enlist them in the struggle for a more just, humane and democratic national arrangement but also to promote and protect human rights in other countries. Our passion, courage of convictions and attitude of dialogue will help us succeed if we reinforce them with an ability to engage in discussion about the facts with rigor and honesty and do not attempt simply to impose our will. In the 1930s, the Spanish philosopher Miguel de Unamuno confronted the fascists who were on the rise with a phrase that is well known to Spanish speakers: "Vencereis pero no convencereis." The play on words is hard to translate into English, but it means: "You may win, but you cannot persuade." The only weapons of the human rights movement are words and peaceful political action; that is precisely why we fight with the arms of reason. We will succeed not so much if we win the debates but if we persuade and convince.

PERSONAL
POSTSCRIPT

My professional career and my private life have always
been intertwined. I have lived far from my parents and
siblings because exile was first imposed on me and later
because I chose to remain abroad. My human rights work had taken
an international bent, and I could do it effectively only from the United
States. All along I have enjoyed support and encouragement from my
relatives, even and most especially when my activities in Argentina (and
perhaps abroad as well, in the early years) put them and their families at
considerable risk. I have always been grateful for that and for the love
that all of them have always given to me. Since 1983, I have returned to
Argentina frequently for visits, and I have had many occasions to experience that affection. My younger sister, Maria del Carmen, died in 2000
after a cruel battle with cancer when she was only fifty-three. Her wid-
ower, children and grandchildren remain very close to me, even though
a son and a daughter and their families are now living abroad; the rest
live in the greater Buenos Aires area. My older sister, Susana, is herself
a human rights activist in Argentina as a psychologist and a university
professor. She is also a volunteer member of a governmental committee against torture and for the preservation of memory of the dirty war
abuses. My brother Julio, his wife and a daughter are all architects, and
his three other children are successful professionals. Susana, Julio and
his family all remain in Mar del Plata. Over the years, there have been
painful disagreements among my siblings, although fortunately never
particularly bad; throughout, I have had excellent, warm relations with
each of them. Maybe the distance has made it easier for me to avoid

becoming involved in those disagreements and having a truly fraternal relationship with them.

My mother, Aurelia, died in 2004 after a short illness. I was in Geneva when I received the news, in my first days as Special Advisor on the Prevention of Genocide. I had visited with her only a few days earlier and had said my painful good-byes, so I continued my trip to The Hague and to Stockholm, where I was to meet with the Swedish prime minister and receive assurances of that country's support for the task with which the United Nations' secretary general, Kofi Annan, had entrusted me. I returned to Mar del Plata to see my father a few days after my mother had been buried and was gratified when he told me that my mother had learned of that assignment and had expressed her pride on what she considered to be my important achievement. I promised myself that I would remember those words as I tried to save lives. She was eighty-seven when she died and had been in good physical and mental health almost until the end. My father, Julio, died in late 2008, when he was one month short of his ninety-fifth birthday. He also had enjoyed excellent mental and physical health literally until the last few days. In his eighties, he had learned to use the Internet. Until the very end, he remained curious about and awed by the progress of science as well as appalled at the cruelty of which human beings can be capable in exercising power. We had disagreed over politics in Argentina, especially when I was a student and a young lawyer; but he always respected me and my choices; his love, affection and support in difficult times were always unconditional. My brother and sister and I were truly blessed to enjoy the company of our parents for so long and in good health.

My children (and now my grandchildren) are an enormous source of pride for me. Juan Francisco (Juanfra) is a lawyer in a large firm in New York, and, as mentioned, he has done his share of pro bono work in the area of human rights and international justice. He studied at the University of Virginia and Columbia Law School and later obtained a master's in law from New York University. After studying at Oberlin and Johns Hopkins, Camilo now works in micro-financing in South America from his base in Lima, Peru; he is following his interests in development economics and social justice. Soledad is an architect from Notre Dame at a prestigious firm in New York City and has recently completed a master's in urban planning at the Massachusetts Institute of Technology. Juanfra and Camilo each have two children, with their wives, Beth and Maria Eva, respectively. I do not know if I should take any credit for my children's achievements, especially because, when they were growing up, I always thought that I was improvising as a parent and was never certain that I was doing it right. For example, I never knew how much I should tell them about what happened to me—or what I did—in Argentina. I generally thought that they would ask when they wanted to know. As a result, there may well be gaps in their knowledge of those years; if they read this book, some of those gaps will be filled, but I am sure that new questions will arise. I would never hide anything from them, but I also do not think I should force on them information that may be unpleasant. In the meantime, I am happy that they have grown up with a sense of a duty to care for what happens to the least privileged among us and that "among us" to them means the whole world and the whole of humanity. Now that they have their own children, I fondly remember my visits with our pediatrician in Mar del Plata, Dr. Adler. (His son is now the prosecutor who has filed the charges against the CNU members.) Dr. Adler always made this insecure young father very proud when he said my sons were "very well stimulated." Whenever I spend time with my grandchildren—Joaquín, age seven; Anahí, age four; Camila, age three; and Javier, age one—I also feel that they are very well stimulated, which means they will grow to live happy, fulfilling lives.

I am naturally gratified that Juanfra, Camilo and Sole feel equally comfortable in considering themselves both American and Argentine. They are world citizens not so much because they travel the globe but because everywhere they feel responsible to do something for others who are less fortunate. Perhaps it sounds like I am saying that they have learned this from me; in fact, every day they teach me lessons. Their tolerance for other people's ideas and their acceptance of diversity because it enriches us all are ideas and sentiments that I wish I had had when I was young.

Juan Francisco was born when I thought of myself as a committed Christian, so we named him for St. Francis of Assisi in tribute to the saint's love for and dedication to the poor. Camilo is named for Father Camilo Torres, a revolutionary priest in Colombia who died in combat in the 1960s, and Camilo Cienfuegos, a Catholic activist who fought with Fidel Castro in Cuba and died in a plane accident only weeks after the triumph of their revolution. Soledad is named for a dear friend of mine, María Antonia Berger, whose nom de guerre was Soledad. In 1972, after a failed escape from a Patagonian prison, she and eighteen other prisoners were shot at point blank range on a naval base. Sixteen perished; María Antonia survived even though one of the assassins shot a "finishing shot" in her face. I met her later, when she was in charge of assistance and solidarity with prisoners, and she asked me to take on the defense of those most recently arrested and to visit them in prison when I could. She called me from Europe when I was already living in the United States; shortly thereafter she was captured upon her return to Argentina and became one of the last few cases of desaparecidos. Our own Soledad was born in Washington a few months later. She likes to tell the story behind her name and says: "The story has profoundly affected my life. For me it forged a connection to my family's past and to those times in Argentina. It reminds me daily to be strong and courageous and to have strong convictions in life."

Beth Formidoni is married to Juanfra. She is New Jersey–born and of Italian and Irish ancestry and was practicing law in New York when they met. Before their wedding she decided to quit the law and became a chef. She worked at an excellent restaurant in Greenwich Village until she started having children, and Camila and Javier are so young that for now Beth has her hands full raising them in Manhattan. María Eva Dorigo is Camilo's wife. They met in Buenos Aires when Camilo was there for a few months after graduating from Oberlin. She is the daughter of Pablo Hermes Dorigo, an accountant and union activist who is counted among the desaparecidos. María Eva was one year old when she lost her father, and her mother died of cancer when María Eva was only sixteen. Camilo met her in Buenos Aires at a meeting of the children of the disappeared. She followed him to the United States and they got married in the late 1990s. They have lived in Washington, New York, Hoboken, Geneva and Lima. María Eva helped Camilo through graduate school at Johns Hopkins, and then she obtained a bachelor's degree at Hunter College in New York. In addition to raising Joaquin and Anahi admirably, she is completing a graduate program at the Catholic University of Peru. Soledad is in a loving relationship with Esteban Gergely, a lawyer in Maryland who is also the son of dear friends of ours. His mother has a sister among the disappeared.

Silvia (Chichela) and I are enormously proud of our three children, and we enjoy the company of our four grandchildren as much as we can. We have been married for forty years and have been together for forty-one years. We started dating in 1970—the same year in which I graduated and started practicing law. Chichela was still in law school, and by July 1972 we already had two sons. Nevertheless, Chichela graduated at the end of that year and briefly practiced law in Mar del Plata before we had to pack and leave in a hurry. She also practiced a bit in Buenos Aires, although after I was arrested, eighteen months of raising the kids alone, visiting me in prison in another city and indefatigably trying to secure my release did not leave much time for a career. Her family and mine helped, but the burden was on her. In my cell, I felt responsible for her plight, as well as surrounded by her love as shown in all these big and small details. In late 1976, seven of my fellow lawyers were arrested and disappeared, and Chichela had to go into exile in Brazil, with two young children and not knowing when—or if—I would be able to join her. The first few years in the United States were hard on her because she had to learn English as an adult, in addition to raising kids and adjusting to an unfamiliar culture. Nevertheless, by the mid-1980s she had obtained an LLM degree (master's in law) and passed the Virginia bar exam. Her example of dedication, hard work and perseverance in the face of adversity definitely rubbed off on our children. How could it be otherwise?

In the meantime, my work for Human Rights Watch had me traveling abroad and within the United States quite frequently. I have continued traveling ever since, and, although we both understand that travel is inevitable in my line of work, it does strain our relationship. Chichela sometimes jokes that these short separations actually have helped keep our marriage together. But business travel is never pleasant, and travel for business related to genocide and torture is hard to reconcile with what we once thought was glamorous, mysterious or exciting about travel. I try not to forget that travel also takes a toll on the loved ones who stay behind, especially on Chichela, whose responsibilities increase while I am gone. My parents once told me that, when we lived in Costa Rica when Sole was a teenager, my daughter once complained that I was never there. I cannot think about that without feeling guilty. Although I travel just as frequently now, my trips tend to be shorter, and I now often have the luxury of declining invitations if they will cut into my weekend time at home.

Chichela and I have had good and exciting times and some hard ones as well. We did decide to stick to our marriage and to make it work, and, for the most part, it seems like we have made it. We do not regret having made difficult choices, even when we felt they might not be the wisest. We never hesitated to make some sacrifices in lifestyle if we thought they were necessary to provide for the best possible education for our children. Some of our relationship problems have been financial in nature, although after what we had gone through, financial instability was not the worst of our problems (and we navigated through hard times anyway). We both wish we could say that our marriage has arrived at a point where everything is sweet and blissful. It has not, but we now have a formula and are sticking to it, and I am happy to say it works.

Writing and reading some early drafts of this book brought back painful memories for both of us. In my case, at least, the pain is a helpful and necessary cathartic exercise, and conducting it with Chichela at my side makes it all worthwhile. That is why this book is humbly, and lovingly, dedicated to her.

ACKNOWLEDGMENTS

Had it not been for Marjory I probably never would have gotten around to writing this book. Her cheerful and gentle insistence persuaded me that the book was worth the effort of writing it and helped me overcome insecurities and doubts that were with me all along. Of course, her contributions to this volume far exceed encouragement: Our conversations about format, tone and substance, chronologies and timelines and ultimately what should be included and excluded have made this a joint enterprise.

I am also indebted to John Silbersack for his work as our agent and for putting us in contact with Palgrave Macmillan, but more emphatically for giving us excellent advice as we progressed from an idea to an outline, to a complete proposal and to a book. We also want to thank Kimberly Whalen at Trident Media Group for introducing us to John. We thank Laura Lancaster, our editor at Palgrave Macmillan, for her innumerable valuable suggestions. We know how different—and how much better—this book is after we incorporated all of her ideas. We also thank her predecessor as our editor, Alessandra Bastagli, for her enthusiasm and support in the early stages of this venture. The copy editing process, directed at Palgrave by Alan Bradshaw, has also greatly improved this product.

Special thanks to Robert Cox for his enthusiasm and help with the title of the book. I am also indebted to Luis Ubiñas, president of the Ford Foundation. At his invitation, I spent the summer of 2009 as a "scholar-in-residence" at Ford, and that provided the opportunity to get started on this book.

Marjory and I are especially grateful to Ian Martin for agreeing to write a foreword to this book, and to Amnesty International-UK for asking him to do so. I have been fortunate to know Ian from the time he was

AI Secretary-General through his many UN positions in the field in Haiti, Timor Leste, Rwanda, Eritrea, Darfur, Bosnia and most recently Nepal. Ian has served with great distinction and has left behind invaluable lessons for all who have worked with him.

WHEN I STARTED DEFENDING political prisoners in Argentina, I met some of the most courageous and dedicated lawyers that one can ever encounter. Among them, Mario Landaburu was an early and decisive influence on me, not only for his knowledge of the law and his creativity, but also for his selfless dedication to helping all others, his wonderful sense of humor and his modesty.

In those years of early exile, when I was desperate to help my friends and the Argentine people overcome the tragedy of the "dirty war," my mentor was Emilio Mignone, the country's foremost human rights leader. His ability to draw strength from the personal tragedy of losing a daughter to "forced disappearance" was an example not only to me, but to generations of human rights activists in Argentina and elsewhere. The concepts of what states owe to victims of mass atrocity and of the worth of the principles we now know as "transitional justice" would not be as well established today if it had not been for Emilio's intellectual and ethical contributions early on, when those ideas clashed with the conventional wisdom of letting bygones be bygones. In those years, his friend Augusto Conte MacDonnell was also a mentor of mine. I am glad to say that, although both of them are long departed, their contributions are well remembered in Argentina today.

I want to mention Tricia Feeney for being an inspiration to me at virtually every stage of my professional life. She was the Amnesty International researcher in charge of Argentina in the 1970s, and responsible for my adoption as a "prisoner of conscience" even before she had met me. Her frustrated attempt to visit me in prison in 1976 and her forceful inquiries about my case caused the military government to allow me to go into exile much earlier than would otherwise have been the case. Tricia and her family have become dear friends to us.

For all my years at Human Rights Watch, I am grateful to Aryeh Neier. In addition to allowing me early on to be a part of an exciting new venture, I learned a lot from his leadership and inventiveness in tackling new human rights problems.

I want to mention three longtime friends from my tenure as executive director at the Inter-American Institute of Human Rights: Pedro Nikken, a noted Venezuelan jurist and human rights activist who was the chair of the Institute's board at the time; Roberto Cuellar, from El Salvador, who worked with me and then succeeded me as director; and my longtime friend Charles Moyer, whose steady hand at administration and good counsel on substance made my work much easier there.

At Notre Dame I had wonderful teaching and research experiences. I am particularly grateful to Guillermo O'Donnell, a world-renowned political scientist, for his warm friendship and also for opening up my understanding of the ethical and political dimensions of justice and accountability and how they should be used to assess the quality of democracy. I want to mention one student in particular: Bernard Duhaime, a Canadian scholar and practitioner. His generosity of spirit and intellectual rigor in pursuit of rights for the most underprivileged and vulnerable among us is exemplary.

During my term as a member of the Inter-American Commission on Human Rights (IACHR) I enjoyed my exchanges with fellow members such as José Zalaquett and Susana Villarán and with the IACHR's staff directors Jorge Taiana (later foreign minister of Argentina) and Santiago Canton. I learned a lot from staff attorneys, among whom I need to mention Eduardo Bertoni, Verónica Gómez and the unforgettable Brian Tittemore who authored the two reports that made me proudest during the year (2002) when I was the Commission's president: the precautionary measures on Guantanamo and the report on Terrorism and Human Rights.

My five years as president of the International Center for Transitional Justice (ICTJ), in New York, were also the occasion for many learning experiences. I wish to remember fondly all my colleagues who worked with me there, approximately 140 at the time I left in 2009. For that reason, I will single out only Pablo de Greiff, ICTJ Director of Research, whose keen intellect and breadth of knowledge is only enhanced by his profound sense of the ethical dimensions of justice.

I am especially indebted to Kofi Annan for appointing me his Special Advisor on the Prevention of Genocide, but more importantly for his moral leadership and insistence in making that task the United Nations' most important responsibility.

My long-time friends Claudio Grossman and Robert K. Goldman allowed me the opportunity to return to full-time teaching in the area of international law and human rights in this most special place of learning for human rights: the Washington College of Law of the American University. Far beyond that, Claudio, Robert and I share multiple advocacy experiences and a warm and lasting friendship.

For my understanding of present-day Argentina I am much indebted to Horacio Verbitsky, the country's foremost investigative journalist and the chair of the board of CELS, the human rights organization founded by Emilio Mignone and Augusto Conte MacDonnell. I also wish to acknowledge the influence on me of successive CELS directors, all of them of a younger generation than me: Martín Abregú, Víctor Abramovich and Gastón Chillier. For keeping me abreast of the state of human rights in Latin America I am grateful to José Miguel Vivanco, a Chilean lawyer who succeeded me as director of the Americas Division of Human Rights Watch. I owe a lot of insights on human rights to three younger attorneys who have worked with me at different times and places: Francisco Cox, Javier Mariezcurrena and Garth Meintjes.

I am grateful to Chichela for her critical reading of early drafts of all the chapters and for helping me remember with accuracy episodes that happened long ago. In almost every case, remembering those events was painful for both of us; nevertheless, her support for this project never wavered. My daughter, Sole, kept asking to read drafts as I produced them and many times reminded me of anecdotes and stories that she thought should be included. My sons and their wives also asked about the progress of our writing, and, altogether, the attitude of my family was a source of invaluable encouragement.

My parents, Aurelia and Julio, died in 2004 and 2008, respectively, and I was blessed to enjoy their lives among us until advanced but fruitful ages. My younger sister María del Carmen died in 2000 when she was only fifty-three. Each of them—and also my living relatives—encouraged me greatly during various stages of my human rights career. I think they would have liked to read this book.

NOTES

CHAPTER 1

1. Montoneros and ERP were the largest and most powerful guerrilla groups in the country. Both were leftist, but as stated, Montoneros identified itself with Peronism, while the ERP was a Marxist organization.
2. Carnival is not an important feast or celebration in Argentina, but it is a long weekend, as Monday and Tuesday of Carnival are nonworking days.

CHAPTER 2

1. UN Commission on Human Rights, Resolution on Torture and Other Cruel, Inhuman or Degrading Treatment or Punishment, E/CN.4/RES/1985/33, March 13, 1985.
2. Juan E. Méndez, "Torture in Latin America," in Kenneth Roth, Minky Worden and Amy Bernstein, eds., *Torture: Does It Make Us Safer? Is It Ever OK?* (New York: New Press, 2005), p. 67.
3. Due to pressures from the military, the government of Raul Alfonsín passed the laws of *punto final* ("full stop") in 1986 and *obediencia debida* ("due obedience") in 1987. Although not explicitly an amnesty, their legal effect was to immunize most defendants from prosecution.
4. *Mapp v. Ohio,* 367 U.S. 643 (1961), *Weeks v. United States,* 232 U.S. 383 (1914). Under this doctrine, in criminal cases courts must exclude all evidence obtained through an illegal search and seizure and also all other evidence—even if regularly obtained—that originated in the illegal search. Judge Kaplan's exclusion of the testimony of a witness in the Ghaliani case mentioned below is an example of this doctrine, because the witness came to be known to the prosecution through Ghailani's confession under torture.
5. Joby Warrick, "CIA Tactics Endorsed in Secret Memos," *Washington Post,* Oct. 15, 2008.
6. Alan Dershowitz, *Why Terrorism Works* (New Haven, CT: Yale University Press, 2002).
7. Supreme Court of Israel sitting as High Court of Justice, Concerning Interrogation Methods Applied by the GGS, Judgment of Sept. 6, 1999.
8. David Rivkin is a former Bush administration official and former appointee to the now-defunct UN Committee of Experts on Human Rights. Rivkin made these remarks at a Wilson Center event in Washington, DC, in October 2007, where I was also a featured speaker. *Legal Standards and the Interrogation of Prisoners in the War on Terror,* Cynthia Arnson and Philippa Strum, editors, Washington: Woodrow Wilson International Center for Scholars, Dec. 2007, pp. 52–53.
9. Chad Bray, "US Won't Appeal Terror Case Ruling," *Wall Street Journal,* Oct. 11, 2010; Warren Richey, "Ahmed Ghailani gets life sentence for Al Qaeda bombing of US embassies, *Christian Science Monitor,* Jan. 25, 2011.

10. "Extraordinary rendition" alludes to the transfer of a detainee to the jurisdiction of an-
    other country without using the extradition process or deportation on immigration law
    grounds. Renditions to face justice are controversial; but "extraordinary" renditions are
    not to face justice but precisely to subject the person to interrogation under torture.
11. Senate Committee on the Armed Forces (Sen. Levin, chair) report, 2008; Report of the
    Department of Justice Office of the Inspector General (on the "torture memos"). A Sen-
    ate Committee on Intelligence report on the CIA is still pending. Also pending is any
    result of the investigations by a Special Prosecutor appointed by the Attorney General.
12. Jay S. Bybee, Assistant Attorney General, *Memorandum for Alberto R. Gonzales,
    Counsel to the President,* Washington, DC, Aug. 1, 2002. Regarding Bush administra-
    tion disavowal of the Bybee memo, see John W. Dean, "The Torture Memo by Judge
    Jay S. Bybee that Haunted Alberto Gonzales' Confirmation Hearing," FindLaw, Jan.
    14, 2005.

CHAPTER 3

1. *La Noche de los Lápices,* Argentina, 1986, directed by Héctor Olivera, produced by
   Fernando Ayala, based on the book by Maria Seoane and the testimony of survivor
   Pablo Díaz.
2. Alejandra Dandan, "El ex director del Buenos Aires Herald Robert Cox también será
   testigo en la causa ESMA," *Página12,* Nov. 23, 2010.
3. "Antonio Pernías reconoció los 'vuelos de la muerte,'" *Página12,* Aug. 26, 2010.
4. IACHR, Report on the Situation of Human Rights in Argentina, OEA/Ser.L/V/II.49,
   doc. 19, corr. 1 (1980).
5. See "A Message for Moscow," *Time,* Feb. 9, 1981. Haig declared that "[i]nternational
   terrorism will take the place of human rights in our concern because it is the ultimate
   abuse of human rights."
6. Cynthia Brown, ed., *With Friends Like These: The Americas Watch Report on Human Rights and United States Foreign Policy in Latin America* (New York: Pantheon,
   1985).
7. Americas Watch, "Honduras: Signs of the "Argentine Method'" (New York, Dec.
   1982).
8. IACourtHR, *Velásquez Rodríguez v. Honduras,* Judgment on Merits, July 29, 1988.
   Series C, No. 4.

CHAPTER 4

1. Committee Against Torture, case of Ahmed Agiza, Sweden, Communication No.
   233/2003, May 24, 2005.
2. UNESCO, Social and Human Sciences, www.unesco.org/.
3. Inter-American Court of Human Rights, *Haitians and Dominicans of Haitian Origin
   v. Dominican Republic,* Provisional Measures, Resolution of Aug. 18, 2000.
4. Inter-American Court of Human Rights, *Yean and Bosico v. Dominican Republic,* Series C, No. 130, Sept. 8, 2005.
5. Inter-American Commission on Human Rights, Annual Report, 2003.
6. International Convention on the Protection of the Rights of All Migrant Workers and
   Members of Their Families, New York, Dec. 18, 1990, entered into force July 1, 2003,
   United Nations Treaty Series, Vol. 2220, p. 3.
7. Protocol to Prevent, Suppress and Punish Trafficking in Persons, Especially Women
   and Children, New York, Nov. 15, 2000, entered into force Dec. 25, 2003, United
   Nations Treaty Series, Vol. 2232, p. 319.

CHAPTER 5

1. Jean J. Kirkpatrick, "Dictatorships and Double Standards," *Commentary,* Nov. 1979.

2. Buckley's retraction appeared in William F. Buckley, Jr., "Lessons from Argentina," *The Washington Post*, June 9, 1985. That was more than what Jeanne Kirkpatrick, the touring legislators and other supporters of Videla, et al, ever did, but Buckley's *mea culpa* was limited and insincere: He blamed Robert Cox, the editor of the *Buenos Aires Herald*, with whom he had met during the Burson Marsteller–sponsored trip, for what he had written. It seems Buckley took very bad notes because, at the time of his junket to Buenos Aires, Cox was already well on the public record criticizing disappearances and the policies of denial and deception of the Argentine government.

3. Robert Parry, "Ronald Reagan, Enabler of Atrocities," Consortiumnews.com, Feb. 6, 2011 ("Reagan joshed that Derian should 'walk a mile in the mocassins' of the Argentine generals before criticizing them"). Parry refers to Martin E. Andersen, *Dossier Secreto* (Boulder, CO: Westview Press, 1993), pp. 19 and 329. See also, Marta Gurvich, "Argentina's Dapper State Terrorist," Consortium.com, Dec. 29, 2010, originally published August 19, 1998.

4. Noted in a Church Committee report. See *Alleged Assassination Plots Involving Foreign Leaders: An Interim Report of the Select Committee to Study Governmental Operations with Respect to Intelligence Activities*, US Senate, Nov. 20, 1975, Washington: GPO, 1975 (Report No. 94–465).

5. Cynthia Brown, ed., *With Friends Like These: The Americas Watch Report on Human Rights and United States Foreign Policy in Latin America* (New York: Pantheon, 1985). I wrote chapters on Argentina, Honduras and Nicaragua for this volume.

6. On Jacobo Timerman's testimony in the Senate, during confirmation hearings for Ernest Lefever, see Molly Ivins' column in *Fort Worth Star-Telegram*, Nov. 14, 1999 (reproduced on creators.com, accessed May 4, 2011, http://www.creators.com/opinion/molly-ivins/molly-ivins-november–14–1999–11–14.html). In later years we would learn what the real import of "quiet diplomacy" was. Declassified State Department cables show that Henry Kissinger urged the Argentine military to finish the job of repression quickly before human rights pressures in Washington made it difficult for the executive branch to defend the regime. In 1978, when he was no longer secretary of state, Kissinger attended the World Cup of Soccer in Buenos Aires, appearing in public with General Videla and the other junta members and providing them with an argument that concerns for their human rights practices were not widely shared, and in any case, they did not amount to isolation from the Western world. Martin E. Andersen, *Dossier Secreto* (Boulder, CO: Westview Press, 1993), p. 279.

7. Congressional Record, House Foreign Affairs, hearings on Nicaragua, 1985.

8. "We love your adherence to democratic principles and to democratic processes." Vice President George H. W. Bush addressing Marcos, on his visit to Manila, 1981, Wikiquote "Ferdinand Marcos," consulted March 27, 2011.

9. UN Human Rights Council, "Human Rights in Palestine and Other Occupied Arab Territories: Report of the UN Fact-Finding Mission to the Gaza Conflict," A/HRC/12/48, Sept. 25, 2009; "United States: Goldstone Report 'Biased' and 'Flawed,'" AIPAC Memo, Nov. 12, 2009.

CHAPTER 6

1. IACHR, Report on the Situation of Human Rights in Argentina, OEA/Ser.L/V/II.49 Doc. 19 corr.1, April 11, 1980.

2. Inter-American Commission on Human Rights, Annual Report 1978, OEA/Ser.L/V/II.47 Doc. 13 rev. 1, June 29, 1979.

3. American Convention on Human Rights, approved Nov. 22, 1969, entered into force July 18, 1979, OAS Treaty Series No. 36. The United States has signed but not ratified the American Convention. See IACHR, *Basic Documents Pertaining to Human Rights in the Inter-American System*, Washington: OAS, 2007, p. 51.

4. IACourtHR, *Angel Manfredo Velásquez Rodríguez v. Honduras*, Sentence of July 29, 1988. Series C, No. 4.

5. *Gomes Lund et al. (Guerrilha do Araguaia) v. Brazil,* Sentence of Nov. 24, 2010, Series C, No. 219.

6. IACHR, *Report on the Situation of Human Rights in Venezuela,* OEA/Ser.L/V/II.118 Doc. 4 rev. 2, Dec. 29, 2003.

7. African Commission on Human and Peoples' Rights, Communication 276 / 2003—Centre for Minority Rights Development (Kenya) and Minority Rights Group International on behalf of *Endorois Welfare Council v. Kenya,* Nov. 25, 2009; Communication 310/2005—*Darfur Relief and Documentation Centre v. Republic of Sudan,* Nov. 25, 2009.

8. *Citizens United v. Federal Election Commission,* 130 S. Ct. 876 (2010).

9. The Defensor del Pueblo is an institution that several Latin American democracies have borrowed from Spain. It is an autonomous administrative agency, sometimes answerable to parliament, that monitors the behavior of all other administrative agencies with regard to the rights of citizens in the manner of an ombudsman's office, makes public comments on the administration's performance and seeks reform of practices deemed contrary to the rights and interests of consumers and citizens. The IIHR promoted the institution and offered training programs to staff members.

10. IACHR Annual Report 1994, Chapter V: "Report on the Compatibility of Desacato Laws with the American Convention on Human Rights," OEA/Ser.L/V.88 Doc. 9 rev. 1, Feb. 17, 1995.

11. *New York Times Co. v Sullivan,* 376 U.S. 255, 84 S.Ct. 710 (1964). Liability for defamation of public figures can be imposed only if the person who uttered the allegedly offensive speech has acted with "actual malice," in the sense that he or she knew the facts expressed to be false or acted in "reckless disregard" for whether they were true or false.

12. European Court of Human Rights, *Lingens v. Austria,* 8 EHRR 407 (1986); and Inter-American Court of Human Rights, *Herrera Ulloa v. Costa Rica,* Judgment (2004).

13. Inter-American Court of Human Rights, *Awas Tingni Community v. Nicaragua,* (2001); *Aloeboetoe et al. v. Suriname* (1993); *Moiwana Community v. Suriname* (2005).

14. IACHR, *Odir Miranda v. El Salvador* (2005).

15. IACHR, *Maria da Penha v. Brazil* (2000).

CHAPTER 7

1. International Court of Justice, *Military and Paramilitary Activities in and against Nicaragua (Nicaragua v. United States of America). Merits, Judgment. I.C.J. Reports 1986,* p. 14.

2. Pedro Linger Gasiglia, *El Mozote: The Massacre 25 Years Later* (Buenos Aires: author's edition, 2007). UN Security Council, *Report of the UN Truth Commission on El Salvador,* S/25500, April 1, 1993. The massacre happened in December 1981 and was reported by Alma Guillermoprieto, "Salvadoran Peasants Say Army Killed Hundreds in Community," *Washington Post,* Jan. 27, 1982; and in a front-page story: Raymond Bonner, "Massacre of Hundreds Reported in Salvador Village," *New York Times,* Jan. 27, 1982.

3. The Americas Watch report of our mission was published in 1990. An expanded version was later published as Juan E. Méndez and Kenneth Anderson, "The Panama Invasion and the Laws of War," *Terrorism and Political Violence* 2, no. 3 (Autumn 1990): 233–257.

4. Mark Bowden, *Black Hawk Down, A Story of Modern War* (New York: Atlantic Monthly Press, 2003).

5. Geneva Convention I, articles 15 and 17.

6. Article 51, Additional Protocol I of 1977. See Robert Block, "Shields," in Roy Gutman, David Rieff and Anthony Dworkin, eds., *Crimes of War 2.0* (New York: W. W. Norton, 2007), pp. 378–381.

7. Middle East Watch, *Needless Deaths in the Gulf War: Civilian Casualties During the Air Campaign and Violations of the Laws of War* (New York: Human Rights Watch, 1991).
8. The HRW report *Indiscriminate Fire: Palestinian Rocket Attacks on Israel and Israeli Artillery Shelling in the Gaza Strip* (June 2007) criticized the use of cluster bombs that spread over large areas and can remain as explosives on the ground as inherently indiscriminate.
9. UN Human Rights Council, Twelfth Session, Report of the UN Fact Finding Mission on the Gaza Conflict, A/HRC/12/48, Sept. 25, 2009.
10. · Memorandum for the President from Attorney General Alberto González, Decision Re: Application of the Geneva Convention on Prisoners of War to the Conflict with Al Qaeda and the Taliban (Jan. 25, 2002).
11. President George W. Bush's Military Order of Nov. 13, 2001: Detention, Treatment, and Trial of Certain Non-Citizens in the War Against Terrorism; 66 FR 57833.
12. Marc Perelman, "From Sarajevo to Guantanamo: The Strange Case of the Algerian Six," *Mother Jones*, Dec. 4, 2007.
13. Brian Tittemore, "Guantanamo Bay and the Precautionary Measures of the Inter-American Commission on Human Rights: A Case for International Oversight in the Struggle Against Terrorism," *Human Rights Law Review* 6, no. 2 (2006): 378–402.
14. *Rasul v. Bush,* 542 U.S. 466 (2004); *Boumediene v. Bush,* 553 U.S. 723 (2008); and *Hamdan v. Rumsfeld,* 548 U.S. 557 (2006).
15. *Rasul v. Bush,* U.S. Supreme Court, 542 U.S. 466, 2004.
16. Inter-American Commission on Human Rights, *Report on Terrorism and Human Rights* (Washington: OAS, 2002).
17. Elizabeth Stubbins Bates and the IBA Task Force, *Terrorism and International Law: Accountability, Remedies and Reform* (Oxford: Oxford University Press, 2011). International Commission of Jurists, *Assessing Damage, Urging Action: Report of the Eminent Jurists Panel on Terrorism, Counter-terrorism and Human Rights* (Geneva: ICJ, 2009).
18. International Bar Association, *Terrorism and International Law* (2001); Bates, *Terrorism and International Law;* International Commission of Jurists, *Assessing Damage, Urging Action, Terrorism and International Law.*
19. Erica Gaston, "The War Over Afghan Civilian Casualties," *Foreign Policy,* March 8, 2011.

CHAPTER 8

1. Aryeh Neier, *War Crimes: Brutality, Genocide, Terror and the Struggle for Justice* (New York: Times Books, 1998).
2. Theo van Boven, Special Rapporteur on Restitution, Compensation and Reparations for Gross and Consistent Violations of Human Rights, *Study concerning the right to restitution, compensation and rehabilitation for victims of gross violations of human rights and fundamental freedoms,* UN ESCOR, Comm'n of Hum. Rts., 45th Session, E/CN.4/Sub.2/1993/9 (1993); Louis Joinet, Special Rapporteur on Impunity, *Question of Impunity of Perpetrators of Violations of Human Rights (Civil and Political Rights): Final Report,* UN ESCOR, Comm'n of Hum. Rts., 48th Session. UN Doc. E/CN.4/Sub. 2/1996/18 (1996); Human Rights Committee, *Comments on Reports Submitted by State Parties under Article 40 of the Covenant,* #10 (Argentina), UN Doc. CCPR/C/79/ Add.46 (1995); Human Rights Committee (Peru), CCPR/C/79/Add.67 (1996); EuCt HR, *Aksoy v. Turkey*–Rep. 1996-VI, fasc. 26 (18.12.96); EuCt HR, *Kurt v. Turkey*– Rep. 1998-III, fasc. 74 (25.5.98); EuCt HR, *Kolk and Kislyiy v. Estonia* (dec.), nos. 23052/04 and 24018/04, ECHR 2006-I–(17.1.2006).
3. CONADEP, *Nunca Mas: Informe de la Comision . . .* (Buenos Aires: EUDEBA, 1984). An English-language version, *Nunca Mas,* was published in 1986 by Farrar Strauss Giroux.
4. The full name in Spanish is *Ley de Caducidad de la Pretensión Punitiva del Estado,* roughly meaning that the ability of the state to exercise punishment had elapsed by the force of events.

5. In the mid-1980s, HRW and AI had joined human rights organizations from the Southern Cone of Latin America to oppose self-amnesties and pseudo-amnesties and to advocate in favor of policies of truth and justice for past human rights violations. This was an important change from previous practices of the human rights movement.

6. Juan E. Méndez, "Truth and Partial Justice in Argentina," an Americas Watch Report, Aug. 1987.

7. Juan E. Méndez, "Truth and Partial Justice in Argentina: An Update," an Americas Watch Report, New York, 1991.

8. Inter-American Court of Human Rights, *Almonacid-Arellano v. Chile,* Judgment (Sept. 26, 2006) and *Gomes Lund e Outros (Guerrilha do Araguaia) v. Brazil* (Nov. 24, 2010).

9. Inter-Am Court HR, *Barrios Altos case (Chumbipuma Aguirre et al. v. Peru),* judgment of March 14, 2001, Series C, No. 75.

10. This is a Maoist insurgent guerrilla organization in Peru, also known as The Shining Path.

11. In the judgment of the *Barrios Altos* case, the Inter-American Court ordered payments of $175,000 to the four survivors and next of kin of the massacre at the hands of the Colina Group and $250,000 to the family of one of the victims in November 2001.

12. Tina Rosenberg, in Alex Boraine, Janet Levy, Ronel Sheffer, eds., *Dealing with the Past: Truth and Reconciliation in South Africa* (Cape Town: IDASA, 1994).

13. South African Truth and Reconciliation Commission Report (Cape Town: Juta Press, 1998).

14. Juan E. Méndez and Garth Meintjes, *Reconciling Amnesties with Universal Jurisdiction,* International Law Forum, 2000.

15. Charles Krauthammer, "Truth, Not Trials," *Washington Post,* Sept. 9, 1994.

CHAPTER 9

1. UN Factfinding Mission on the Gaza conflict ("Goldstone Report"), Human Rights Council (Sept. 2009), UN DOC A/HRC/12/48 Much credit for the selection of Cassese and Goldstone goes to Swedish jurist Hans Corell who, as UN Legal Advisor, would not settle for political appointments and insisted on the highest judicial qualifications and integrity for these jobs.

2. Alison died in a plane crash near Buffalo in January 2009. I was then president of ICTJ and had had the occasion to work with her further. Like so many colleagues at HRW and elsewhere, I felt that, with her death, Rwandans of all identities had lost a great champion and that the international community at large had been deprived of a powerful voice to prevent genocide and to protect human dignity everywhere.

3. The UN Special Rapporteur on Extra-judicial Executions, Bacre Waly Ndiaye, had warned in April 1993 of genocidal acts against the Tutsi, echoing the conclusions of a nongovernmental fact-finding mission that had been issued a few weeks earlier. William A. Schabas, *Genocide in International Law,* 2nd ed. (New York: Cambridge University Press, 2009), p. 9.

4. ICJ, Legal Consequences of the Construction of a Wall in the Occupied Palestinian Territory, Advisory Opinion, 2003.

5. International Center for Transitional Justice, *Forgotten Voices: A Population-Based Survey on Attitudes about Peace and Justice in Northern Uganda* (July 2005); *When the War Ends: A Population-Based Survey on Attitudes about Peace, Justice, and Social Reconstruction in Northern Uganda* (Dec. 2007).

CHAPTER 10

1. Arnold Toynbee, "A Summary of Armenian History up to and including 1915," cited in Frank Chalk and Kurt Jonassohn, *The History and Sociology of Genocide* (New Haven, CT: Yale University Press, 1990), p. 270.

2. Frank Chalk and Kurt Jonassohn, *The History and Sociology of Genocide: Analyses and Case Studies* (New Haven, CT: Yale University Press, 1990), p. 366.

3. Lemkin was a Polish scholar in international criminal law who coined the word "genocide" in his *Axis Rule in Occupied Europe,* published in 1944. Cited in William A. Schabas, *Genocide in International Law,* 2nd ed. (New York: Cambridge University Press, 2009), p. 17.

4. Ben Kiernan, *The Pol Pot Regime,* 2nd ed. (New Haven, CT: Yale University Press, 2002).

5. Article II, Convention on the Prevention and Punishment of the Crime of Genocide, approved Dec. 9, 1948, entered into force 1951.

6. *Prosecutor v. Jean-Paul Akayesu,* International Criminal Tribunal for Rwanda, judgment (Sept. 1998).

7. The only exception is Guatemala, where some killings of the Maya population in the early 1980s were characterized as genocide. *Guatemala: Memoria del Silencio,* Report of the UN Commission on Historical Clarification, Feb. 25, 2009.

8. Report of the International Commission of Inquiry on Darfur to the United Nations Secretary General (Jan. 2005). The Commission of Inquiry was led by Antonio Cassese.

9. UN General Assembly, 2005 *Summit Outcome,* A/60/L.1, Sept. 20, 2005, paragraphs 138 and 139.

10. Among many other useful compilations, see Chalk and Jonassohn; John L. Davies and Ted Robert Gurr, *Preventive Measures* (New York: Rowman & Littlefield, 1998); Eric D. Weitz, *A Century of Genocide* (Princeton, NJ: Princeton University Press, 2003); David Hamburg, *Preventing Genocide* (Boulder, CO: Paradigm, 2010).

11. Report of the International Commission of Inquiry on Darfur to the United Nations Secretary General (Jan. 2005); UN Security Council Resolution 1564 (Sept. 2004).

12. Office of the Special Advisor on the Prevention of Genocide, *Note to Secretary-General: End of Mission Report,* April 2007 (unpublished); Toby Mendel, *Study on International Standards Relating to Incitement to Genocide or Racial Hatred,* April 2006 (unpublished).

CHAPTER 11

1. European Ct H.R., *MSS v. Belgium and Greece,* Grand Chamber judgment, Jan. 21, 2011.

INDEX

Abramovich, Victor, 105
Abrams, Elliott, 60, 127
Abu Ghraib, 45, 134
Afghanistan, 131–2, 134, 136, 196
African Commission on Human and Peoples'
    Rights, 98, 106
African Court of Justice, 98, 106
African National Congress (ANC), 152–3
African Rights, 170–1
African Union, 95, 171, 180–1, 196, 217
African Union/United Nations Hybrid Operation
    in Darfur (UNAMID), 171
Aidid, Mohamed, 130
Alfonsín, Raúl, 139–44, 233n3
Alianza Anticomunista Argentina (Triple A), 7,
    10–1
Alien Rights Law Project, 68, 72
Alien Tort Claims Act, 169–70
Allis-Chalmers, 84–5
Almonacid-Arellano v. Chile, 148
American Civil Liberties Union, 44, 134, 216
American Convention on Human Rights, 74,
    101, 103, 146, 148
American Service-Members' Protection Act, 173
Americas Watch, 60. *See also* Human Rights
    Watch (HRW)
amnesty, 6, 38, 40, 103, 138, 140, 143–8, 152–4,
    158–9, 167–8, 199
Amnesty International (AI), 1, 23–24, 32, 40, 48,
    54, 68, 79–80, 94, 190, 238n5
Anderson, Ken, 128–9
Annan, Kofi, 155, 189, 200, 202–3, 224
apartheid, 84, 91–2, 151–3, 167
arbitrary arrest and detention. *See* prolonged
    arbitrary arrest
Argentina:
    Carnival in, 20–1, 233n2
    constitution of, 25
    democratization and, 138–41, 164
    dirty war in, 42, 45, 60, 84, 192, 205
    disappearances in, 47–64, 100, 139, 209
    exiles from, 18–23, 48–9, 53, 57, 59, 65, 69,
        71, 80–3, 98, 227
    habeas corpus in, 4

JM's arrest and imprisonment in, 3–4, 10,
    12–20, 34–8, 65, 149, 207
JM's return to, 139–40
junta in, 14–5, 20, 25, 38, 40, 47–52, 56–60,
    82–6, 100, 110, 139–44
pseudoamnesty laws in, 146–8
state of emergency invoked in, 7, 25, 27
See also Peronism and Peronists
Argentine Airlines, 21–2
Argentine Information Service Center, 83
Arpaio, Joe, 70
Assembly of First Nations (AFN), 160
Astiz, Alfredo, 54–5
Atlacatl Battalion, 127
Awas Tingni v. Nicaragua, 112
Aylwin, Patricio, 145

Bagram Prison, 134
Bangladesh, 187
Barayagwiza, Jean-Bosco, 169–70
Barreiro, Ernesto, 177
Barrios Altos case, 147–8, 238n11
al-Bashir, Omar, 155–6, 173, 180–1, 196–8
Belgium, 169, 179–80, 216
Berger, Maria Antonia, 225
Bernal, Reiniero, 4–6
Bizimungu, Augustin, 170
black sites, 63, 215
Black Hawk Down, 129
Bosnia, 134, 159, 165–6, 188
Boumedienne v. Bush, 134
Brazil, 18, 21–2, 26, 48, 61, 69, 73, 84, 99,
    102–3, 114, 147, 227
Brown, Cynthia, 140
Brutus, Dennis, 32
Buckley, William, 85–86, 235n2
Burkhalter, Holly, 93
Bush, George H. W., 95
Bush, George W., 42, 45, 63, 197, 214–6
Bush (George W.) administration, 42–6, 132–6,
    173–4, 202, 214–6, 233n8

Cabo, Dardo, 19, 149
Caducidad. *See* Ley de Caducidad